Starting at Sea Level

Starting

At

Sea

Level

Terry L. Noble

Foggy River Books
MCLEOD, MONTANA
2007

Frontispiece: Crab pound with shedding floats (some in the water and some drying on racks). Soft crab packing shanties in the background. Photograph by A. Aubrey Bodine. Copyright © Jennifer B. Bodine. Courtesy of A AubreyBodine. com.

FOGGY RIVER BOOKS
P. O. Box 520
McLeod, MT 59052

Visit our website: FoggyRiverBooks.com

ISBN: 978-0-9793603-0-5

Library of Congress Control Number: 2007922723

Contents

Author's Note

THE EVENTS DESCRIBED ON THE FOLLOWING PAGES ARE REAL, BUT A BIT of literary license was used in telling them. Not all incidents are presented in the exact order in which they occurred. Some were shifted over a year chronologically to produce a more coherent story. Although true names were used for most people in this book, pseudonyms were chosen for others where it seemed appropriate. In a quest for simplification, my memories of two people were combined to create one of the characters.

I have nothing but warm feelings for the individuals who appear in this narrative. The people of Somerset were the most decent I have ever known. I hope that in the process of telling my story, I have done justice to theirs.

Acknowledgments

MY FATHER AND HIS FELLOW OFFICERS TAUGHT ME MUCH ABOUT THE Chesapeake oyster conflict, but for information on the early years of the struggle, I turned to *The Oyster Wars of Chesapeake Bay* by John R. Wennersten, Tidewater Publishing. It was a valuable resource.

I owe a debt of gratitude to my wife, Aileen, for all her invaluable assistance during the development of this book. Without her morale boosts along the way, the project may never have been completed.

Special thanks go to my mother, Kathleen Noble, and my cousin, Robert Shockley, for providing historical information about our family and the Oriole community. Together, they helped to clarify my early childhood memories.

Thanks also go to my brother, Danny, and to Johnny Bates, Billy Bates, Beauchamp Bloodsworth, James Henderson, Ellsworth Hoffman, Dr. Leroy Johnson, Nancy Reid Johnson, Elmo Powell and Richard Tyler for allowing me to use their names in telling this story.

Finally, I want to express my appreciation to all the people who read the manuscript and offered advice and encouragement. Your input made it a better book. Special recognition goes to Evelyn VanGinhoven and Carolyn Crittenden for their excellent editing.

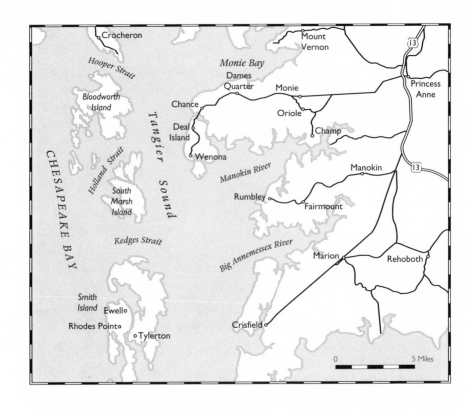

Crocheron

Hooper Strait

Bloodworth
Island

Tangier Sound

CHESAPEAKE BAY

Holland Strait

South
Marsh
Island

Kedges Strait

Smith
Island Ewell○

Rhodes Point○
                ○Tylerton

Mount
Vernon

Monie Bay
Dames
Quarter   Monie

Chance

Oriole

Deal
Island   Champ

○Wenona

Manokin River

Princess
Anne

13

13

Manokin

Rumbley○
              Fairmount

Big Annemessex River

Marion   Rehoboth

Crisfield○

0   5 Miles

WESTERN SOMERSET COUNTY
My World as a Young Boy

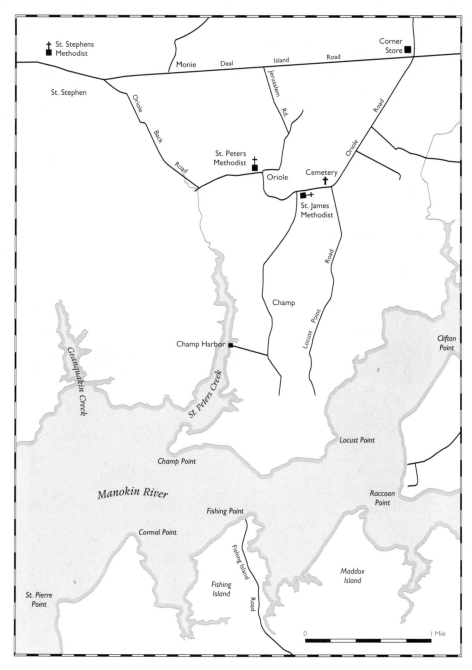

† St. Stephens
■ Methodist

Corner
Store ■

Monie   Deal   Island   Road

Jerusalem Rd.

St. Stephen

Oriole

Oriole Road

Back

Road

St. Peters
Methodist †
■

Oriole

Cemetery †

St. James
Methodist ■ †

Road

Champ

Locust Point Road

Champ Harbor ■

Clifton
Point

Geanquakin Creek

St. Peters Creek

Locust Point

Champ Point

Raccoon
Point

Manokin River

Fishing Point

Cormal Point

Fishing Island

Fishing Island Road

Maddox
Island

St. Pierre
Point

Fishing
Island

0   1 Mile

ORIOLE, CHAMP, AND MANOKIN RIVER
The Center of My World

1. The Perfect Day

 I FOUGHT FOR BALANCE ON THE TINY DECK AS THE SKIFF abruptly changed direction. My father, standing on the deck at the other end, appeared unconcerned with my fate. He poled forcefully to the left, sending my part of the little boat careening the opposite way. I teetered on the gunnel, using the handle of my crab net like a tightrope walker's pole. Somehow I managed to stay dry.

I knew the old man would be happy to see me fall overboard—it was a one-sided game we had been playing since I was a small boy. But I was older now and not about to give him the pleasure. In fact, I had done nothing in over a year that pleased him.

When my father was satisfied with the skiff's position, he maneuvered his net in behind the crab he had been pursuing. It was a large male known as a Jimmy. The ten-foot-long net handle bowed as he swept the animal off a mat of eelgrass. The force of the onrushing water flipped the crab onto its back, pinning it in the shallow string bag. With one continuous motion, my father brought his prey to the surface and dumped it into the skiff. At an inch over six feet and muscular, he was surprisingly agile. Twenty years on the water had made his balance on any boat nearly perfect.

It was a hot August morning, sultry on land but glorious on the flats of the Chesapeake. My father and I had been dipnetting blue crabs since dawn. We were working the shallows of the Manokin River, a

1

tidal finger of the Bay. The day was perfect for crabbing, with clear water, no wind and a low tide an hour after sunrise. This was our first time alone together in months. My senior year of high school had been turbulent, leaving us in perpetual conflict. In the past, a day on the river had always brought a truce. I hoped it would again.

The sun was gaining on the hazy blue sky and I could feel its heat on my bare back. In the skiff, crabs were scuttling about the mud and eelgrass that covered the boat's wooden bottom, looking for space in the limited shade. There was a constant waving and snapping of claws as they sparred for position. A few were locked in combat with their pincers clamped on to opponents' limbs. A number of legs had already been lopped off. For a moment I watched two Jimmies intimidate each other, extending their claws to make themselves seem larger. Like most crab fights, this one appeared senseless; they could have passed each other without doing battle.

Something under the water near the skiff caught my eye. It was a tiny patch of blue in a clump of grass. I brought my net up beside the vegetation. A doubler, a male crab carrying his mate, burst out the other side. The Jimmy swam for cover using his paddle-shaped back legs while clutching the female with his six crawling legs. As my net drew close, he attacked it with his claws while continuing to swim. It was a brave but losing effort. I scooped up the pair and brought them to the boat.

The female was a peeler, a crab about to shed its old shell. More valuable than a Jimmy, a peeler could be used for fish bait, or held in a float until it backed out of its shell as a soft crab.

"Is she rank?" my father said.

I held up the female so he could see the triangle of shell covering her reproductive parts. The normal white color had been replaced with lines of red and blue. "Look at that apron," I said.

He nodded his head. "Yeah, she'll shed tonight."

I dislocated the hinged portion of the female's claws to prevent her from biting, and placed her in a basket with other peelers. I had just finished covering them all with wet eelgrass when my father barked an order.

"Cover those crabs good, I don't want them getting hot." Immediately I felt annoyed. Why did he always have to tell me what to do? I had covered the crabs better than he ever would have. I glared at him but said nothing. Sunburned scalp was showing through the thin spots in his dark, wavy hair. I smiled inside. He pretended not to care about losing his hair, but I knew better.

My next crab, a small male peeler, was buried in the mud with just its eyes sticking out. As I approached with my net, it shot out of its hiding place. I blocked its escape but it quickly darted in three directions, stirring up a cloud of mud. For a short time it disappeared, until the incoming tide cleared the water. Then I could see the animal reburied in the soft bottom with only the outline of its shell visible.

I caught the little male but he was not ready to surrender. As I swung my net through the air toward the skiff, he scrambled over the rim and fell back toward the water. My father had been watching the action. He turned instantly and caught the crab in midair, like a lacrosse player receiving a pass. A half smile came to his face.

"If I have to net them for you, there's not much reason to have you along," he said.

"Looks like more crabs in my end of the skiff than yours," I said.

"Surely you're not going to count those snots you've been catching," he said. Snots were peelers a long way from shedding, and they had little value.

"If you think they're worthless, let me keep the money they'll bring when we sell them."

"It won't be enough to buy a soda," he countered. His smile had grown wider.

"Right, you know you're whipped, you might as well admit it," I said. There was no answer. He just turned and poled toward the next patch of grass. The banter had lightened the mood and I was thankful for it.

Our skiff wasn't large, just sixteen feet long, with barely twelve inches of freeboard. Pointed at both ends, it had no place for a motor, but it was perfect for netting crabs. My father was an expert at poling it. Working from just one side, he kept the little boat on a straight track by touching his net handle to the gunnel on every stroke. Still, it was not easy for him. The bullet fired that night on the Potomac River had severed a nerve, leaving his right arm partially paralyzed. He never talked about it, but I knew he had to concentrate to grip the net handle.

It soon was midmorning and our crabbing day was almost over. My father caught another doubler and sat down to separate the pair.

"Let's eat and then cull off," he said.

I pulled a paper sack of sandwiches out from under my deck. The bologna was warm and a little slimy.

"You should have fried it," he said, with his mouth full. I had made the sandwiches in the early morning while he cooked breakfast.

"If you don't like it, I'll eat yours," I shot back.

He took another bite. "It's not that bad."

Culling meant sorting through the crabs roaming the boat's bottom. Most of them had been caught when the action was fast and there was no time to grade them. Culling was a tricky business—our hands would always be in range of several sets of snapping claws. My father never wore gloves for the job, and he said they were only necessary for timid people. He had developed a hand motion that seemed to mesmerize crabs and they seldom bit him. My technique was not as good, but I never wore gloves in his presence, preferring sore fingers to his ridicule.

I began working through the catch in my end, putting the keepers in baskets and tossing the rest overboard. The soft crabs were easy; with their rubbery claws they were unable to bite. The hard crabs were another matter. Those I pinned to the boat bottom with my foot before grabbing them. The only safe hold on a blue crab was to firmly grasp its back leg near where it attached to the body. Any weakness in the grip would allow the animal to twist around and reach a finger with one of its claws.

Not long into the cull, there was a problem. I was wearing my old canvas tennis shoes with no socks, and there was a hole worn in each one where my little toe stuck out. Two medium-sized crabs were lying together under the boat seat and as I trapped one with my foot, the other one saw my exposed pink flesh and grabbed it. The animal clamped down hard; its pincers began to cut through my skin. I had suffered through many crab bites but none had ever hurt so badly. I held my foot still, knowing that jerking it away would only make the wound worse.

My father was busy trying to determine if a small male crab was a peeler. He was holding it up to the sun, looking for a tell-tale red line on its back leg. He was unaware of my plight and I was glad. If he discovered what was happening, he would only laugh and then tell everyone in the neighborhood. As his oldest son, I was expected to be tough. There had never been any sympathy for small injuries.

I remained still and the crab slowly released its grip. When it let go, I wiped my bloody toe on my pants leg and resumed culling. I pinned my attacker with the bailing scoop, instead of my foot. He was undersized and I turned him loose.

When my father was finished sorting, he looked at the tide. "Let's make one more drift up Geanquakin Creek," he said.

"The breeze is picking up, we'd better put out some oil," I said. "It would improve the visibility. Mix it up."

We had brought along a mayonnaise jar containing a small amount of linseed oil. I filled the jar with water and shook it vigorously, careful to keep my finger over the nail hole punched in the lid. When the contents were mixed, I sprinkled some over the water around the skiff. An oily sheen soon covered the surface, calming the ripples and eliminating the glare. Where a few minutes before it had been difficult to see bottom, now everything was visible. We began to float along in the slick, netting crabs at a fast pace.

The drift ended and my father was poling us back into the river when I spotted a soft crab in deeper water. It was lying in the grass behind its cast off shell. I quickly pushed the boat around for a better angle of attack. A scuffling sound to my rear caused me to look back. I had caught my father off balance and he was thrashing the air with his net, fighting to stay aboard. When one foot slipped off the deck, the outcome was no longer in doubt. His fall started slowly but rapidly picked up speed. He smacked the water hard, stretched out like a breaching whale. The splash was huge, sending spray all the way to my end of the boat.

This was a new turn of events; I had never caused my father to fall in before. For an instant I felt panic, worried about what his mood would be when he surfaced. He had a waterman's pride in not falling overboard, and if his friends found out they would harass him for weeks.

My father stayed under for a long time and I began to wonder why. The ripples from the splash had obscured my vision. He had fallen into the hole at the creek mouth but the water was only five feet deep.

Suddenly I felt a hand grasp my ankle. He had swum under the skiff and come up behind me. I looked down, and he was grinning, unaware that three strands of eelgrass were draped over his head.

"Payback is coming," he said. He jerked on my leg, but not hard enough to pull me in.

"Why? I can't help it if you're clumsy." He pulled my foot a little closer to the deck edge.

"You've muddied the water and I can't see my crab," I protested.

"It doesn't matter, we've got enough. The tide is getting up—let's go home." He released his grip on my ankle and swam to his end of the skiff.

On the trip home I poled while my father sorted the last of the catch. For the first half mile I followed the river shore, working against a rising south wind. After I turned into St. Peter's Creek, the wind and tide were at my back and the next half mile passed quickly. Soon we were in the harbor at the waterfront community of Champ.

The harbor had always been an exciting place; my greatest adventures had all begun there. It was located at a spot where the solid land ended and the marsh began. Barely a hundred yards wide, it was sheltered on the west by a pine woods. From the east bank, two weathered crab wharves ran out toward the channel. One of them was turned up at the end, like the ramp to a motorcycle jump. Heavy ice and a rising tide had lifted its pilings out of the mud the previous winter.

Each crab wharf was attached to the shore by a wooden shanty. Every summer, thousands of soft crabs were packed there for shipment to Baltimore. Attached to the end of one shanty was a tiny store that was covered in corrugated metal and painted lemon yellow. The proprietor sold groceries, gas, and marine supplies. To my relief, he had recently taken down a reward poster for information leading to my arrest. It was another thing I had to tell my father about someday.

There was a third wharf, a substantial structure built by the county for oyster buyers. In the winter, they drove their trucks onto it, to load the day's catch. In the summer it saw little activity, except as a diving platform for me and my friends.

On the creek bank, between the wharves, was a row of wooden skiffs. They were used by the watermen to commute to their larger work boats, which were moored out in the channel. Those graceful, gasoline-powered vessels were the pride of the community, and each was tied to a large wooden stake, settled into the creek bottom by its owner. As we came into the harbor they were swinging gently back and forth in the wind. It was Saturday afternoon and their work was over for the week.

I guided our skiff up to the first wharf and my father unloaded our baskets of crabs. We had decided to sell half of them and eat the rest. It had been a good day. Once again the river had eased the tension between us and I hoped the feeling would last, but I doubted its chances. Maybe it didn't matter; in a few weeks I would be leaving home for good.

2. Romance on the Train

THE RELATIONSHIP BETWEEN ME AND MY FATHER WAS not always strained. In fact, for a long time it was nearly perfect. He gave me the opportunity to grow up as he had, roaming the land and waterways near Oriole, a small village on Maryland's lower Eastern Shore. Even as a child, I knew I was fortunate to be growing up in that Chesapeake Bay environment during the 1950s and 1960s. It offered all the adventure that a boy required with little exposure to the darker side of life. What I did not recognize was how the people of our small community were guiding my rush toward manhood. I was unaware of the battle for my future between the sirens of the Bay and the practical farmers who saw something in me worth saving. When I rebelled against my father's control, other men, from humble watermen to senators, stepped in to give me direction. I had the love of an intelligent, witty mother, and a bossy, supportive aunt, but still I managed to find trouble enough for my frustrated high school principal to predict that I was headed for the state penitentiary.

Our county was Somerset and it is tidewater country, a verdant area of small farms and woodlots, divided by serpentine, marshy rivers. It is a flat land with much of its elevation in single digits. The high spot in our area was a sandy rise in a farmer's field; at sixteen feet above sea level, it was called "Pike's Peak." In many communities, when a hurricane arrived, someone's boat would likely wind up in your yard. Occasionally, coffins floated up and were deposited around low lying neighborhoods. If the deceased made it all the way to his former residence, it was a sign of a troubled soul.

Land as low and flat as ours always had problems with standing water. Our world was crisscrossed with drainage ditches, each tilted imperceptibly downhill toward the river. They were dug to make the land tillable and the quality of the ditches usually determined the productivity of a farm. Even with all that drainage, we wore boots in the wet season.

Before there were effective control programs, mosquitoes could make our lives miserable. In wet summers astonishing numbers hatched, and some evenings giant clouds of the insects appeared over the marsh. Sometimes a parent would drive the neighborhood kids out to witness the spectacle. The high-pitched whine from millions of wings seemed threatening as we watched from the car. Usually we would speculate about what would happen if they all descended on us at once. How many seconds until we were drained of blood? What would we look like with all those holes?

During the warm months, there were always mosquitoes in our yard but they were local insects and somewhat domesticated. My friends and I had learned to ignore their attacks. But on evenings when the marsh mosquitoes ascended and the wind was right, tens of thousands of the insects arrived in our neighborhood. Our backyard ballgame went on as usual, but each of us participated in the same strange dance—rhythmically wiping our arms and legs with our hands and then slapping ourselves on the back.

Inevitably, "Aack, I swallowed a skeeter," came from one of the players. Everyone knew that it meant time out. Our ground rules stated that if the ingestion occurred while running to first base, the batter got another turn at the plate.

In spite of the mosquitoes, native Americans had lived in the area for thousands of years before Captain John Smith made contact with them in 1608. These Algonquian-speaking people lived along rivers that still bear their tribal names—Pocomoke, Annemesssex, Manokin and Monie. My friends and I saw proof of their existence in the arrowheads we discovered along the river shore. I sometimes found delicate bird points on the beach, lying in the debris left behind by the high tide, and I tried to picture the hunter that had lost it. Usually I imagined him crawling through the marsh grass, stalking a Canada goose.

The Indians hunted and grew corn and squash, but the bulk of their diet must have been seafood. They left behind huge piles of oyster shells called middens. Artifacts indicate that at some point they lived and cooked atop the shells. Once, I explored a midden that was being dug up and trucked away for road fill and there were pottery shards throughout most of its six foot depth. I loved oysters and wondered how long it would take to eat that many.

The county's first white settlement was founded in 1662. By the mideighteenth century, slave-holding plantations controlled much of the best farmland. The wealthy planters built stately homes along the river, and many were still standing during my childhood. They were owned by an eclectic group of people, all moneyed refugees from someplace else, looking for a quieter life on the tidewater. They seldom socialized with the natives, preferring each others' company to ours. As a consequence, my neighbors sometimes ridiculed the "big house" owners, making fun of their agricultural practices and ineptness with boats.

When I was a boy most of the men I knew farmed or worked the water, catching crabs in summer and oysters in the winter. Some of my father's relatives were also carpenters and boat builders. Several skipjacks—the famous sail-powered oyster boats—were constructed in the community before I was born.

My father chose another path; he was Captain Tom Noble, Supervisor of Inspectors for the Maryland Tidewater Fisheries Commission. He was a marine policeman, charged with enforcing the state's seafood harvesting laws. Dad had joined the force shortly after being discharged from the Navy at the end of World War II. He started as an inspector but was soon promoted to district supervisor. When he went to work on what everyone called the police boat, he was issued a uniform and a .38 caliber revolver. The boat's only armament was a high caliber military surplus rifle but he soon supplemented that with his own automatic shotgun. In the coming years he would need them all. With rising shellfish prices, the oyster wars that had plagued the Bay for almost a century, flared up again.

Land on the bay side of the county is divided into narrow strips by the rivers. Our strip, one of the widest, is bordered on the north by the Wicomico River and on the south by the Manokin River. A state highway runs down the middle, from the county seat of Princess Anne to the waterfront community of Deal Island. Our house was located on Oriole Road, a thin ribbon of asphalt connecting the villages of Oriole and Champ to Deal Island Road. It was one of seven homes in a little neighborhood that had no name.

We lived in a white bungalow built by my parents after Dad started work on the police boat. The contractor was Harry Noble, a relative, and his chief carpenter was my grandfather, Tom Noble, Sr. The house cost $4,800 and my parents worried if they would ever be able to pay off the mortgage with my father's $30 per week salary.

The building lot was donated to my parents by my father's older sister Hilda, and her husband, Milbert Shockley. Their farm bordered our yard on two sides. My father and some neighbors cut the trees off the lot and grubbed out the stumps with axes and hoes. Two large oak trees were left on each side of the house for shade. One had limbs perfectly spaced for climbing, and it became my refuge and lookout tower. From its top branches, I could survey the river and neighboring farms.

The side yard was filled by our large vegetable garden and I often helped my father plant sweet corn and lima beans. One of my best early memories is of receiving his praise for my work. His approval was easy to come by then.

Our backyard contained no trees or shrubbery in the early years; my father loved baseball and thought every kid should have a place to play. It became the neighborhood diamond even though it was a bit cramped. For a while, a corner of the back steps served as third base but after two broken dining room windows, the base was moved further from the house.

Behind the ball field was a strip of land that my father had once used to raise livestock. When I was seven, my mother convinced him to plant a strawberry patch there for her to manage. Strawberries had once been the largest crop in the county, and they were still profitable on small acreages. For two years my mother marketed her berries, obviously delighted to have her own income. She seemed happier during the strawberry season than at any other time of year. Her joy ended the day my father announced that he planned to build a chicken house on the strawberry land. I overheard the conversation.

"No, Thomas," my mother said. The dismay in her voice was palpable but my father had made up his mind. He wanted more income than his salary alone could provide.

"Milbert is making good money growing chickens—a lot more than your berries bring in," he said.

"Who is going to work in the chicken house?" she said.

"I will, when I'm not on the boat. Maybe you can help out during the day."

Her jaw tightened, "Not on your life."

Dad looked surprised when she put down the cake she had been making and left the house.

* * *

My mother continued to protest, but in the end she signed the note for the chicken house. In a few weeks, they stood together in the backyard watching as a big yellow grader leveled her strawberry patch. After a few minutes, she turned and went inside. The slamming screen door was notice to my father; he had started a feud that would not end for years.

From that summer on, there was a chicken house standing eighty feet from my bedroom window. On warm evenings, I went to sleep listening to the subdued night time sounds of five thousand chickens. Usually it was peaceful, but occasionally a bird would stick its head through the guard on a ventilation fan. I would be jolted awake by a loud "WHANG." The sound of disturbed chickens would fill the air until the decapitated bird completed its struggle. Eventually, better fan guards eliminated the problem. But for a couple summers, my sleep was fitful and I never forgot that "whang."

The closest town for business and shopping was Princess Anne, five miles away. Founded in 1733 and named after the daughter of King George II, it was sited as far up the Manokin River as small, eighteenth century sailing vessels could navigate. It became a center for commerce and county government. The tree-covered streets were lined with impressive, historic houses that my school bus passed every day. The thing I remember most about them was that they were always being painted.

At one time during my childhood, the two-block-long business district had two each of movie theatres, grocery stores, hardware stores, and pharmacies. There were also men's and women's clothing stores and a shoe store. An imposing Greek Revival style courthouse sat on the corner of the main intersection, near the town's only stoplight. Nearby was the Washington Hotel, which was built in 1744 and is still in operation.

The elementary school, a two-story brick structure with four white columns, was located in a residential neighborhood on the west side of town. Surrounding it was a large, tree-shaded playground. The high school was on the north end of Main Street. It was a brick rectangle, framed on each side of the entrance by enormous pecan trees.

If you turned left from our driveway, Oriole Road ran for a mile through fields and woodlots until it reached the cemetery turn. There the asphalt made a sharp right bend around the graveyard where my father's ancestors were buried. It was the new cemetery, started after the old one next to the church filled up. The land was picked because it was two feet higher than the old site. It wasn't selected to get the occupants closer to heaven, but just a little further out of the water.

Down the road from our cemetery was what was then known as the "colored church"–St. James Methodist. Across from it was a hardwood grove, where one Sunday every September more than a thousand people gathered for their annual camp meeting. The faithful came from Baltimore, Philadelphia, and towns in New Jersey. As kids, it was the largest crowd any of us had ever seen. After church, we stood on the roadside to watch the line of cars and buses go by. The celebration lasted all day and the sound of hymns floated our way until after dark.

At the camp ground, the road divided with a spur going left to Champ. It was a watermen's community, and their houses were strung out along the road to the harbor. Many yards contained evidence of the owners trade: boats on blocks, stacks of crab pots or oyster tongs on racks. The wharves were located at the end of the road on the last dry ground. Few people made an effort to farm in Champ, the land being just too low.

Oriole began just past the Champ turnoff. It was a larger community but showing signs of decline; seafood and boat building were fading.

During my early childhood it had three struggling general stores. Mostly they had become social clubs for the men who gathered there every evening to tell stories and play dominoes. My father went occasionally and once he took me along. I remember sitting on a nail keg in the dim light, beside a pot-bellied stove, while my father and his friends talked. Eventually, television and lonely wives ended the store culture.

Our church, St. Peter's Methodist, was the most prominent building in the community. It was white clapboard with a steep roof and a square bell tower over the entrance. The minister was a fire and brimstone preaching Irishman. He had been a hard drinker in his youth, but "saw the light" one day when he was thrown out of a British pub and landed sprawled in the street. He was middle-aged when he got to our church, portly and bald up the middle, with long white hair on the sides. One Sunday, while at full volume, his false teeth flew out. The reverend caught them in his hand, never missing a word. My friends and I fell over in our back pew, dying with laughter. Despite the dirty looks from our parents, the giggling didn't stop until the service ended. On the way home, I received a long lecture from my mother on proper church behavior.

I attended St. Peter's Methodist almost every Sunday until I was sixteen. The parables and bible stories I was taught there helped me develop a code to live by. And it was fun to hear those sunburned farmers and watermen sing hymns, enthusiastically, in no particular key. But as I got older, my interest in organized religion diminished and I spent less time at church.

Next to the church was the home of my father's uncle, Sigsbee Noble. As a patriotic gesture, he had been named after Captain Charles Sigsbee of the battleship *Maine*, which was sunk near the time of his birth. He was a spry man and his ready smile gave the impression that he enjoyed life. Uncle Sigsbee was a well-known boat carpenter, having built many power boats, mostly bateaus and box sterns. As the seafood industry declined, he turned more to farming and began growing strawberries and tomatoes. He never gave up boat building completely; usually there was a skiff or runabout under construction in his backyard.

My father grew up in Oriole during the Great Depression and his family struggled like most of their neighbors. No one went hungry—there were vegetables from the garden and seafood was plentiful—but cash was hard to find. With carpentry jobs scarce, my grandfather turned to the Bay for income. He walked miles across the marsh in freezing weather, trapping muskrats for a few dollars. In the summer he caught diamondback terrapins, a small aquatic turtle used in a dish in fashionable Baltimore restaurants. At their peak, terrapins brought a dollar per inch of length. Wages were a dollar per day, making a six-inch turtle the equivalent to a week's pay. Their numbers rapidly declined, bringing them close to extinction. Somewhere along the way, the terrapin became the mascot of the University of Maryland.

During my father's childhood there were few restrictions placed on children in Oriole. They were free to play in anyone's yard and go into the house for food, even if no one was home. They had free run of the woods and creeks; "no trespassing" signs were nonexistent. Boys were allowed to be mischievous as long as they did not destroy property. One of my father's friends was not fond of school. Occasionally, he would throw a handful of .22 caliber bullets into the woodstove that heated the one room building. By the time they finished exploding, the teacher would be so rattled that she would cancel classes for the day.

I do not remember my paternal grandfather, who died when I was two, but he must have been a caring man. When my father was a child, he was prone to earaches. On nights when they were bad, my grandfather would get out of bed, pull on his hip boots and go down to the creek to gather mussels. He would heat the shellfish on the woodstove until they opened and then pour the warm liquid into my father's ear. Dad said it gave instant relief that lasted all night.

My father's mother was a round, kind woman, who according to Mom, spoiled me at every opportunity. As a good Methodist, she was opposed to all drinking, gambling, dancing and swearing. Once when I was four years old, I went fishing in the ditch in front of our house. It was full to the top with runoff from a large storm. My only tackle was a silver lure with three feet of line attached, and I stood on our driveway bridge, dangling it in the water. There should have been no fish in the ditch, but soon I felt a hard tug on the line. I jerked back and a large white perch, weighing nearly a pound, flipped up onto the bridge.

I grabbed my prize and ran to our house yelling, "I caught a Goddamned ten pound rock." Rock was short for rockfish or striped bass; it was the only fish name I knew. My bad language was probably the result of my night at the store. When my grandmother found out what I had said, she surprised everyone by not being upset. She just laughed and praised me for catching such a nice fish. From that day on I became a fisherman and exaggerating the size of my catch became a habit.

After high school, my father got a job forty miles from home at the Dupont nylon factory in Delaware. Other young men from Oriole worked there, usually to accumulate money to buy a boat or some farm equipment. Few stayed for very long. A childhood in the outdoors made it hard to work behind factory walls.

With a little money in his pocket, my father began to date. He met a pretty, blonde Deal Island girl named Kathleen Thomas, and they started to go out. Her father, Willie Thomas, was a waterman and her mother, Ruth, was a Methodist. Whenever I asked about my parents' dating, Mom would begin the story.

"The attraction between us was strong, but my mother's rules got in the way," she said. "If we went out, I had to be home by ten. If he visited me at the house, he had to leave by ten."

At that point my father would break in. "Miss Ruth would start winding her noisy old clock at 9:45. If I wasn't gone by ten, she would come down the stairs and say, 'Young man, I've worked hard today and it's time for you to go.'"

My parents dated for almost a year before my father got tired of the restrictions and quit calling.

"I was hurt and mad," Mom said. "He shouldn't have given up on me like that."

In a few months, the Japanese bombed Pearl Harbor and my father enlisted in the Navy. He spent the next two years on a landing craft in the South Pacific. He landed troops for more than one invasion, but after the war he mostly talked about the beauty of the islands. Our album contained photographs of Dad and his buddies having fun on leave in Australia. One photograph from his first tour had been enlarged and it hung on the wall in my bedroom. In it, a tall skinny kid that looked a bit like my father was holding a fishing rod and standing beside a huge shark.

After my father went off to war, my mother broke free of Grandma's restraints and moved to Baltimore where she took a job building airplanes at the Glenn L. Martin factory. Her excitement showed every time she talked about living in the city and working on the war effort.

After a year in the Pacific, my father was lonely and he started to write to the girl he had dropped. My mother was still angry and she seldom answered him, but he persisted. Near the end of his tour, he suggested in a letter that they get married. Mom was surprised and not sure how to respond since she already had a new boyfriend. She wrote back but didn't mention his proposal.

Shortly after that, my mother moved to a new apartment on St. Paul's Street. A few days later, when she went back to her old residence to pick up mail, there was a telegram from my father, stating that he was in San Diego and would see her soon. Mom faced a dilemma; he was on his way and she was still unsure of her feelings.

Three days later, another telegram arrived at her old address—Dad was in Chicago and would meet her the next day at the B & O Train Station in Baltimore. The pressure on my mother was building, and she called her older sister for advice.

I think you should see him," my aunt said. "He deserves that, he's been off to war."

"All right, I'll meet him for a few minutes," my mother said.

The next day, Mom went to the station to meet the train. She sat on a wooden bench in the waiting room, looking carefully at every sailor coming through the door from the trains. It had been two years, and she was afraid she might not recognize him. An hour went by and my father never appeared. Mom gave up and went back to her apartment, unaware that Baltimore had two B & O stations.

My father's train arrived on time at the other station, but no one was there to greet him. Not willing to give up, he hailed a cab and went to my mother's apartment, only to be told that she had moved. "Somewhere on St. Paul's Street," the neighbors said, but no one knew the address. He directed the cab to St. Paul's Street and began asking everyone he saw if they knew Kathleen Thomas.

"I ran into every building with women's clothes hanging on the line, but I couldn't find her," he always said.

In the meantime, my mother returned to her apartment building and told her landlord about my father's failure to show. This kind man immediately realized the problem, and drove her to the correct station. They searched the waiting area and the landlord lifted the hats from the faces of sleeping sailors. Each time he asked, "Is this him?" Each time my mother answered, "No."

When it was clear that my father was not to be found, the landlord returned to his building. Mom decided to wait at the station a little longer. As darkness fell outside, she sat alone, surprised to be feeling a sense of loss. She was about to leave when a sailor walked through the door with a seabag on his shoulder, obscuring his face. Something about the way he moved looked familiar. Mom stood up and the sailor turned—it was my father.

By then they were surprised to see each other. The first few minutes were awkward but things warmed up quickly. My father never revealed what he said, but it must have been one of his best moments. After they talked for a while, Mom agreed to accompany him that night on the late train to Princess Anne. Somewhere in the darkness, rolling down the Eastern Shore, he asked her for her ring size. She told him, and three days later they were married.

After several months of temporary duty, my father was ordered to the Port of New York. He and my mother arrived in the city on New Year's Day, 1945. For the next four months they boarded with a Russian-Jewish family, while Dad waited for orders back to the Pacific. It was a cold, snowy winter, but Mom always spoke fondly of that time.

In April, my father shipped out to Pearl Harbor to begin training for the final assault on Japan. It was a tearful separation; my mother was pregnant, and they were both aware of the risks of the invasion. Mom went back to Oriole, moved in with her in-laws, and waited. To everyone's relief, the war ended without the invasion.

Soon after the Japanese surrendered, my father caught a ride back to the States on the battleship *North Carolina*. During the trip he slept in a hammock on deck, exposed to weather, just happy to be going home. He hoped to arrive before I was born, but he was three days late. When he saw me for the first time, my head was still misshapen by the obstetrical forceps.

"Do you think he will ever be normal?" he asked my Aunt Hilda. She reassured him that I would be. But during my teenage years he must have wondered if those doctors had done some permanent damage.

* * *

In August of the year I was five, the first complicating event occurred in my relationship with Dad. I was staying with the Shockleys while my mother was in the hospital. By then my aunt and uncle were like second parents. Their white, two-story farmhouse had become as familiar as my own.

My Aunt Hilda was a talkative, full-figured woman. When she hugged me, I disappeared into her large bosoms where sometimes there was no air. She was the unofficial boss of our extended family, quick to give praise or encouragement, but not afraid to criticize if it was needed.

My Uncle Milbert was a gentle man with a warm smile. His stout body suffered from years of farm work, causing him to walk bent over like a man leaning into a gale. The Shockleys had two sons. The older one, my cousin Harry, was married and lived on his own farm a mile away. Their younger boy, Bobby, was only four years older than I. I looked up to him and followed wherever he led.

Bobby and I were sitting at the kitchen table, putting together a puzzle, when the phone rang. My aunt got up to answer it and Milbert stirred from his after-lunch nap in his easy chair. After a brief phone conversation my aunt turned toward me.

"Terry, you have a new baby brother," she said.

That sounded interesting. I had no idea my mother had been pregnant; all I had been told was that she was getting fat. "Where is he now?" I asked.

"At the hospital, your mother will bring him home in a few days. They're going to call him Danny."

I stood up and started for the back door. "I'm going to build him a crab net," I said.

My aunt laughed. "He won't be able to use it for a while."

I went out to my uncle's shop and looked for materials, but I couldn't find any wire strong enough to make the rim. After a while I gave up, realizing it was beyond my abilities. I may not have known how to build a crab net, but I knew every boy needed one.

3. The Schooner Hits a Storm

 IT WAS SUNDAY AND MY FATHER WAS DRIVING OUR family to my grandparents' house on Deal Island. I loved the trip because there were always some interesting animals to see. I stared out the window as the road took us through woods and cornfields and past the little cluster of houses in Jerusalem and Monie. At the village of St. Stephens the pine trees ended and the open marsh began. It was midsummer and the sea of bright green marsh grass seemed to have no end. I spotted a brood of young ducks in a small pond beside the road and pointed them out to my father.

After two miles on the marsh, the road ran on higher land for a short distance through the village of Dames Quarter. From there it was on the marsh again until Chance, a slightly larger community with two stores. At Chance the road crossed the Deal Island Bridge, which was an old wooden structure with loose boards that clapped and rumbled as cars passed over them. The noise was so loud that drivers sometimes stopped and backed off, afraid that it might collapse.

From the top of the high, arching bridge there was a good view of Deal Island harbor and out across Tangier Sound to the far islands. My father slowed the car and called my attention to the conditions on the Sound.

"Terry, there's an ebb tide and a fresh southwest wind pushing against it. See how high those waves are building? It's rough out there today."

"Why do you always do that? He's so young?" my mother said.

"I'm trying to keep him alive, Kathleen. I've pulled too many drowning victims out of the water. Someday he's going to be on the Sound alone."

Mom looked at me with a strange expression.

Once across the bridge, the road wound through the community of Deal Island, past the watermen's houses, the red brick school and the impressive white church. At the far end of the island sat Wenona, a separate village with its own post office and harbor. My grandparents Willie and Ruth Thomas lived there in a white two-story house. Their yard was separated from the road by a row of hedge. Beside the house was a large maple tree, with a porch swing hanging from its biggest limb. In the backyard were a grape arbor and a shed for storing boat equipment. Behind that was the vegetable garden, a sandy patch that my grandfather had carved out of a myrtle and pine thicket.

My grandfather was sitting in his swing when we pulled into the driveway. He was a jovial man with a hearty laugh and a funny story never far away. His hair was graying but his arms and shoulders were heavily muscled from his work on the water.

"Howdy T," he said with a smile, as I got out of the car. "You're just in time, Ruth has dinner almost ready. We're having turnips." He knew I hated turnips and he laughed when I grimaced.

Mom greeted her father and then went inside to help with the meal. Dad and I sat in the swing with Grandpa. Danny played in the grass with a toy tractor.

"Captain Willie, how was your catch this week?" my father asked. He and Grandpa usually talked about crabs, oysters, or the weather.

"Kind of slack, the first run of peelers is over," Grandpa said. "That's why we're only having beans with those turnips." My father laughed. I could tell he liked Grandpa but I was never sure how he felt about Grandma.

Dad decided to change the subject. "I'm having trouble with Luke again," he said, referring to a waterman they both knew. "I hate to fine him, but he's regularly keeping undersize crabs."

"You're going to have to do it, Tom. That whole family is crooked; his old man would steal lightning and grab at thunder. A fine or jail is the only thing that will get his attention." My grandfather had strong opinions when it came to some of his fellow watermen.

Dad was considering his advice when my grandmother called us to dinner. Grandma was plump, with white hair and wire rimmed glasses that made her look like a stern Mrs. Claus. Her life was devoted to Methodism, and she went to church every day of the week and twice on Sunday. My grandfather never went to church except on very special occasions.

As I walked into the kitchen, Grandma hugged me and whispered in my ear. "Terry, do you know the Lord?"

"I'm not sure," I said.

"You should be sure; it's very important if you want to get to heaven."

Grandma released me and we went into the dining room where she said a long prayer before the meal. Her food was never very good. She thought it was a sin to cook on Sunday, so she cooked the meal on Saturday and warmed it up. The only bright spot was her homemade bread, which is mostly what I ate.

Grandma had a lot of illnesses and she talked about them often. One shelf in her cupboard was full of medicine bottles. Dad said they were mostly sugar pills prescribed by the doctor in Dames Quarter.

After the meal, the men went out to the back porch to talk and I followed them. There was no reason to go outdoors, because if I ran or made any noise, Grandma would come out and stop me. "Remember the Sabbath and keep it holy," she always said.

My grandfather sat down in his wooden rocker and carefully filled his pipe. He struck a large kitchen match by dragging it under the chair arm. With a few puffs, the pipe began to glow and the sweet smell of Sir Walter Raleigh tobacco filled the air. Now he was ready to talk.

"Tom, are we going to have any oysters this fall?"

"I think so; I took the state biologist for a survey last week. The Sound looked good but they were scarce farther up the Manokin."

"Are there any spat on the shells that the state planted near Piney Island?"

I knew the state bought discarded shells from the shucking houses and put them back on the river bottom as a place for baby oysters (spat) to attach.

"They're covered up with them," Dad said.

My grandfather took a few more deep puffs from his pipe. "You know we have a right smart number of oysters here, but it's nothing like I saw in Mississippi," he said. "When I was dredging on that schooner out of Biloxi, we used to fill the hold and pile them high on the deck every day."

"How old were you then?" I wondered why my father asked; we had both heard the story before.

"Seventeen. I learned a lot about sailing and a lot about the world in Biloxi."

My grandfather loved to talk about his time down south. Except for that year, he had lived his whole life on Deal Island. He never owned a car—he walked the two hundred yards to his boat every morning.

"It was hard to get out of that harbor," Grandpa said. "Too many shoals. But after I had been there a month, the Captain started letting me take the helm. I was the only one he trusted. He only let me have her if the wind was fair. If it was against us, he did the job and he was a master at it."

"Did you ever run into any storms?" Dad said. I listened closely, waiting for my favorite part.

"Aye, we did. One day when we were loaded with oysters, a wind came up out of nowhere. Before we could do anything, it ripped the mainsail and tore away the jib. In a few moments, seas were washing over the deck. We tied ourselves to the rail to keep from going overboard."

"How did you keep her afloat?" Dad said.

"The captain didn't want to run before the wind and end up farther out in the Gulf, so we put out the anchor with all the rope we had. It kept her heading into the wind while we shoveled the oysters overboard to lighten the load. It was a bad time; she wallowed in those seas all night. In the morning the wind moderated and we managed to limp home."

I was still picturing the storm when my grandmother walked in. She was ready for her second trip to church; the collection jar for her ladies bible class was under her arm.

"There goes Ruth off to get her soul saved," Grandpa teased. My father stifled a laugh.

"You'd do well to go with me," she said.

"And sit down with that bunch of hypocrites? No thanks. Besides, lightning would hit the steeple if I walked in."

"You'll regret it on judgment day," she said as she went out the door.

Grandpa looked at us and smiled. "If I had the money she's given to that church, I could buy a big house."

Grandpa and Dad talked for a while and Mom joined them, but before long it was time to leave. On the trip home I thought about my grandparents—they seemed to love each other, but I couldn't understand how they were so different.

4. Gunfire on the River

ON THE CHESAPEAKE, MEN FOUGHT AND DIED OVER oysters for nearly a hundred years. Their collective battles, large and small, came to be known as the Oyster Wars. As a Tidewater Fisheries Commission (TFC) officer in the 1950s, my father fought in some of the last skirmishes.

Oysters have been a valuable commodity on the Bay for more than two hundred years. The industry began to develop in the early 1800s, and in those days a waterman's catch was limited only by his ambition and the weather. Immediately after the Civil War, a decreased harvest in New England waters and the advent of steam canning produced a boom in the Bay oyster business.

An entrepreneur named John Crisfield pushed a railroad south through Somerset County to Somers Cove and founded the town of Crisfield. With its proximity to the lower reaches of Tangier Sound, it quickly became a center for the shucking and packing of oysters. A gold rush atmosphere developed as people moved in to make their fortunes. Crisfield soon resembled a western mining town and was well supplied with saloons and brothels. It is fitting that many of the oysters canned there were shipped west to feed miners in the Colorado gold fields. The county's other waterfront communities had oyster packing houses but none of them could rival Crisfield's volume.

In the early years of the industry, the oysters were all harvested with tongs—two opposing rakes with hinged, wooden shafts up to thirty feet long. A waterman lowered his tongs over the side of his boat until they were resting on the river bottom. By opening and closing the shafts, he could collect a small pile of oysters in the rakes. When they were full, he brought them to the surface and dumped them onto a culling platform. Watermen repeated the procedure a hundred or more times each day, and it was all done by muscle power. When the culling board was full, oysters that were large enough to keep were separated from smaller ones and empty shells by breaking them apart with a culling hammer.

In the late nineteenth century a new type of oystering came to the Bay. Large sailing vessels pulling heavy steel dredges began to work the oyster beds. These dredges, pronounced "drudges" by watermen, had teeth that tore deep into the bottom, stripping the beds. Some of the boats were owned by local watermen, but many were the property of New Englanders or the large packing houses in Baltimore. Eventually, over seven hundred dredge boats were at work on the Bay.

Oyster beds were quickly being depleted, and Maryland passed laws restricting dredging to the deeper water, away from the rivers. Most dredge boat captains ignored the law and continued to raid the shallow water beds reserved for tongers. They dared anyone to stop them. Their crews intimidated individual tongers, who could see their livelihood disappearing.

The tongers began to fight back by carrying rifles on their boats and firing at dredgers with small cannons mounted on shore. Before long, most boats on the Bay were armed. By 1870, Maryland had formed the Oyster Navy to protect the dwindling shellfish stocks. They fought pitched battles with the dredgers using machine guns and cannons. Men were killed on both sides, and a number of vessels were sunk, but the state had too few boats and the destruction of the oyster beds continued. Dredgers and tongers went on murdering each other; their corpses were regularly found floating in the Bay.

The Oyster Wars continued with varying intensity into the twentieth century. In the twenties and thirties, oyster prices were low and the violence diminished. A few illegal dredgers continued to work but they switched from sail to power boats. During World War II, many of the state's oyster patrol boats were loaned to the Coast Guard, which reduced enforcement. By then the Oyster Navy had been replaced by the Tidewater Fisheries Commission. At that time, many of the TFC officers were older and not aggressive on patrol. Some would not go out at night when most of the illegal activity occurred.

After World War II, oyster prices increased and there was renewed interest in protecting Maryland's remaining beds. The TFC began hiring returning servicemen who were willing to fight to establish the state's control over its natural resources. My father was one of them. In 1945, Dad and his fellow officers were faced with rough, independent watermen who had been doing things their own way for generations. Some of their fathers and grandfathers had fought in earlier battles of the Oyster Wars. Many believed that any living thing in the Bay should be theirs to plunder as they saw fit.

During the oyster season, there was always tension in our house— I could sense it in my mother's voice. My parents often spoke in low conversations that I was not allowed to hear. They did their best to shelter me from the conflict my father faced on the water, but as I got older, I found out about events past and present. Much of the information came from Dad's fellow officers who often stopped by our house after work. Whenever I could, I listened from another room as they talked with my father. Their respect for him was obvious, even to a boy. I usually picked up a few details about a particular arrest or a boat chase. Later, I would ask my father about the incident and sometimes he would tell me the story. Slowly, I began to understand what life was like for him away from home.

When Dad started work with the TFC, many watermen resented having their boats boarded and their catch inspected. The rougher ones routinely dared the older officers to step foot on their vessel. The challenge was seldom accepted. My father had been on the job only a few months when he was first challenged. The older training officer pulled their patrol boat up beside an oysterman, and Dad requested to board.

"Go to hell, you're not coming on my boat," the man said.

My father never tolerated anyone cursing him. He jumped aboard and hit the man with his fist, knocking him down onto the pile of oysters. After a similar incident with another young officer, word spread that there was new blood in the TFC.

Early in my father's career, a new type of illegal dredging developed called handscraping. The men doing it used fast power boats and small hand pulled dredges. They worked at night on oyster beds reserved for tongers. In a few hours they caught as many oysters as a tonger did in a week.

Late on a cold, still December night, my father and his mate were on the Manokin River searching for handscrapers. They had received information that some were working near Fishing Island. The officers approached the area slowly with all lights off, their only illumination were the stars twinkling in the clear sky. Dad cut the patrol boat's engine to listen for any sound in the darkness. He could hear the low rumble of a boat motor nearby.

My father eased his boat toward the sound and turned on his searchlight when he thought they were close. The beam caught two oystermen, not thirty yards away, in the act of pulling their dredge aboard. They were surprised by the light but quickly recovered. With two steps, the dredger reached the wheel of his boat and pushed the throttle open. The engine roared and the vessel picked up speed.

Dad gave his mate the helm and stepped out of the cabin with his rifle. His plan was to shoot the fleeing boat's engine and crack the block; it was the only method a single patrol boat had for stopping a fast handscraper. As usual, the boat's identification numbers were covered. If it got away there would be no way to find it. My father waited for an opportunity to shoot, but the men stood between him and their engine. Frustrated, and not ready to kill a man over an oyster, he went back to the helm.

By now the boats were a hundred yards apart, speeding down the river. It was obvious the handscraper was faster and the distance between them was widening. The oystermen were still visible in the searchlight beam, and Dad and his mate could see the men taunting them, waving goodbye. At that point the lawbreakers must have felt confident, but they made a mistake. Unable to see the outline of the shore because of the light, they turned inside of Cormal Point and headed up a dead-end creek. The little waterway quickly narrowed and the marsh closed in on both sides. My father thought he had them trapped, and he turned his boat sideways across the creek to block their escape.

The oystermen realized their error and tried a sharp left turn, but the creek was too narrow. The bow of their boat smacked into the marsh, continuing several feet up onto the muddy bank. With the impact, the men fell forward but they soon scrambled to their feet. The mate jumped ashore and ran off into the darkness. The captain, unwilling to give up his boat, reversed his engine at full power. A column of muddy water erupted from the stern. Slowly the vessel eased off the bank. It regained forward momentum, and picked up speed coming down the creek.

"Damn, I think he's going to ram us," my father's mate yelled.

Dad, having the same idea, grabbed his shotgun and stepped up on to the washboard. When the oncoming craft was fifty yards out, he began to empty the five-shot automatic directly at the little cabin where the waterman was crouched. On the fifth shot, the handscraper turned, passing within three feet of the rear of the patrol boat. He made his escape out of the creek. My father and his mate resumed the chase, but again the boat outran them. It eventually reached the limit of their searchlight beam and disappeared. They continued on the same course for a while but saw nothing. Reluctantly, they gave up for the night.

Shortly after dawn they were back on the river, searching. After checking the major harbors with no success, they began looking in more out-of-the-way places. Within a few hours, they found the boat hidden far up a small marsh creek, called a gut. Its wooden cabin had been shredded by shotgun pellets. With that as identification, my father confiscated the boat and towed it back to Champ. The state would later sell it.

No one was ever arrested for the events of that evening, but it was a major loss for the oysterman and an early victory for my father.

5. Grandpa Bites a Crab

OYSTER SEASON CLOSED IN THE MIDDLE OF APRIL, ALONG with the packing houses. Illegal dredgers stopped work because there was no place to sell their catch. To my father, spring meant a break from night patrols and more time at home. Crabbing began in May and it was a relaxed time, with little danger of violence. The tension in his face melted away with the warm sun.

Even with the mild weather, life for commercial crabbers was not easy. All three methods of crabbing—pots, scrapes and trotlines—required hard or unpleasant work. Everyday, crab potters pulled hundreds of their chicken wire traps to the surface by hand. They rebaited them while trying to avoid the stinging tentacles of jellyfish caught in the wire. On windy days, salt spray mixed with bits of jellyfish turned their faces bright red.

Scrapers caught their crabs by pulling toothless dredges (scrapes) over the grassy flats. Their boats were specially designed for shallow water. Crabs and other marine life, as well as grass dislodged from the bottom, were caught in the net on the back of the scrape. When the waterman judged the net to be full, he hauled the heavy scrape aboard by hand, dumping the contents into a cull box on the boat's washboard. This act was the hardest physical labor found in any form of crabbing.

Trotliners made their living by setting long lines on the bottom with baits tied at three-foot intervals. Bait was usually a piece of salted eel or a hog choker, a small flounderlike fish. Less desirable was the salted cow's stomach called tripe. To me, trotlining was the most exciting because it required the waterman to net each crab as the line brought it to the surface. It was an art and a lot of the catch could be lost if you were clumsy at it. The unpleasant part occurred at days end when the line had to be rebaited. By then, the pieces of eel and hog choker had been reduced to skeletons. Loosening the knots holding the baits was difficult with fingers already raw from crab bites. The most painful part for the trotliner was plunging his hands into the salt of the bait barrel. After the initial shock, they ignored the discomfort and got on with the chore that was keeping them from dinner.

In spite of the hard work and discomfort, it would have been difficult to find a crabber willing to give up his job as long as he could make a living. They loved being on the water and they loved having the prospect of a big day's catch. But my father said the main reason they were there was because no one was telling them what to do.

* * *

During the summer that I was eight, my father often took me to work with him, usually on days that he planned to stay in port. He had just gotten a new patrol boat named *Somerset*. At forty-one feet, with twin gas engines, it was the fastest TFC vessel on Tangier Sound. Dad spent several weeks getting the new vessel in top shape; he and his fellow officers had to do their own painting and maintenance.

While my father was working, I always had free run of the harbor and spent most of my time crabbing. At low tide I waded the shallows, dipnetting; as the tide rose I set baited lines from the wharves. Each time I caught a crab, I put it in my rusty bucket and carried it back to Dad. He would examine it and tell me where it was in its life cycle. Slowly, I learned to tell rank peelers from snots and hard crabs from buckrams. The latter were crabs that had recently been soft and were rehardening. Their new, shiny-white undershells would buckle when squeezed, and their meat was watery, which prevented them from being sold.

No matter what type of crab I brought to my father, he always had some praise for me. It was never lavish, but just a "not bad" was enough to send me off with a grin, determined to catch something even better.

Later in the day, I would wander into the crab picking house to watch the women at work. They sat at tables piled high with steamed crabs, talking constantly, seemingly paying no attention as their hands operated knives separating the white meat from the skeletons. If one of them spotted me, I would usually be teased until my face turned red, then someone would make amends by getting me a soda.

From there, I would walk out back to watch the man empty the big crab steamer. He would open a valve, letting out a large cloud of steam, and the smell of cooked hard crabs would almost overwhelm me. After the steam pressure was down, he would open the cooker and roll out the wire basket containing nearly twenty bushels of the bright red crustaceans. I would help him push it out to the edge of the dock, where the crabs were allowed to cool in the breeze coming off the sound.

At the other end of the picking house, there was a pile of discarded crab parts called chum. Periodically, a truck would haul it away to the fertilizer plant. If it was left too long, the odor could make anyone gag. In the spring, our school bus would occasionally meet a load on its way out and our driver would yell "chum truck." We would all scramble to close the windows before the bus filled with the smell.

Sometimes, in the summer, my father would take me out on patrol. On those mornings, we would rise at dawn and leave for Deal Island without eating. During the trip across the Sound, the mate would take the helm and Dad would cook bacon and eggs in the little galley. Usually we would eat in Holland Straits, a passage through the outer marsh islands where many of the scrapers worked. I never forgot those breakfasts, sitting in the early morning sun, watching the crab boats with the gulls whirling around them.

One day my father pointed out a white speck in the distance that he said was my grandfather's boat. His ability to identify vessels always impressed me; he seemed to know every one on the Sound.

"Would you like to go aboard Captain Willie's boat while I check the crabbers?" he said. I quickly agreed, always glad to see my grandfather.

As we approached Grandpa's boat, it was running about one-third speed, dragging two crab scrapes behind it. He was bent over the washboard culling his catch and he looked up as we drew near. The water was shallow and the *Somerset's* propellers churned mud as the mate brought her alongside. My father and I stood on the washboard.

"Captain Willie, can you take him for a while?" Dad asked.

"T, come aboard," my grandfather said. His deep voice boomed loud, almost drowning out the engines.

As the two vessels ran side by side, Dad lifted me under my arms and handed me across the water to Grandpa. I had no fear, these were two men I could count on. When I was safely aboard, my grandfather put me down.

"I don't have much to eat. Ruth just gave me a pack of saltine crackers this morning," he said. I knew he wasn't telling the truth.

My grandfather adjusted his straw hat and went back to work, his corncob pipe clenched in his teeth. He stepped onto the washboard and began to pull in a scrape, working hand over hand down the manila rope. Muscles bulged in his arms as he drew it on board. The net bag was full of eelgrass and he struggled to dump it. When it was empty I went over to help him cull.

I had just begun to pick through the grass, looking for crabs, when I felt a sharp pain in my index finger. A small drop of blood appeared on the tip, as though a doctor had pricked it for a blood sample. Grandpa saw me squeeze it.

"Looks like a grass shrimp got you," he said. "They flick their tail and drive the point on the front of their shell into your skin." He showed me the inch-long animal wiggling on the washboard.

"I wish he was big enough to eat," I said.

"Don't feel bad," he said. "A sook got me good this morning." A sook was a mature female crab, distinguished by her bright red claw tips. They were quick to bite and slow to let go.

"She pinched my index finger with one claw and when I tried to get her off, she caught my other index finger with her second claw." He showed me his injured fingers.

"What did you do?" I said.

"Well, there I was trapped, unable to use either hand. I tried everything—laying her on the washboard, holding her under water. Nothing worked, she just clamped down harder."

"How did you get her to let go?"

"The boat was running and the scrapes were out, so I had to do something soon. After a couple minutes, I took a big bite right out of the middle of her. In a few seconds the claws started to relax and I could pull free."

I was beginning to suspect that he was teasing and telling me another tall tale. "What happened to the crab?" I asked.

"Behind that basket." He pointed to the front of the boat's cockpit.

I moved the basket and found a dead sook with a semicircle missing from the front of its body. The eyes, mouth parts and brain were gone.

"You weren't kidding. How did she taste?"

"Kinda salty," he said, grinning. "You want something to eat? I'd like to get that taste out of my mouth." He pulled the scrapes aboard and stopped the engine. We culled off, and shared a sandwich and some conversation about school.

After our break, Grandpa let me keep the little fish I found while culling. I filled a bucket with water and it was soon occupied by baby eels, oyster toads, and flounders. He had another bucket in which he kept busters. They were peelers that had already begun to shed. Their old shell had popped open and the rubbery back of the soft crab was visible. Busters could only shed in water and would die if handled like typical peelers. For an hour, I regularly changed their water and watched as two soft crabs backed out of their old shells.

In the early afternoon, Dad returned and I was handed back aboard the patrol boat.

"Did he give you any trouble?" Dad said.

"No, Tom, he's good help but he eats too much."

"At least I didn't eat any raw crabs," I said. Grandpa laughed and my father looked puzzled.

On the return trip across the Sound, Dad and his mate were talking about a man they had just ticketed for keeping undersized crabs.

"Did you ever have to arrest Grandpa?" I said.

"No, son, I've checked his catch a few times and he's straight as they come." Happy with his answer, I crawled into a bunk and lay down. The gentle roll of the *Somerset* carried me into a contented sleep.

6. Angry Mob on Smith Island

 THE THIRD GRADE SHOULD HAVE BEEN A BREEZE—MY teacher was young and attractive and she liked me. My grades were good and I was given important jobs like washing the blackboard. And it would have been a great year, if not for Savilla Powell, the principal.

Mrs. Powell was tall and straight, with well-permed gray hair and thick glasses. She had a fondness for bright red lipstick and sweaters and shoes that matched it. The school was a quiet and orderly place; she spanked without hesitation and usually without warning. During my first two years under Mrs. Powell's rule, I did nothing to attract her attention. But in the third grade I sometimes noticed her staring at me on the playground, as though she disapproved of my behavior.

There was a new boy in our class that year named Louis. He was older and stronger, but we became playground friends. One day we were on the far side of the schoolyard, playing rough on the seesaws, when Louis decided to get clever. While I was at the highest point, he stepped off his end, letting me crash to the ground. He laughed as I lay there rubbing my bruised backside.

I got up and ran toward him, seeing nothing funny in the situation. Just as I was about to tackle his upper body, he ducked and I slid over his back, landing against a pecan tree. I realized that this kid was tricky and playing with him was painful.

On my next try, I hit Louis a bit lower and managed to get him to the ground. We wrestled in the grass for a while, neither of us able to pin the other. Suddenly he stopped fighting and looked over my shoulder with fear in his eyes. I rolled over and saw Mrs. Powell breaking a switch off a nearby tree. Her upper lip was curling as it often did when she was mad. We jumped to our feet as she strode toward us.

"You know there is a rule against fighting. I'm going to teach you a lesson you won't forget."

There was a swishing sound, followed by a "pop" as she brought the switch down on Louis's pants. It must have hurt more than he expected because he hopped in the air and let out a yelp. I snickered without thinking.

"Funny, is it?" she said, turning my way. Her first blow convinced me there was nothing humorous.

"Get into the school right now," she said.

We started walking and she switched us every few steps. We walked faster but she kept up with us, in her red high heels. By the time we got to the school, the backs of our legs were burning but neither of us cried. She took us to the auditorium and pointed at two chairs.

"You're going to sit there during every recess for the next two weeks."

My spirits fell even further; being confined indoors all day was as bad as being switched.

That afternoon on the school bus, I pleaded with the neighborhood kids to keep my whipping a secret. My father had promised me another one at home if I ever got one at school. The teachers had my father's full support. Thankfully, the kids' code of silence held and he never found out.

* * *

Tangier Sound is separated from the Bay by a low-lying chain of islands. Two of them are inhabited: Smith Island in Maryland and Tangier Island in Virginia. Smith Island residents lived isolated lives, eight miles from the mainland, relying entirely on seafood harvesting for income. More than any other watermen, they believed the state should leave them alone to work the Bay as they saw fit. In 1883, their ancestors had fought a major gun battle with a Virginia police boat that pursued illegal dredgers back to the island. Twenty-five men with rifles set up fortifications and held the policemen at bay. Eventually the officers gave up and sailed away.

In the 1950s, Smith Islanders intimidated less aggressive TFC officers by putting out an illegal dredge near the police boat and daring
the officers to try to arrest them. One of my father's mates said, "When
we first started, the farther you got from Deal Island, the less law there
was, and by the time you got to the bay side of Smith Island, there
wasn't any."

One day in December of my third grade year, I got off the school bus
and saw our car in the driveway, indicating my father was home early. I
went into the house and found my parents arguing.

"Thomas you don't have to go over there, those Smith Islanders
might kill you," Mom said.

"I don't care. I saw him handscraping today and I would have
arrested him if those other boats hadn't interfered," my father said.
He was chewing on the inside of his lip like he always did when he
was mad.

"But why do you want to risk your life over an oyster?"

"It's not just that, Kathleen—he cursed me this afternoon and we're
going to arrest him tomorrow." There was finality in Dad's tone; he had
decided on a course of action, and my mother knew it was useless to
argue more. He picked up his paper and went to the living room.

It would be some time before I found out the details of that day and
the one that followed. It seems that my father and his mate had spotted
a Smith Islander handscraping in Kedges Strait, a passage just north of
the island. His mate at the time was Roland Muir, another war veteran
from Oriole. They had begun pursuit, but the dredger ran his boat in
among other Smith Island vessels working nearby. Those boats surrounded the lawbreaker, preventing my father from getting close
enough to board. It was a tense situation; the officers were outnum-
bered five to one. To get to the man, they would have to fight their way
across several boats and maybe use their weapons. Dad could identify the dredger and his boat, so he decided to withdraw and arrest the
man later.

Backing down was not easy for my father. As he forced the *Somerset* through the seas toward Deal Island, he regretted his choice and
his anger grew. Once in the harbor, he called the TFC office in Annapolis for support. They promised to call him at home later in the day. I
had interrupted my parents' conversation just after the call. Head-

quarters had decided to send just one man to help with the arrest, and he was coming the next day by seaplane. My mother was upset because there would only be three officers to go ashore on Smith Island to face an unknown resistance. In later years they would have the support of the state police, but not this time.

The following day was Saturday and my father knew the dredger would be back in the port by noon. He had arranged to meet the seaplane at one o'clock. As he brought the *Somerset* into Smith Island, the view was idyllic with the December sun shining on the white clapboard houses. The plane was anchored just outside the harbor, bobbing in a light breeze. It had arrived an hour early and the islanders were alerted. A group of thirty men were gathered on the shore near the wharf. Dad eased the patrol boat up to the seaplane's pontoon; his superior officer, Mr. Sutton, grabbed the bow rail and awkwardly pulled himself aboard. He worked his way down the washboard, past the cabin, to the cockpit.

"Tom, it looks like we've got a welcoming committee," he said.

"Yeah, and I'm not sure what they might do. So far, I haven't seen any guns," my father said.

"How do you think we ought to play this?" the superior officer asked nervously. He kept looking back toward the crowd.

"It will be best to leave Roland on the boat with the rifle. You and I will just have to go ashore and confront them."

"Do you think they will attack us?"

"It's very possible, are you ready to fight?" my father said. He studied his boss for signs of fear.

"Tom, I'm more of a talker than a fighter."

"Well I damn sure hope your tongue is in tune today," Dad said.

My father brought the *Somerset* up to the end of the longest wharf. Mr. Sutton tied one bow rope to a piling using a quick release knot. Roland sat down on the cabin roof with his rifle. Dad gave his mate instructions in a voice loud enough to be heard on shore. "If they attack us, fire the first shot over their heads; if they don't stop, empty the rifle into the crowd."

Roland was having doubts. "Tom, do we have to do this?" he asked quietly.

"Hell yes—I'm tired of them flaunting the law."

When the two officers reached shore, they were surrounded by angry watermen. The mob threatened them with physical violence and yelled about how the state was interfering with a man's ability to make a living. Dad and his boss held their ground.

"The oyster laws protect everyone, including you men. If the beds are destroyed your way of life will change forever," Mr. Sutton said. "This man was handscraping in an area reserved for tongers and he has to be arrested."

"You're never going to take a man off this island," one hothead shouted.

"Oh yes we are," my father said, stepping forward. The crowd backed up a little.

The confrontation lasted for half an hour while Roland waited nervously. Mr. Sutton's tongue must have been in tune, because in the end, the dredger surrendered without a fight. It was an important message to Smith Islanders that their isolated home was no longer a refuge from the law. They still escaped there often enough, disappearing in the web of marshy creeks during pursuit, but after that day, they knew if they were identified, someone might come ashore to get them.

My father liked many Smith Islanders and he respected their self-reliant attitudes. His problems were always with the hard-core group that refused to honor any oyster conservation laws. But, regardless of whether they were good guys or outlaws, when their boats were missing, Dad and his fellow officers went out to search, night or day, often in terrible weather. In those days the Coast Guard didn't conduct searches on the Bay; there was no helicopter to fly out and look for the missing.

One morning, a month after the dredger's arrest, Dad received a call that two Smith Island tonging boats were three days overdue. The men's wives reported that they had probably been working in the Kedges Strait area. The weather was extremely cold and most of the Sound was frozen over. My father's wooden patrol boat was not much of an icebreaker. The sheet metal attached along its sides only provided limited protection. He wasn't sure if he could get to the men but it was his duty to try.

Before leaving Deal Island, Dad stocked the galley with groceries, aware that he and Roland could be trapped by the ice for days. Slowly, the *Somerset* cut its way out of the harbor and into the Sound. After a mile, the hard ice turned to slush and my father increased his speed a little. For a while the going was easier, but as they neared South Marsh Island the ice again turned solid. This time it was thicker.

My father slowed the *Somerset's* engines and inched along, listening to the ice scrape along the hull, hoping that the metal sheeting would hold. If it didn't, the boat would be damaged or might even sink. After a tense hour, they rounded a marsh point and found the two boats, trapped in a small area of open water.

To the officers' amazement, the watermen were still tonging, even though their boats were almost covered with oysters. Uncertain of their fate, but with nothing else to do, they had just continued working. Their supplies were down to a can of beans, some crackers and less than a gallon of fresh water.

For the remainder of that day the *Somerset* broke ice, leading the boats back to their village on Smith Island. It was the same harbor where the officers had been threatened a month before. This time the people on the shore appeared happy to see them.

7. Endless Supply of Nails

 MY MOTHER ALWAYS TOOK CARE OF MY EVERY NEED. SHE provided a warm environment that I could come home to when I tired of my adventures in the outdoors. She cooked my favorite foods anytime I asked. When I arrived home from school, Mom was always there, usually with a slice of cake and a glass of milk on the table. She nursed me through stomach aches, measles and chicken pox. Even with all her efforts, by age eight my attention was entirely focused on the men in the community. I wanted to be around them, to hear their conversation or help them with their work.

As time went on, men other than my father began to affect what I was to become. One of the first was Pud Pusey, a retired logger who owned the school bus I rode on. He was a short, stocky man who seemed to have a cigar permanently attached to his lips. I had seen him a few times at the store, but his gruff demeanor made me keep my distance. One morning as I ran up the bus steps, I was surprised to find him behind the wheel. Our regular driver was sick and he was filling in. As I came aboard, he said nothing; he just watched me and chewed on his cigar. I quickly moved to a seat, noticing that the bus was quieter than usual. My cousin Bobby got on at the next stop and sat down beside me.

"Don't misbehave," he said. "If you do, Mr. Pusey will put you off along the road and you'll have to walk home." Mr. Pusey had once been the regular driver and stories of his reputation had been passed down. The trip to and from school that day was about as quiet as church.

In a few weeks school was over for the year. One day in mid-summer, my father and I stopped by Oriole's last remaining store for a soda. While Dad talked to the owner about his lack of customers, I wandered among the groceries. The bell on the door jingled and Mr. Pusey came in. He glanced at me and walked over to the hardware section. I moved toward the meat case and stared at its only contents, some shriveled up sausages. In a minute, I was startled by a tap on my shoulder and I turned around to see Mr. Pusey standing behind me.

"Here boy," he said, handing me a bag of nails. "Do you think you can make use of these?"

"Yes sir," I stammered, not sure what he meant.

"I figured a boy your age can find something to build. When you use those up, I'll get you some more."

"Thanks," I said, looking into the bag of shiny sixpenny nails. Mr. Pusey chuckled and winked at my father.

On the drive home, Dad had a warning for me. "It was nice of him to give you those nails but don't let me find any in my tires."

For the next two weeks, I pestered my father to help me build something. Carpentry work didn't seem to appeal to him but he finally relented. Together, we constructed a wooden box-trap for rabbits. He let me do most of the sawing and nailing. It was too early in the year to be trapping rabbits, but I pleaded and he agreed to help me set it in the Shockleys' woods.

"You have to turn loose any you catch, they still have babies," he said.

The next morning the door of the trap was down and a hole was chewed through it. I had caught a squirrel, but he had let himself out. Since I needed to build a new door, I decided to build an additional trap. It took most of a day for me to make a lopsided copy of the original version, but I was proud of it. The rabbits must have liked it too, because I caught my first one in it.

I never knew why Mr. Pusey started giving me nails but he made good on his promise to keep me supplied. Every few months, he would see me playing in the yard and stop his old pickup out front. He never said much; he just gave me a cigar-laden grin and handed me a bag of nails through the truck window. His generosity had a lasting impact. With an unlimited supply of nails, I was always looking for scrap lumber and finding new projects. Pud started me on a building habit that I was never able to break.

* * *

One summer my father moored the *Somerset* at Wenona harbor, which gave me a new waterfront to explore. I spent much of my time at the crab shanties, watching the men pack the soft crabs for shipment. After sorting them by size, they laid them out in rows in wooden boxes. Each layer of crabs was covered with wet eelgrass to help them survive the trip to Baltimore.

The shanty men seemed to like me, probably because my grandparents lived in Wenona. A couple of them regularly asked about my mother, and they seemed unhappy with my father for taking her off the Island. One of the shanty owners, Mr. Webster, sometimes took me out in his skiff as he checked his floats for new soft crabs. Floats were wooden cages moored in shallow water, each containing fifty or more peelers waiting to shed. They were enclosed by a wooden fence, called a pound, that blocked waves and protected the crabs as they backed out of their shells.

I always watched carefully as Mr. Webster moved his net among the peelers, lifting out the soft crabs. I learned to identify them by their color and sluggish movements. He began to let me catch some. One day, I was able to pick out all of the soft crabs in a float with no mistakes.

"You're getting good at this, maybe I'll give you a job in a few years," he said. "Would you like to be a crab shedder?"

"Yeah, it's fun."

I had never thought much about what I would do as an adult, but Mr. Webster had planted a seed; after that I considered crab shedding as a possibility.

* * *

On days when I did not go to work with my father, I could usually be found on the Shockley farm, playing catch with Bobby or helping him with some chore Milbert had assigned. Often we were joined by the Bates brothers—two skinny, white-haired boys like me, who lived on the neighboring farm. Billy was a year older than I and Johnny was three years older. When the four of us were together, much of our time was spent playing cowboys and Indians in the barn. It would have collapsed into a pile of splinters if all the imaginary bullets we fired had been real.

One July day, I was hanging around as Milbert assembled a crew to haul bales of wheat straw. He always hired neighborhood boys to help with farm chores and they liked working for him. The group ranged in age from eighteen down to nine or ten; I could hardly wait to be old enough to join. Johnny and Billy were already members. If the older boys were involved in something—work or play or mischief—I wanted to be there.

On this hot afternoon, my uncle was one person short of a full crew. My cousin Harry had been baling for two hours and there were already over a hundred bales on the ground. Thunder clouds were building over the Bay and my uncle needed to get his straw in the barn before the rain. He took a long look at me.

"Terry, how would you like to drive the truck?"

I was shocked and thrilled, but there was a problem. "I don't know how to drive," I said.

"I'll show you what to do; you just have to steer between the rows of bales."

Milbert opened the door to the farm truck, a dark green 1947 Ford. I climbed in and slid over to the middle of the seat; he sat behind the wheel and started the engine. My heart was racing as he gave me instructions. I tried to concentrate, but the world appeared fuzzy, his voice coming from far away. When he was finished, he set the throttle and let out the clutch. The truck started to roll and he stepped onto the running board.

"You'd better start driving," he said with a smile. He motioned for me to slide behind the wheel. "Now just don't hit a bale. At the end of the field, I'll help you make the turn."

He stepped off the running board and disappeared from view. The old truck lumbered along at walking speed. Up ahead, the bales seemed too close together for the wheels to pass between them. I tried to steer in a straight line, but the truck always went toward one bale or another. I struggled with the wheel and somehow managed to miss them. The pressure was intense.

Occasionally, one of the boys picking up bales on the ground would come forward enough to be visible at my side window. They would look at me and laugh. Finally, Bobby stepped on the running board and calmed my nerves.

"Relax, you're doing okay," he said. "But loosen up on that wheel, your fingers are turning white."

After that, my tension subsided a little. I began to notice the sweet smell of the straw. It felt good to be part of the crew. A bumble bee came in the open window and bounced across the windshield. It sounded angry and I was glad when it found a way out.

My fear started to return as the truck approached the end of the field—I could see bales blocking my path and there was no opening to make a turn. Beyond the bales was a large ditch. Where was Milbert?

In desperation I veered left but I felt the rear wheels go over a bale. The truck rocked and the boys on the back yelled something I couldn't understand. I was sure the entire load must have spilled. The only part of my uncle's instructions still in my head were "If you want to stop, turn off the switch." It was my only option; my legs were too short to reach the pedals. Another bale was approaching fast. I fumbled around the steering column for the switch lever and found it. When I flipped it off, the slow-moving truck stopped immediately. Just as it came to rest, Milbert opened the door.

"I hit a bale, did the load fall off?" I blurted out.

"Don't worry, only two fell off and we can easily rebale the one you ran over," he said.

"Why didn't you come back?"

"Harry was having trouble with the baler and I had to help him fix it," he explained. "You did a fine job driving. Turned off the switch just like I said. I think you're going to be a good man at the wheel." My uncle always had a way of making people feel better about themselves.

I continued to drive for the rest of the afternoon and it went smoothly. During a soda break, the older boys teased me about hitting the bale. Their comments were good natured and they helped to ease my embarrassment. At the end of the day, I felt like a regular member of the crew and I was proud and anxious to tell my parents. I didn't see how life could be any better.

8. Rescue in the Strawberry Patch

FROM THE TIME I WAS NINE, DAD SEEMED DETERMINED to accomplish two things: teach me to work so I would become a productive member of society and keep me under control to prevent me from embarrassing the family. He started the work training early with help from Uncle Milbert and some other neighbors. My father insisted that I do useful labor for any money received—there was never any allowance at our house. "One of the most important things a boy can learn is the value of a dollar," he said more regularly than I cared to hear.

When the next spring came, I needed some cash. My truck driving wages were long gone, spent on a necklace for a cute fourth grade girl with a pony tail. She was my first real girlfriend. I was broke and the church bus trip to Ocean City was just over a month away. I wanted to accumulate money to play the arcade games on the boardwalk. One night at supper I brought up the subject.

"Dad, I need money."

"What for?"

I explained my reason. He shook his head and smiled. "Why don't you pick strawberries for Uncle Sigsbee? He's paying ten cents a quart. You could make a couple dollars tomorrow."

"Tomorrow is a school day," I said.

"Well don't go to school," he said matter-of-factly.

That was all I needed to hear; making money and skipping school was too attractive to refuse. Older kids often missed school to pick strawberries during the harvest. It was still an important crop, and most farmers had at least one field of berries for springtime income.

The next morning, my mother woke me at six. She had breakfast on the table by the time I finished dressing. I ate quickly; pickers had to be in the field by seven. It was a cool May morning with a mist off the river and I shivered as I pedaled my bike toward the farm. I was uneasy, having never picked for anyone except my mother before.

When I arrived at the field, the smell of ripe strawberries filled the air. Twenty-five pickers were already there, an equal mixture of blacks and whites. Most of them were gathered around Sigsbee's partner, Preston Lawrence, who was handing out baskets and assigning rows. Preston was a tall, lanky man who sang in the church choir. He was a part-time barber and had cut my hair for years. I stood at the back of the group while he took care of the others. Some were already in the field, placing empty baskets in their rows. They were moving slowly, the way people do when they know another day of hard work lies ahead.

When Preston finished, he looked at me.

"Master Noble, do you want to pick today?"

"Yes, I need to make some money."

"Oh my blessed, don't we all. Follow me and I'll get you started." He handed me a short stack of quart baskets and we walked to where the green rows began. He picked a few berries and held them in his open hand. "Don't pick any smaller than this one and none greener than that one," he said, pointing as he spoke. "Pick both of your rows as you go down the field, and don't put any stems in the basket."

"Yes sir."

"I expect you to finish these rows before you quit."

"I can do it," I said, not really sure.

He smiled and patted me on the shoulder. "Good luck."

Nothing grows much lower to the ground than strawberries, and to get at them I worked on my knees. After half an hour, my legs were aching and I had filled only one basket. Worse, I was only a few feet from my starting point. I was beginning to wonder how I would ever finish the rows. A black woman, wearing a long dress and a straw hat, was working the rows next to mine. Her name was Leezy Maddox. She was already a third of the way down the field. On her way to the packing shanty, carrying a tray with baskets full of berries, she stopped. "Boy, you've got to pick faster than that. Keep both hands working or you'll never get done." She set her tray on the ground and began to pick in my rows. I watched how her hands raced through the green leaves. In a moment, she dropped two handfuls of fruit into my basket. It was encouraging to see it fill up so fast. "Try it like that," she said.

I barely knew this woman even though she and her husband, Clemmon, were our closest black neighbors. Whenever I stopped by their house, she stayed inside while her husband and I sat on the porch, talking about fishing and how he wanted me to catch him a big snapping turtle to eat. I had already caught two in a ditch near our house. Clemmon was a tall, well-built man with an easy laugh. Always a snazzy dresser, he was fond of Panama hats and shiny brown and white shoes.

After receiving Leezy's instructions, I filled the baskets a bit faster, but I was still the slowest picker in the field. The day began to warm and I removed my top shirt. It wasn't long before the skin on my forearms began to sting. Leezy walked by again and saw me rubbing them.

"It's that dog fennel weed causing your arms to sting. It doesn't usually bother colored people but white folks get a rash," she said with sympathy. She pointed out the white flowering plant growing in the space between my rows.

I went back to work, trying to avoid the fennel, but I was getting hungry so I ate a berry. It tasted good and I ate more. For a while I ate more than I put in my basket. That ended when my stomach began to churn. With stinging arms and a bellyache, my enthusiasm for strawberry picking hit a new low.

To ease my stomach, I stretched out on the ground for a few minutes. When I looked up again, there was a full basket of berries sitting between my rows. Clemmon had come over to talk with Leezy, and he had decided to help me out. He filled two more of my baskets before going back to his part of the field.

The sight of those full quarts lifted my spirits and I became determined to finish. I went back to work and began to feel better. By late morning I finally reached the end of the field. Clemmon and Leezy had just finished their second set of rows and they were sitting by their car having a snack. After collecting my pay, I walked over to them.

"Here's the money for picking those baskets," I extended my hand with three dimes.

"No boy, you keep it," Clemmon said. "It looked like you needed some encouragement."

"Did you make enough money?" Leezy asked.

"Two dollars and thirty cents."

"That will buy a lot of candy," she said.

"I'm saving it for Ocean City."

"Hot damn, now that's some fun," Clemmon said in a loud voice. Leezy frowned and he quieted down.

I thanked them both and walked to my bike. My pants legs were red and sticky with smashed strawberries. My muscles were stiff as I pedaled home, but I had a sense of satisfaction. I had learned something about work, and that we had some nice neighbors. Nothing I missed at school that day could have been more important.

* * *

Summer came and I spent my money at Ocean City carefully. For the first and only time in my life, I won a prize—actually two—in the claw machine. I spent twenty-five cents trying to pick up a fancy water pistol, but on each attempt it slipped out of the claw before making it to the chute. During one try, another boy distracted me and the claw fell into some prizes that didn't interest me. When the mechanical fingers closed, they were gripping a fancy address book and a ceramic duck. To my amazement, the claw maintained its hold on both items. That evening I gave them to my mother, and she seemed happy to have them.

* * *

I took fewer trips on the police boat that summer and spent more time on my uncle's farm. Only once did I go aboard my grandfather's boat.

"T, come aboard and visit me," he yelled out, as we pulled up beside him that day. I was older then, and I jumped onto the washboard without help. I wobbled a little but he pretended not to notice.

"How are the crabs running?" I asked.

"Not bad—twenty peelers in each scrape on the last two licks." He placed the wooden lid back on his peeler basket.

"You're doing good," I said.

"I had a little problem this morning, though." He chuckled and I knew a story was coming. "When I was halfway across the sound, I smelled smoke."

"What happened?" I knew that fire on a boat could be serious trouble.

"First, I checked the engine and it was okay. Then I searched through the cabin and couldn't find anything."

"Where was the fire?" I said, impatiently. It didn't matter—my grandfather would never rush his stories.

"I walked all the way around the boat and saw nothing wrong, so I went back to the cabin. This time I pulled everything out—life preservers, groceries, extra rope—but I couldn't find the fire."

"It must have gone out," I said.

"Nope, when I went back to the helm, the smell of smoke was even stronger."

By then I was growing frustrated. "Where was it?" I demanded.

He smiled before going on. "I didn't find it until I saw a wisp of smoke come down over my hat brim. I snatched the hat off and sure enough, it was on fire." As he spoke, he removed his straw hat and showed me a black hole burned in the crown. "I guess a spark from my pipe must have blown up there." He chuckled again. "I sure felt dumb."

* * *

My brother, Danny, turned four that year, and he was a cute kid with a smile no one could resist. He was fun to have around, but I noticed he was spending way too much time with my father. In the evening, when Dad read the paper, Danny sat on his lap. Sometimes when my father went to the store, he took my brother instead of me. Once, the two of them even went out on the *Somerset* without me. I had an uneasy feeling that my world was changing

In time I began to try harder to please my mother. She often complained that Dad would not do household repairs or yard work. Sometimes at supper she would run down a list of projects for him to do, but he generally just kept eating and made no comment. To gain Mom's favor, I began to take over any of the chores that were within my abilities.

For a long time my mother had been pressing Dad to repair the driveway. Like most local roads, its foundation was oyster shells and beach sand. With our heavy rains and poor drainage, it always had potholes.

It was a quarter mile from our driveway to the junction of Oriole and Deal Island Roads. Across the intersection was the Corner Store, a combination of garage, gas station and grocery. With the decline of Oriole stores, it had become the daytime meeting place for local men. During the winter, when no field work was possible, many farmers hung out there for hours each day. Watermen only showed up if the weather was too severe for them to take out their boats. Even in the busy summer season, farmers managed to come in at least once a day to catch up on the news. I sometimes rode my bike there to pick up bread or milk for my mother. If there was change, I would buy a soda and a candy bar, and listen to the men talk. I always stood in the back, trying to be inconspicuous; if they noticed me, I would be teased about girlfriends or anything else that would make me blush.

One day I noticed a small pile of crushed stone by the edge of the store parking lot. It had been left behind by state highway workers after a road repair job. I asked Mr. Wilson, the store owner, if I could have some.

"The state is done with it, so I suppose it's mine now," he said. "How do you plan to haul it?"

"With my old Express wagon."

"In that case, you can have all the stone you can haul," he said, grinning.

An hour later, I returned to the store with the wagon, towing it behind my bike with a rope. The men inside looked amused as I passed the open front door. Using my father's shovel, I piled as much stone on the wagon as it could carry. When I jumped on my bike and tried to leave, my load was too heavy to move. I stood on a pedal and pushed down with all my weight and strength, until I lost my balance and the bike fell over. That brought a roar of laughter from inside the store.

Embarrassed, I tried pushing the bike and it slowly began to move. When it was rolling, I jumped on and began to pedal. The bike wobbled crazily as I fought to gain speed. There were hoots from the store crowd as I struggled across the parking lot. Eventually, I acquired enough forward momentum to travel in a straight line.

It took only a few minutes to go home and unload the stone. Soon,

I was back at the store for another load. The men seemed surprised to see me. That afternoon, when I returned for the tenth load, their reaction was reduced to, "Here he comes again."

The next day was Friday and I worked on the driveway all day. My father was returning from a week of training with other TFC officers and even though I had done the job for my mother, I still wanted to impress him. When he drove up, I was waiting in the yard. All the potholes were filled and there was a layer of stone down each car track.

"You did all this?" he said.

"I hauled it with my wagon."

"Not bad," he said, walking toward the house. I followed after him, pleased. "Not bad," was his second highest compliment, just behind "pretty good."

I am not sure if my work endeared me to my father because he had to hear about it several times over the next twenty-four hours. My mother brought it up as soon as we walked into the house. "Aren't you embarrassed that your son had to do your work?"

"No, the exercise will do him good. What's for supper?" he said.

The next day, when Dad and I went to the store, the jokes started immediately. It was always a place where a man had to verbally fight his way in to be part of the group. On this day, the crowd had more ammunition than usual.

"Aren't you ashamed, sending your son out to steal road material from the state?" Scoot Barnes said. He was a wisecracking farmer with a son in my class at school.

"No, considering the little bit that the state pays me, I deserve it," my father said.

"I told him it was alright to take some stone, but I didn't know he was going to get it all," Mr. Wilson said, winking at me.

"That was your mistake; he's a Noble and he knows how to get things done," Dad said. That comment made me feel proud.

"It's a shame to make a young boy work that hard. I'll bet you don't even give him an allowance," one of the other neighbors said.

"I allow him to eat at my table," Dad countered. That was his standard answer concerning allowances.

The sparring went on for a few minutes and my father took a lot of jabs before the subject turned to fishing.

9. Hurricanes Don't Quit

"THAT HURRICANE IS COMING OUR WAY," DAD ANNOUNCED from the living room, where he was watching television. "It will be here sometime tomorrow afternoon."

I walked in to see what he was talking about. "What's a hurricane like?" I asked. It was October 1954 and I had never experienced one.

"It's a storm, a lot worse than any you've seen. It will probably blow down a lot of trees and maybe some houses."

"I hope it does come here," I said. The prospect seemed exciting. My father gave me an annoyed look and turned his attention back to the screen. The news broadcast ended, and there was no more information about the hurricane again that evening.

When I awoke in the morning, low, fast-moving clouds covered the sky. A strong breeze was blowing out of the southeast. Dad had left the house early to move the *Somerset* from Wenona to Champ. He thought St. Peter's Creek would be a more secure harbor. The morning radio announcer at WBOC in Salisbury, Maryland, said Hurricane Hazel was on her way and winds might exceed ninety miles per hour.

At midmorning I rode my bike to the Shockley farm, fighting ever increasing wind gusts. I helped Milbert and Bobby nail the chicken house doors and windows shut. The rattling of the farm buildings was disturbing. The cattle corralled in the pound beside the barn were restless and bawling.

By early afternoon, the sky was darker, but the warm air made the situation seem less threatening. Bobby and I stayed outside, marveling at how the wind would support us when we leaned into it with our shirts open. After one strong gust blew us backwards, Aunt Hilda yelled out the window that I should go home.

As I rode down the Shockley lane with the tailwind, my bike seemed rocket-propelled, reaching a speed that I had never approached before. I was enjoying the wildness of the storm when disaster struck—a gust came in from the side and blew me over. It was one of my worst wrecks; when I finished sliding, I was face down in the lane with a mouthful of sand. I got up slowly and walked my bike the rest of the way home.

My father had returned from mooring his boat at Champ but he still seemed worried. He had placed the *Somerset* in the middle of the harbor with two palm-type anchors off the bow, each with 150 feet of rope. To hold the stern, he had sunk a large grapnel in the mud and attached it with 100 feet of line. Even with those precautions, he was not sure what would happen.

"If it's anything like that typhoon I went through in the Pacific, it will be bad," he said.

As the afternoon went on, the wind increased but there was little rain. We stayed indoors and looked out at the bending trees. My father's mother, Grandma Lena, recently paralyzed by a stroke, was in a hospital bed in our dining room. As the wind noise grew louder, she became concerned and I sat with her.

About three o'clock my father called out from the living room. "Louie Reid is leading his horses up the road, something must be wrong." Louie was a bachelor farmer who lived alone in a big house across the field toward the river.

"His barn has blown down. It's almost flat," Mom said, as she looked out the kitchen window.

Louie treated his pair of retired draft horses as friends and he planned to care for them until they died. As he led them past our house on his way to my uncle's barn, the nervous animals were dancing sideways on the road. He was a small, wiry man and he looked even smaller between the big horses. There was a cut on the gray gelding's hip, and blood ran down all the way to his hoof. As I watched, Louie struggled to keep them moving.

The wind increased and after dark its howl became frightening. The power was off and our single oil lamp was not much comfort. The house shuddered with every gust and tree limbs pelted the roof. During a lightning flash, Dad saw the oak tree in our front yard go down. We were sitting in the kitchen and there was a much bigger tree just across the driveway from us. My father thought it might fall and decided to move us to the other side of the house. As we made our way to the back bedroom, my grandmother began to cry, fearing she would be left alone. Dad sent us on to safety and stayed with Grandma. At that point, I just wanted someone to make the hurricane go away.

For two more hours we huddled in the dark until the wind subsided. Danny fell asleep. Thankfully, the other tree never fell and our house had only minor damage. After the storm, my parents and I walked around the yard in the dark, shocked by the warm feel of the air. There was a red glow in the northern sky from a fire; the flames reflecting off the low clouds produced a menacing light. A neighbor said Scoot Barnes's chicken house had blown down and sparks from the coal stoves had set his hay shed on fire.

Dad took our only flashlight and left to check on the *Somerset*, it was over an hour before he returned.

"How was your boat?" Mom asked as he came through the door.

"I don't know, I didn't get that far," he said in a worried tone. "There was water on the road at the cemetery turn so I started wading. Not far past the colored church, it was nearly up to my waist. I went on for a while but it was no use, I was still a mile from the harbor."

"Did you see anyone else?" I asked.

"No, the people on Champ must be trapped in the second story of their houses."

My parents sat at the table and continued to talk about the storm, but with the danger to our family over, I fell into a deep sleep.

By morning, the water had retreated and my father drove to Champ. All the houses had been flooded but they were still standing and no one had drowned. What he saw at the harbor amazed him—of twenty-four boats moored in the creek, only the *Somerset* remained afloat. All the rest, including another police boat, were on land, scattered about in the marsh, fields and yards.

In our neighborhood, many trees were down and most roofs damaged but the houses were intact. The phone and power were off and our news came by word of mouth. We received a message that my grandparents on Deal Island were okay.

The next day, my father and some watermen planned an attempt to get the stranded boats back into the water. He took me along and when we arrived at the wharf, his mate and eight watermen were standing there in the warm October sun. Dad suggested using the *Somerset* to pull the boats off the shore. Some of the men were skeptical, but my father's experience in the war—dragging landing craft off the beaches—convinced them to give it a try.

Dad poled our skiff out to the patrol boat, while the watermen walked up the creek bank carrying small logs to use as rollers. When the *Somerset's* engines had finished their warm-up, we headed up the creek toward the first stranded boat. It was not far from the water's edge, resting on high ground beside a grove of locust trees. The men on shore had already placed rollers in front of it.

As we eased into the shallows, the mate threw a heavy rope toward the bank but it fell short. Seeing my chance to help, I jumped overboard and carried the line to the waiting men. They fastened the rope to the oyster boat and Dad backed the *Somerset* into deeper water. As the line was drawing tight, the men used large poles to pry the boat upright, onto its keelson.

When everything was ready, my father pulled the *Somerset's* throttles to full reverse. The engines growled and muddy water churned at her stern. The bow post creaked from the strain of the rope. Slowly, the stranded boat eased onto the first roller and it began to turn. The progress became quicker after it reached the second roller, and the vessel moved smoothly toward the water. As it slid into the creek undamaged, cheers went up from the usually quiet watermen. My heart swelled; I felt I was part of important work.

It took three days to return all the boats back to the water and I did not miss a minute of it. Some of them were so far inland that a bulldozer was used to move them closer to shore before the *Somerset* could do its work. In the end, we refloated them all with little damage.

* * *

Six weeks later, on an evening in late November, the tropical air of hurricane Hazel was a distant memory. A hard, biting wind was blowing out of the north as the first major cold front of the winter hit the Bay. The blow had started around noon and the temperature dropped quickly. Because of the deteriorating weather, most of the oystermen quit work early. Dad and his mate returned to Deal Island harbor well before dark. During supper, my father mentioned the rough conditions they had encountered on the Sound. High seas and poor visibility from wind-driven spray had made it a difficult crossing.

After the meal, my parents were watching television and I was building a crane with my Erector Set. Danny had taken some of the parts and was refusing to give them back. The phone rang and my father answered it. Mom and I listened to one side of the conversation; it was like so many we had heard before.

"When did they leave?"

"Where were they headed?"

"What boat were they in?"

"It'll be hard to find them in this weather but I'll try."

Dad returned to the living room and told us what we already knew—he was going out on a search. Two Deal Island men had left the harbor in mid-afternoon on a boat called the *Marvalo*. They were hauling shucked oysters across the Sound to a packing house in the village of Crocheron. The men were hours overdue and their families were worried.

"Thomas, don't go now, wait for the wind to die down," Mom pleaded. "You've never been out on a night this bad."

"If I was out there, I'd want someone looking for me," Dad said. He began to gather up his warmest clothes. Before leaving home he called Ellsworth Hoffman, another police boat captain, to help him look for the missing boat.

The two officers went out on the *Somerset* and searched all night in the heavy seas. By morning, ice covered the patrol boat. Just after dawn, they found a log floating vertically in the channel leading to Deal Island. It was rare to find floating timber in the lower Chesapeake; Dad figured it must have washed off the shore in the hurricane flood.

A short time later, the officers received a radio message that the body of one of the men was on the beach. They went to the location and arrived before the coroner. The body was lying at the water's edge with a life ring nearby. It appeared the man had made it to shore alive, but had died from exposure. My father photographed the scene and picked up the life ring.

One night a week later, he laid some photographs on the table where I was doing homework. "I want you to see what can happen out there," he said. They were the saddest pictures I had ever seen. In one the man was lying face down, half-covered by sand from the waves lapping on shore. His feet were bare, and I thought about how cold they must have been in that icy water. The other photo showed the body rolled over; beside it was the perfect imprint it had made in the sand. The man had been good looking and about my father's age.

"I don't want you to wind up that way," Dad said. "Remember this when you're older. I've hung the life ring in the attic as a reminder."

A dredger found the body of the second man two months later, after it floated to the surface. The *Marvalo* was located not far out of Deal Island harbor in less than twenty feet of water. When she was raised to the surface, there was a hole punched in the bottom, exactly as a log would have done. Hurricane Hazel had claimed two more victims, a month and a half after it had blown through.

My father was involved in many drowning cases, but this one affected him more than most. He believed he had passed the two men struggling in the water that afternoon, but had not seen them because of salt spray on the *Somerset*'s windows. There had been no report of an overdue boat and he had no reason to be looking for anyone in the water. The fact that he may have saved them, if only he had been more observant, always haunted him.

10. Drive Me to Distraction

 DURING THE WINTER OF 1955, TFC OFFICERS CONTINUED to arrest watermen for illegally handscraping. My father spent a lot of time in court but he often came home frustrated. He complained about certain magistrates that were quick to find the lawbreakers not guilty. These lower court judges were appointed to office by the party in power and they had no legal training. After losing a case where he had more than enough evidence, my father came home angry.

"He doesn't know a damn thing about the law but he knows how to count votes," Dad said about the magistrate. "On Election Day all of those watermen vote and he's thinking about his job, not the loss of the oyster industry." My father went on complaining, unaware that an opportunity to change the situation would soon come along.

Early on a gray morning in January, Dad and his mate surprised a handscraper at work on the upper Manokin. As the patrol boat approached, the oysterman cut the rope attached to the dredge and gunned his engine. The officers gave chase, and when they passed near the location of the dredge, my father threw out a marker buoy, hoping to find the device later for evidence. The pursuit continued and the *Somerset* steadily gained on the fleeing vessel. After a short run, the dredger cut his engines and Dad jumped aboard to write out a citation.

The man insisted that he had not been handscraping or running from the patrol boat, but simply hurrying along to his favorite tong-

59

ing spot. He loudly proclaimed his innocence and promised to fight the case in court. My father found the piece of rope cut loose from the dredge, still tied to the boat's rear cleat. He took it as evidence, not sure how it would be used.

For the next two days, my father and his mate dragged a grapnel over the river bottom trying to hook the dredge. Finally, they found it with the other piece of the rope still attached. If the two pieces could be shown to match, Dad thought he would win the case. He asked his boss in Annapolis to call the FBI lab, even though they had never been used in an oyster-poaching case.

The Bureau agreed to examine the evidence, and in a few weeks a large brown envelope arrived at our house. It contained pictures of the rope taken through a microscope. Woven between the manila strands was a tiny strip of paper printed with the manufacturer's name. The cut ends of that paper matched perfectly.

On the day of the trial, an FBI expert came down from Washington, D.C., to testify. The magistrate was intimidated by having the FBI in his courtroom. It did not take him long to issue a guilty verdict. After that, TFC personnel found it easier to prosecute cases. The magistrates got the message—the officers were serious about the oyster laws.

* * *

North of the Virginia line, Maryland owned the bottom of the Bay and all its tidal tributaries. In the 1950s, the state ran a program to lease barren areas of river bottom to individuals for the establishment of private oyster beds. It was legal to harvest undersize oysters on bars where they were plentiful and transport them to the leased bottom, locally called oyster grounds. These seed oysters were scattered on the lease in the hope that they would grow and reproduce. If the shellfish became large enough, they could be sold on the open market.

Even though my father had been promoted to District Supervisor, his salary was still low. He thought an oyster lease could supplement his income, and he convinced Milbert to be his partner on ten acres in Geanquakin Creek. The plan was for my uncle to catch seed oysters in Holland Straits during the winter when farm work was slack. After searching without success for a boat large enough to cross the Sound, they decided to build one. They asked Sigsbee for advice and he designed a bateau, thirty feet long with a box stern. My father had no time to help with construction, so he hired Preston Lawrence to do his part. Milbert and Preston set up their boatyard in a grove of trees near the Shockleys' garage.

By that winter, Bobby, Johnny, Billy and I had become a tight group, playing and adventuring together after school and on Saturdays. We were together so much, Milbert began to call us "the crew." As the youngest member, I felt privileged to be around the older boys. In the fall, most of our time had been devoted to building pushcarts, which were like wooden go-carts without motors. The older boys supplied the construction knowledge and I provided the nails. Always in need of wheels, they convinced me to remove the set from my old Express wagon. Except for hauling the stone, I had not used it for years, but my father was unhappy when he found it upside down in the yard with bare axles.

On our flat land there was a basic problem with the carts—if one of us rode, someone else had to push. For a few weeks we willingly propelled each other around the Shockleys' farm, crashing into buildings and running into ditches. Occasionally, the driver steered through cow manure, which coated the pusher in a green spray. Eventually we tired of the carts, and I returned the wheels to my wagon, putting it aside for my brother.

After the boat construction got underway, the four of us went to the site every afternoon. We saw the keelson laid and watched the bottom planks being screwed in place. It was not long before we wanted a boat of our own, and Bobby asked Milbert if we could build one.

"Why don't you use my old muskrat trapping skiff? It's still tied up down in the gut." He was referring to the small marsh creek, which formed the eastern boundary of the Shockley farm. He was trying to prevent us from borrowing his tools and ruining good lumber. Getting a ready-made boat seemed like a good deal to us.

On the following Saturday morning, we set off to the gut. It was a cloudy March day but nothing could dampen our spirits. Bobby led the way across the muskrat marsh. It was riddled with holes, and by the time we reached the water's edge, the Bates brothers and I had been in mud to our knees. Bobby was the only one still clean and dry. The skiff had sunk and it was hard to locate. A half-rotted length of rope tied to a myrtle bush led under water to our boat. We pulled on the rope, trying to bring the skiff ashore, but the hemp parted and we staggered backward. Bobby, in the rear of the line, lost his balance and fell into a particularly muddy spot. The rest of us fell on top of him and he almost disappeared into the ooze. After that, none of us worried about the condition of our clothes.

We waded into the gut, and lifted and tipped our skiff to dump out the water. When we set it back down on the surface, it did not leak a drop. Johnny found an old board to use as a pole and we all climbed in for our first voyage. We stood upright, laughing and fighting for balance as the little boat rocked from side to side. My father had always made me sit down in a skiff but now I was doing what I wanted.

We followed the gut through the marsh and into swampy woodland. The water became shallow and we had to wade to make progress. Soon, the creek became a man-made ditch, straight with piles of dirt on both sides, and the skiff began to drag on the sandy bottom. We stopped for a rest, believing our outing was over, until Bobby made a suggestion.

"Let's build a dam to make the water higher."

"How do we make a dam?" I asked.

"Remember that stump we passed? We could pile logs in front of it."

Johnny and Billy liked the idea so we went back downstream and began work. For an hour we dragged fallen trees and branches to the gut and jammed them in front of the stump. We covered those with armfuls of leaves and pine needles. By the time the dam began to seal, we were all exhausted.

"Tomorrow we'll have our own lake," Bobby said. As we walked home, the wind freshened from the northeast and rain began to fall.

On Sunday, it poured all day and we postponed our boat outing. When I boarded the school bus on Monday morning, it was still raining. During the ride to school, I noticed the ditches along Deal Island Road were full and running over. That afternoon on the return trip, the road was covered with four inches of water. Our driver eased through it at a slow roll. No one in the crew gave it much thought; the sun had come out and we were anxious to get to our boat.

At home, I changed quickly and headed to the Shockley farm. As I pedaled into their yard, I saw a yellow State Roads Department truck parked by the barn. Three serious-looking men in wet clothes were standing beside it talking to Milbert and Bobby. My cousin was staring at the ground. Sensing trouble, I stood behind the magnolia tree and listened.

"What ever gave you the idea that you could dam up that creek?" the oldest man said. "It drains hundreds of acres along Deal Island Road."

"We just wanted to use our boat," Bobby mumbled.

"Do you know how hard we have to work to keep these ditches open?" the man said.

About that time the Bates boys rode across the field on their bikes; seeing the Roads Department truck, they braked hard and slid to a stop beside the cow pound. For another minute Bobby took the heat alone, but soon guilt forced the three of us to walk up beside him. Having new culprits to lecture gave the man renewed energy. For fifteen minutes, we received a large dose of "you boys ought to know better." At the end he said, "Next time, the sheriff will come to see you."

As soon as the men drove away, we ran to the creek. The dam was gone and water was rushing through. Our boat had been tied to a tree but somehow the knot had come undone and it had washed away. We never found it.

I decided not to tell my father about the men in the yellow truck. When I arrived home for supper, he was already halfway through his plate of chicken and dumplings.

"Dammed up the creek did you?" he said, as I sat down to eat.

"Yes," I muttered. I expected to get another lecture but his attitude surprised me.

"I wouldn't worry about it. That bunch of State Roads freeloaders needed to do some honest work. Usually all they do is drive down the road ten miles per hour with a little asphalt in their truck. I've never seen them put out more than two shovelsful in a day." Roads Department employees were paid more than my father for his dangerous work and he was unhappy about it.

The next afternoon all the members of our crew went back to the boatyard to watch Milbert and Preston fasten planks on the oyster boat's sides. We moaned about the loss of our skiff and this time my uncle gave in.

"Okay, you can build your boat but no more dams," he said. "You can use some of the old boards in my shed."

We set to work immediately and two days later, our first skiff was complete. Barely ten feet long and square at both ends, it was not pretty but we were proud of it. For its first voyage, we launched it in the ditch in front of the barn. Our spirits dropped when water began to pour in at every seam. Preston walked over to look at our sinking creation.

"It reminds me of that old Jules Verne book, *Twenty Thousand Leaks,*" he said with a chuckle. "But if you'll leave it in the water a few days, the boards will swell and it will be fine."

He was right; in three days the leaks had stopped and we prepared to put the boat to use. Our mothers ordered us not to come home covered with marsh mud again; they insisted we find some place other than the gut to navigate. A gravel pit on the Bates farm seemed like the logical choice. It was nearly an acre in size, with water not over three feet deep, and my father said it was a safe place for us to be reckless with a boat.

For the next three months, we went to the pit at every opportunity. Early on, we discovered that one boat was not enough, so we built a second one. Two boats allowed us to race and engage in mock naval warfare. We regularly crashed them together and attempted to board the opposing vessel to throw its occupants overboard. Since I was the smallest, I usually was the first to go. My mother's patience was pushed to the limit as I came home wet every day. One afternoon as I was headed out the door, she said, "This has to stop. If I hear 'going to the pit' one more time I'll scream."

My father was just coming in from work, and he paused to lay a nice sea trout in the kitchen sink. "Let him go, Kathleen, he's just being a boy." He often said that when I was engaged in some kind of wildness that didn't upset the neighbors or damage property. As strict as he was about those things, he remembered his childhood and wanted me to have the same freedom.

Our time on the pit ended the first Saturday in July. That was the day my father's cousin drove down from Baltimore to the Shockley farm, bringing along her two sons who were about our age. Bobby and I called them our cousins. Their mother was a talkative woman who loved to brag about her involvement in city politics. She never seemed to enjoy being in the country. Mom once said, "She feels it's her duty to visit what she considers to be her primitive relatives."

The cousins liked being on the farm, and they were willing to try any escapade Bobby and I dreamed up, but their mother seldom let them get far from the house. She always worried about them messing up their clothes. On that day, they were wearing matching white shirts and twill pants pressed to perfection, and their shiny black dress shoes were better than any we wore to church.

The adults, including my parents, sat on the Shockleys' porch and talked. I was bored and suggested that Bobby and I take the cousins to the pit. Our parents were skeptical, but we promised only to show the boys our boats. As we left the yard, their mother called out, "Boys, don't mess up your shoes."

When we arrived at the pit, the Bates brothers were already out in their skiff. Bobby and I climbed into our boat and poled out to meet them. In a few moments a race was underway. For a while our cousins stood on the bank looking neat, but they soon asked for a ride. Bobby and I decided it was okay to show the boys our boats out on the water.

The Bates brothers loaned me their boat and I took the youngest cousin with me. The older one got in with Bobby. We maneuvered around the pit with our passengers standing in the bows like two George Washingtons crossing the Delaware. Everything was fine until Johnny decided to make things more interesting. He threw a bowling ball size chunk of orange clay from the high bank and it landed near our boat. The splash was large but only a few drops of water hit us. If only I had kept quiet, the boys would have made it home without a blemish, but I couldn't resist a taunt.

"What a weak shot, you missed by a mile," I said.

"Okay, how about this one?" Johnny said, launching a ball of clay high into the air. For a moment it was lost in the sun, but it reappeared heading straight for our skiff. It struck dead center, knocking a board completely off the bottom. There was no time to pole for shore. My cousin looked down in disbelief as the water rose over his nice shoes. He remained speechless as the boat filled and we sank to the bottom. We waded ashore, pulling our submerged craft behind us while the other boys laughed until they were out of breath.

Once on shore, my city relative forgot about his wet clothes and only wanted revenge. He gathered up small, hard pieces of clay for ammo. I temporarily repaired the boat by nailing the board on with a rock.

By the time we returned to the water, the Bates brothers were attacking Bobby's vessel. We defended him by pelting them with clay. My city cousin had a good arm and he scored solid hits that must have hurt. Even though we kept the Bates brothers ducking, Billy struck the other boat, knocking a board loose. Bobby poled furiously but his skiff sank a few feet from shore.

With both cousins involved, the battle intensified. The Bates boys went out in their boat and we sank them while they pelted us with clay. We continued to fight, taking turns on the land and in the boats. We quit when the skiffs were too damaged to repair without tools. By then every square inch of our clothes was soaked and covered with orange clay.

We left the pit exhilarated and talking loudly about the action. Our cousins had fought well and earned our respect. When we neared the Shockley house, the mood changed as we began to consider our parents' reaction. The boys had left there looking like models in the Sears catalog; they were returning looking more like flood victims.

Bobby and I let the cousins lead the way up the sidewalk. The squishing sounds made by their shoes announced their arrival. They were halfway to the porch when their mother cried out, "What happened to you?"

"The boats accidentally bumped together and we tipped over," the younger cousin said. Not a bad story, I thought, but I doubted they would accept it. Bobby and I stepped behind a lilac bush and tried to disappear.

"Look at your clothes and shoes, they're ruined," she said. I began to slink away toward the side yard.

"Bobby, come here this instant," my aunt Hilda said in a stern voice.

"Terry, you come too," Dad said. He didn't really sound mad; more like he was going along with his sister to ease their cousin's indignation. Just to be safe, I entered the porch with my head down.

"How could you let this happen?" my aunt said. "The way you boys act, people will think we're heathens. You and those boats are going to drive me to distraction." I never knew where distraction was located but my aunt often threatened to go there. "You aren't going near that gravel pit for a month," she said. My father agreed.

Our cousins soon departed for Baltimore wearing some of Bobby's clothes; it would be years before they returned. With the other activities of summer, our interest in the boats diminished. When the month-long ban was over, we repaired them, but they were seldom used after that. There would be other, bigger boats in my future.

11. Mom Threatens Rebellion

 LATE THAT SUMMER CONSTRUCTION GOT UNDERWAY on the chicken house. I hung around the building site and watched the men work. Sigsbee was the chief carpenter and Dad hired two neighbors to help him. One was Louie Reid, the farmer whose barn had blown down in the hurricane.

Louie's house had once been the finest in the area; most of the rooms remained just as they were when his parents died. I sometimes looked in the parlor window at the Tiffany lamps and blue velvet chairs; it was like no other room I had ever seen. He occupied only the cluttered kitchen and a second floor bedroom. Occasionally, I would pass through his yard at night and see him sitting at the kitchen table beside a flickering oil lamp. It was a lonely scene and I always hurried to the warmth of our house. Even though Louie owned a productive farm, he was willing to work for wages. Mom said he did it to be around other people.

One afternoon I was hanging around the chicken house site as my father unloaded lumber from my uncle's truck. He saw me idling and thought I should be doing something useful.

"Terry, pick up all those little pieces of wood left behind by the carpenters," he ordered. "Pile them outside so I can burn them."

I looked at the hundreds of bits of sawed-off boards littering the dirt floor. "It will take me forever," I said.

"You had better get started then, forever is a long time."

I began to pick up the scrap lumber, carrying it in a small bucket to the burn site. After a half hour, only a small part of the floor was cleared. The August sun was beating down; I was hot and discouraged and wanted to quit. I did not mind doing some jobs like hauling stone for the driveway, because it was my idea and I did it when I felt like it. Driving the truck for Milbert was fun, because the other boys were there. But I had not yet learned the discipline of working alone, on command, in unpleasant conditions.

I walked over to the truck. "Dad, your job is better than mine. I want to help you," I said.

"Son, no job is better or more important than another. It's all work and it all has to be done. This lumber is too heavy for you to handle. Go back and finish what you started."

I returned to picking up scrap, thinking about what my father had said. I resolved to do my job and not complain.

In a short time Dad finished his work and went to the house. Not long after that, the carpenters quit for the day and Louie came over to where I was working.

"Boy, you'll never finish just using that little bucket; you're spending too much time walking to the pile. Carry all you can on each trip." He gathered up two half-bushel tomato baskets that the carpenters had been using for lunchtime seats and we began to fill them with discarded pieces of wood. Having his help lifted my spirits and my pace quickened. He worked fast and I tried to match his speed. In a short time, the job was finished.

"Thanks," I said, as we dumped the last basket on the pile.

"You're welcome Master Noble. You've got a few things to learn about work but you'll figure them out." He walked toward his house and I wondered what it was like to have no one at home to cook supper.

* * *

In the fall I entered the fifth grade. School was fun but I always looked forward to going hunting with my BB gun in the afternoons. My father allowed me to shoot blackbirds, sparrows and starlings, which were considered pests by farmers. I spent hundreds of hours stalking them and at that time there was nothing else I liked better.

On a rainy Saturday, when I could not hunt, boredom led me to poke around in our attic. In the back corner I found a box of my father's old books. I opened one about a boy named Tom Swift, and in five minutes I was hooked. Over the next year, I read them all—more Tom Swift, the Hardy Boys, *The Call of the Wild* and others. Whenever my life seemed dull, I went to that box for another dose of excitement.

One afternoon my father came in from the construction site while I was deep into a book.

"Where's Terry? I have some work for him," I heard him say to Mom.

"In his room, reading."

There was a pause and I expected a knock on my door. Instead, he went back outside saying, "Okay, let him be. I can do it myself."

I was happy to get back to my story of the north woods.

Those books must have been important to my father, because a reprieve like that happened several times. They were the only things for which he let me avoid work.

The books caused me to dream of adventures in the wilderness with only my dog for company. The problem was I did not have a dog; our old male Chesapeake Bay retriever had died in the spring. My parents were not anxious to replace him; he had been a hard-headed animal that was fond of digging holes in the yard. It was good news when the Bates family's Chesapeake had a litter of puppies. After many hints from me, my parents brought home a little brown puppy that we named Cindy. She would become my friend and hunting companion.

* * *

Milbert and Preston finished work on the oyster boat hull and installed a six-cylinder engine salvaged from a wrecked car. They built a small cabin at the bow to give the tongers a place to warm up in cold weather. The vessel was steered by a five-foot-long tiller attached directly to the rudder.

Milbert was not a waterman, so he took Clemmon Maddox as his mate on his one trip across the Sound to tong seed oysters. Clemmon had worked several winters on oyster boats and my uncle valued his experience. They caught a load of seed and brought it back to the lease, but that evening Milbert decided he was a farmer and not the man for crossing the Sound. He rented the boat out to other tongers and they delivered seed oysters as part of their payment. My uncle never had much to say about his day as a tonger.

* * *

In November, the school had problems with its furnace and we got an unexpected day off. My father surprised me by asking if I wanted to accompany him to work. I had never been out on the *Somerset* during the oyster season, but there had been a lull in illegal dredging and he did not expect trouble.

"Every morning Roland and I have been trolling on our way into Holland Straits and we've been catching some nice rock," he said. Fishing was enough to make me forget about sleeping in and I agreed to go along.

Dawn was breaking on a crisp, windless morning as we left Deal Island harbor. "It's slick cam out here this morning," my father said, using the waterman's phrase for totally calm. After a smooth crossing, we put out our bucktail lures near a tiny marsh island at the entrance to Holland Straits. I had never trolled before and I wasn't sure what to expect. Dad ran the *Somerset* close to the island, and as our lures passed the marsh bank, we hooked fish on all three lines. They were identical three-pound striped bass. We made another pass by the island and caught three more. On our third try, we did not get a strike. "That's it for the day," Dad said. "After two passes they get wise." I was disappointed that the action had ended so soon.

With the fishing over, we headed down the east shore of South Marsh Island. Near its southern tip, Dad spotted something white floating on the water and slowed the patrol boat. It turned out to be feathers, a line of them as wide as the *Somerset,* extending across the water and around the next point of land.

Dad increased our speed and we followed the trail of down along the south end of the island. At Sedgy Point it turned toward Spring Island and we continued to track it, more than curious about what lay ahead. On the far side of the next island, after miles of feathers, we got our answer. Up ahead, a Smith Island tonging boat was cruising slowly with two men sitting on its stern. One was picking a Canada goose and the other a black duck. Their oyster culling board was lined with naked waterfowl.

"Morning Captain, looks like you had some luck," Dad called out.

"Aye Tom, we did. I had my trap set on South Marsh last night and, by God, they filled her up," the older man said. He was sturdily built with a ruddy face and a thick island brogue. Feathers continued to fly as he talked. Duck trapping was illegal but the man seemed unconcerned with the *Somerset's* arrival. He knew that TFC officers were not charged with enforcing waterfowl laws; that was the job of state and federal game wardens.

"We've been following your trail," Dad said.

"We wanted to get them picked before we started oystering," the waterman explained. He laid the plucked goose on the culling board and began stripping feathers from a black duck.

"How many did you get?" Roland asked.

"Six geese and twenty two ducks."

"That's quite a haul."

"Yeah, I've got a sale for all of them in Crisfield."

Selling waterfowl was also illegal. My father smiled and shook his head.

"Be sure you don't keep any undersized oysters," Dad said.

"Sure Tom, you know I wouldn't break the law," the waterman said with a grin.

My father pulled away from the tonging boat and steered toward Holland's Island. On the way he explained that the men were descendants of market hunters. Their ancestors had legally killed thousands of ducks and geese each year in the early part of the century. They were just carrying on their family business. "Laws don't change peoples' habits overnight, especially out here," he said.

Holland's Island was a partially wooded strip of land that had once supported a community with dozens of homes. The Bay's ceaseless erosion had greatly reduced the island's size, forcing the former inhabitants to the mainland. Only one house remained, a white two-story that served as headquarters for the Holland's Island Gunning Club.

Dad eased the *Somerset* up to the gunning club dock. Their caretaker, a lanky weathered individual, walked down to meet us. He was wearing an oilskin coat and hip boots rolled down to his knees.

"Hi Charlie, what's for lunch?" Dad said.

"Oysters. What did you think it would be?"

"I was thinking about codfish cakes."

"I hope you brought them along if you're planning on eating them," the caretaker said. His broken grin indicated the tooth fairy had been busy.

"Have you seen handscrapers working anywhere?" Dad asked.

"Yeah, they were thicker than gulls in Kedges Strait earlier this week. They're mostly working in the afternoons."

"Where were they from?"

"Smith Island."

"Damn it, won't they ever quit?" Daid said. There was real agitation in his voice. Charlie looked as though he regretted answering my father. He soon changed the subject to duck hunting which improved Dad's mood. They were discussing where he might shoot some pintail ducks, when a helicopter appeared to the west, coming over the Bay.

In those days, helicopters were a rare sight. This one was headed for Bloodsworth Island, a marshy piece of land used by the Navy as a target range. Our windows at home often rattled as the shells and bombs exploded there. At night we watched the parachute flares float slowly down to earth. The Navy usually suspended shelling in the fall, so the waterfowl would not be disturbed. My father wondered aloud what a helicopter was doing there in November.

The aircraft reached the island shore and began to hover. Something appeared to be falling from it, and Dad grabbed his binoculars to see if they were about to crash. He could see yellow flashes along its underside and feared it might be on fire. When the helicopter turned, he got a good view of the action. What he saw amazed him—two sailors were shoveling corn out the side door.

"They aren't having trouble, they're baiting ducks," he said. "Some of the Navy brass from Patuxent are going hunting." He was referring to Patuxent Naval Air Station twenty miles away across the bay. Dad watched as wind from the aircraft's rotors spread hundreds of pounds of corn like it was coming from a giant lawn seeder.

Baiting waterfowl was illegal, but many hunters still used corn to attract birds and give them better tasting meat. Ducks that ate eelgrass or bottom-dwelling animals often tasted fishy, but corn-fed ones were delicious. As Dad and his mate watched the baiting, they were not so much offended by the game law violation as they were in awe of its scale.

"The Navy is doing things in a big way," Dad said. "They're planning on attracting every duck in the area."

"Those damn admirals are getting greedy," Charlie said. "They're going to out-bait our club. I don't have any more corn coming until next week." In the 1950s, pursuit of ducks on the outer islands was still a free-for-all.

A few days later, my father and Roland went after the handscrapers in Kedges Strait. Ellsworth Hoffman and his mate rode with them on the *Somerset* to help with the arrests. They surprised a group of illegal dredgers right where Charlie said they would be. When the patrol boat appeared, the watermen began to flee back toward Smith Island. The wind was calm and it became a full throttle race toward Ewell, the closest harbor. Unlike handscrapers on some other parts of the Bay, most Smith Islanders had not invested in fast boats, counting on their isolation to protect them.

The *Somerset* quickly overtook the slowest vessel and Ellsworth jumped aboard it. My father left his friend behind to write the citation and fight if necessary.

In a short time, the patrol boat caught up with a second dredger and Ellsworth's mate boarded it. Seeing that two boats had been overtaken, the islanders abandoned their straight run for home and scattered. Some headed out into the Bay, but my father pursued a boat making for a creek on the north end of the island. The man was hoping to hide in the network of interconnecting waterways, but he misjudged the *Somerset*'s speed. When the patrol boat beat him to the creek entrance, he shut down his engine and surrendered.

"You guys are always trying to stop a man from making a living," the waterman yelled.

"If it wasn't for us you'd catch the last oyster and then complain the state did nothing to protect the beds," my father shot back.

The man sat down on his washboard in resignation. Roland stepped aboard to complete the arrest.

"Finish up here, I want one more," my father said. He scanned the Bay with his binoculars and saw that one of the fleeing boats had turned back toward the island. He pushed the patrol boat back up to full speed and headed for Ewell. The high tide allowed him to run close to the marsh bank, cutting the distance to the harbor. As the police boat roared down the shore, its wake surged over the spartina grass tossing it violently.

My father knew that running his boat's aging engines at full throttle for so long was risky. The needle on one temperature gauge was already pushing the red line. He decided there was no choice but to keep up his speed; if the islander made it to the harbor there would likely be another crowd of angry watermen to face.

Both vessels continued the race to the entrance of Ewell. The *Somerset* got there first and my father positioned his boat to block the narrow waterway. The waterman maintained his speed and headed straight for the patrol boat. Dad reached for his shotgun, but the man throttled back and turned to avoid a collision. He surrendered without a fight, but complained bitterly about the state meddling in his business.

Dad cruised back through Kedges Straits, picking up his fellow officers along the way. The men were jubilant as they started across the Sound—four handscrapers in one day was a record. As they celebrated, they were unaware that their lives were at risk. Unbeknownst to them, the long chase had shaken loose an exhaust manifold on one of the engines. Carbon monoxide was filling the cabin. They made it to the harbor without a problem, but when they stepped out of the cabin into the cold, fresh air, all of them got headaches instantly.

My father arrived home with nausea and a pounding head, too sick to eat supper. He tried to sleep but his symptoms worsened. Mom drove him to the hospital in Salisbury and they were surprised to find two of the other officers already there. The three men spent the night in oxygen tents while Ellsworth suffered at home. In a few days, all of them recovered, but the incident started a call among TFC personnel for the state to buy faster and more reliable boats. Later that winter, events on the Potomac River would increase the demand for better equipment.

Not long after my father got out of the hospital, baby chicks were scheduled for delivery to the new chicken house. I skipped school to help get the building ready for their arrival. Louie and I spread fresh wood shavings over the floor while my father lit gas-fired heaters called brooders. The brooders needed to be at incubator temperature when the chicks arrived; if they were chilled for even half an hour, they would grow slowly. When the shavings were finished, we placed cardboard trays with feed around the brooders and surrounded them with a ring of watering jars. The birds would not have to move more than a few feet to eat or drink.

On chick delivery day my father had an unexpected call to be in court. When I came to breakfast that morning, there was tension in the kitchen.

"You forced me to accept this chicken house and now you expect me to work in it on the first day?" Mom said.

"They changed the court date—I can't do anything about it," Dad said. He got up from the table and looked out the window at nothing in particular.

"Maybe you should have thought about what could happen before you built it."

My father put on his green uniform coat and closed the brass buttons before heading out the door.

"I'm not doing anything when these chickens arrive," she called after him.

It worried me that I may have to do the job alone.

The chicks came from the hatchery in a converted school bus that everyone called the biddie bus. The seats had been removed, and the interior was stacked with boxes containing the day-old birds. As the vehicle rolled to a stop, my mother stepped out the back door, putting on her old gardening coat. She never said so, but I think she could not resist seeing five thousand baby chicks.

The driver opened the emergency door and pushed a stack of boxes toward us. The birds were all peeping, searching for their mothers, and the noise made talking difficult. Mom and I began carrying boxes into the chicken house; along the way the occupants lightly picked at our fingers through air holes in the cardboard.

As instructed, we dumped the chicks on top of the feed trays, and in a few moments the little yellow balls were picking and scratching at the food. By the time the bus was empty, some of the birds were looking for a drink. They lined up around the water jars, dipping their beaks and then tilting their heads back to swallow.

After eating and drinking, most of the chicks went under the brooder to rest, but some began to explore their new world. I lay down in the shavings to watch them from their level and in a little while I was surrounded; one baby picked at my earlobe while another tugged at my hair. A few jumped onto my arms and legs and sat down. It was pleasant lying with those little animals in the warmth of the brooder.

When I got up to leave, two dozen chicks started to follow me—they had decided I was their mother. I had to run away to keep from leading them too far from the heat.

My mother was busy refilling water jars even though they were less than half-empty. After we finished that chore, she decided to move the feed trays closer to the brooders. When everything was to her satisfaction, we went to the house for lunch. Early in the afternoon, she was back with the chickens putting out more feed. The day was almost over when my father came home.

"How did it go?" he asked my mother, hesitantly.

"I only went out there because my name is on the loan," she said. "Somebody has to make your chicken house pay off."

"You won't have to do it again. I can take care of the chickens before and after work and on weekends." My mother seemed unconvinced.

Dad could not keep his promise for long. One Sunday two weeks before Christmas, he received a call from the chairman of the TFC. As he listened he paced the floor, stretching the phone cord to its limit. When the conversation was over, he gave us the news. "They've assigned me to the Potomac River for the rest of the winter. I have to take the boat across the Bay tomorrow. Looks like I'll only get home every other weekend."

My mother looked shocked. "Why are they doing this?"

"Hand scraping is about under control in the Sound, but it's still wide open on the Potomac. The boss said I did a good job here and they need help over there."

"That's not the only reason," Mom said. "Part of it is this chicken house. They don't like you having any outside income and they're punishing you." She may have been right. My father's immediate supervisor was a man from Deal Island who held the title of Chief Inspector. He wore a uniform but spent most of his time at the office in Annapolis. He was a cautious man who resented my father's charge-ahead style, and they had clashed over how Dad's job should be done.

"You know he's made comments about 'Noble, the chicken farmer' to Ellsworth and some of the others," Mom said. My father looked troubled as he thought over what she had said. "And who is going to take care of the chickens?" she went on.

"You'll have to do it, Milbert and Terry can help you."

She stared at him in disbelief at the turn of events. Dad went to their bedroom and started packing for his stay on the Potomac.

* * *

Just after World War II, a large oyster bed was discovered on the Potomac just downstream from the U.S. 301 bridge. The shellfish were plentiful there and illegal dredgers could make the equivalent of two weeks' wages, in just a few hours. As usual, the poachers worked at night to avoid detection.

Maryland owned the bottom of the Potomac River up to the Virginia shore as the result of a land grant from the King of England. Virginia watermen were legally permitted to tong oysters there, but an agreement signed in the late 1700s said that lawbreakers would be tried in their home state. The agreement caused an awkward law enforcement problem and the states battled over this issue for years. Virginia did little to protect the oyster beds because they didn't own them. TFC officers could not go ashore in Virginia to make an arrest, and that state's police officers were not always helpful. If Maryland officers captured a Virginia man on the water, Virginia prosecutors often put out little effort to make the case.

In 1955, more than 100 illegal dredgers were operating on the lower Potomac. Many of the boats were based in creeks near Colonial Beach, Virginia. Most of them were small, shallow draft vessels faster than the Maryland patrol boats. They escaped by running far up the creeks where the larger boats could not follow. The local papers had begun calling them the "Mosquito Fleet."

Not all the Virginia dredgers preferred small boats; one man had converted a World War II German patrol boat into a handscraper. Even with a load of oysters, it could outrun anything on the river. Maryland boats had pursued it several times, but the Virginian just waved good-bye as he left them in his wake.

* * *

The day my father departed for the Potomac, Mom began caring for the chickens and I helped after school. The feed came in hundred-pound sacks, and she was not strong enough to dump them into the feed cart. A lot of her time was spent scooping feed from the bags to the cart and then to the feeders. Nancy Reid, a neighbor who had been my playmate when I was five, took an interest in the chickens and stopped by regularly after school. We discovered that the two of us working together could dump the bags. It became our job to keep the cart full for my mother. As the chickens grew larger they began to eat more, and we lifted 500 to 700 pounds every day. Each week we grew stronger and the job got easier, but it was the start of a lot of heavy lifting I would do for the benefit of chickens.

My father came home for two days at Christmas, and for that short time, we were a whole family again. That brief visit reminded me of how much I missed him. When his mate pulled into our driveway to pick him up for the return trip to the Potomac, I went to my room and read a comic book, not wanting to see him leave.

My big present that Christmas was a chemistry set and it was a diversion from the sadness. Danny was only five, but he took a real interest in science. My brother watched intently as I mixed up the formulas in the instruction book; he liked to see the solutions bubble or change color. The fun started when we began to mix chemicals randomly. Sometimes I let him chose the compounds to use in the experiment. He would point to several vials that appealed to him and I would mix a little of each in a test tube. Some mixtures boiled over and others exploded. Twice we had small fires on the tabletop. My mother never complained, except once when we produced a smell so strong everyone had to leave the house.

One afternoon Danny and I were experimenting on the card table in the dining room while Mom was cooking supper. Our first batch that day was dull—nothing but a slight color change took place when I mixed the chemicals. I tried heating the tube with the kit's alcohol burner, and for a while there appeared to be no reaction, but then a few bubbles appeared at the bottom. I heated it some more and, without warning, the entire mixture erupted from the tube, hitting the ceiling with a "splat."

Mom heard the sound and rushed in from the kitchen. Danny and I were staring up at the brown dripping mess on the ceiling. "It was his idea," we said in unison.

"Never mind, move your stuff so I can clean it up," she said.

Mom scrubbed the ceiling three times but the brown stain would not go away. After a few days she painted over it. In a week it was back and she painted it again. In two weeks the spot was beginning to reappear and she covered it one more time, but it was no use. We would look at that stain for years, until my father tore out part of the ceiling while installing a new furnace. After the incident, Mom ordered us to follow the instructions in the chemistry set manual. None of those experiments was very exciting and we soon put the set away in the attic.

During the remainder of that winter, my father came home as often as his boss would allow. On those weekends he and my mother talked mostly about the chicken house, but sometimes they discussed the action on the Potomac. I overheard a few of those conversations and it was obvious my father was frustrated. The Virginia dredgers were regularly escaping to their home waters and making it almost impossible for the TFC officers to arrest them.

Most of the boat chases occurred near the town of Colonial Beach. One of the fastest Virginia vessels was named the *Gray Ghost,* and it always outran the Maryland patrol boats whenever they pursued it. One January night, well after midnight, Dad and his mate surprised three oystermen handscraping in it. When the searchlight came on, the men sprang into action and got their boat underway. Dad positioned himself on the *Somerset's* bow with a rifle while his mate took the helm. He hoped to get a shot at the fleeing boat's engine, but two watermen draped themselves over the engine box to protect it. They were gambling that he would not shoot them to protect oysters and they were right.

But the watermen had been greedy that night, loading their boat heavily with oysters, which slowed her speed. As the vessel fled toward the Virginia shore, the *Somerset* was able to keep up. While his mate trained the light on the handscraper, my father began to shoot at the boat along its waterline. If he could not stop her, he at least wanted to do some damage. The shooting must have rattled the men, because as they approached Colonial Beach, two of them dove into the frigid water and swam to shore.

The chase continued until the remaining oysterman decided to beach his boat on the edge of town. He jumped ashore and disappeared among the houses where the officers could not pursue him. Part of the vessel was resting on Virginia soil but its stern was in Maryland waters. Dad hooked a line to the boat and used the *Somerset* to pull it off the beach. A week later he towed it to Deal Island, hoping the state would be able to use it as a patrol boat, but it leaked so much from bullet holes, they eventually scuttled it.

Not long after that, my father was involved in another chase near Colonial Beach where the fleeing dredger poured gasoline on the water in front of the *Somerset* and tried to ignite it. Luckily, his matches blew out before they hit the surface. My father continued the pursuit, but the man ran his boat into one of the small creeks and escaped. No one was ever arrested for that attempt on an officer's life. The situation on the Potomac was getting more dangerous and everyone knew it.

12. At the Harbor Alone

 THE WINTER ENDED AND MY FATHER CAME HOME FROM the Potomac. Crabbing season began and our family went back to its old routines. Despite a few disease problems in the birds, my mother was successful with her first flock of chickens. When Dad returned, he took over the chores of feeding and caring for the new flock. Mom said she was glad to be free of the chicken house, but I noticed she walked through it every day, compiling a list of things my father was overlooking. Usually it mentioned leaking water troughs, feeders that needed adjusting, or a brooder not quite up to temperature. Dad fixed the things he thought were important but never completed her entire list. Before the second flock was sold, she was convinced that she could do a better job with the chickens.

In the early summer Milbert allowed me to join his chicken house clean-out crew—it was a big day in my life. This crew was a group of young men and boys who shoveled out the manure after the chickens were sold. Bobby and the Bates brothers were members, but until that summer I was considered too small to do the job. I would have done the work for nothing, but my uncle paid me sixty-five cents per hour, same as the older boys, even though I was doing less. He must have considered my wages an investment in the future. None of the others complained; they had been treated the same way when they started.

Some people would have considered chicken house clean-out just a dirty job, but I could not have been happier. I was proving my worth to adults, building my muscles, and earning spending money. The older boys were there and it was where I wanted to be. I was disappointed Milbert that only needed us a few days at a time.

* * *

One hot morning in July, my father decided to take Danny with him on the *Somerset.* I asked to go along but he said no. Seeing the disappointment in my face, he suggested I ride my bike to Champ and set crab lines around the wharves. I had never been allowed to go to the harbor alone, and the excitement of it took some of the sting out of his invitation to my brother.

On the way to Champ, I picked up deposit soda bottles along the roadside to get money for crab bait. Mom had placed my chicken house wages in a new savings account she had opened in my name.

At the harbor, I set nine bottles on the counter in the little store and told the proprietor, Mr. Albert Dashiell, that I needed crab bait. He was a kindly, white-haired gentleman who controlled most of the business on St. Peter's Creek. His store was the only source of groceries, boat supplies, gas and bait.

"Follow me, Master Noble," he said. We walked out of the store and through a covered porch that connected it to the wharf. The porch was a pleasant spot where watermen sat and talked when their workday was over. Halfway down the wharf was the bait shack.

"I only have tripe today," Mr. Albert said. He removed the canvas cover from the wooden barrel containing the salted cow's stomach. I leaned over for a look but the odor drove me back. He suppressed a laugh. "Boy, you've got to get used to this if you're going to crab."

"I've used hog chokers before and they don't stink so bad," I said.

"Tripe does have a flavor you don't forget." He pulled a rusty butcher knife from a crack in the wall and sliced off a chunk. "Here you go, eighteen cents worth," he said, handing me the bait. "It's a pleasure doing business with you. If you catch any crabs I'll buy them."

I did catch crabs that day but I also got hungry. Mr. Albert began to run an account for me that I paid off with crabs—two peelers or a large soft shell would buy a candy bar, three Jimmies would get me a soda. I spent most of the money I earned buying snacks in the store.

My day wasn't very profitable but it was fun. I went to Champ regularly after that.

* * *

The trips to the harbor were not my biggest excitement for the summer. That began one evening during a ballgame, when a biplane, something we had never seen before, roared low over our house. All the players stopped to watch as it dipped below the trees and appeared to go down near Clemmon Maddox's house. Eight of us, including the Bates boys, mounted our bikes and raced off to the scene.

When we arrived the plane was landing, rolling unharmed through the newly mowed field across from Clemmon's house. The pilot was seated in the open cockpit, wearing a flying cap and goggles. He taxied near to where we were standing and cut the engine. When he removed his flying gear, we saw a handsome, dark-haired man with a crew cut, whom Johnny recognized as Beauchamp Bloodsworth, a local World War II veteran who was making his living as a crop duster.

He climbed down from the plane and walked toward us. "I'm going to be flying out of this field for the next month," he announced. We stood speechless and stunned that an aircraft had landed in our neighborhood. "Would you like to see the airplane?" he asked. We all moved forward at once and he put up his hand. "Hold it, make a line. You can all have a turn."

Beauchamp helped each of us onto the plane's wing and showed us the cockpit and how to move the control stick. Just as he finished, his wife drove up in a pickup truck filled with bags of insecticide. She was an attractive, blonde-haired woman about my mother's age.

"Got a ground crew, huh?" she said.

He winked at us and smiled. "Yeah, it looks like a good one."

"Are you going up tonight?" she said.

"Just one trip."

Beauchamp began loading the plane, and the Bates brothers and I volunteered to help. We opened the bags of dust and handed them up to him. He stood on the lower wing and dumped the white powder into the hopper. When it was full, he walked to the front of the plane and spun the wooden propeller. The engine coughed once and then began to run smoothly. He climbed into the cockpit and taxied to the runway with us following at a safe distance. When he brought the engine up to full throttle, the roar caused some of the boys in our group to cheer. We all stood in awe as the plane raced down the grass strip and lifted off.

Our pilot returned in half an hour with his dust hopper empty. He drove two metal stakes into the ground and tied his airplane to them. After thanking us for our help, he promised to return the next day when the wind died down.

The following afternoon no one wanted to play ball. We hung around under the beech tree in our front yard, waiting for Beauchamp. When his truck appeared, we jumped on our bikes and followed it to the airfield. That became our daily ritual, broken only if thunderstorms prevented him from flying. As the days passed, some of the kids stopped going, but the Bates boys and I always showed up. Bobby dropped by whenever he was free from farm work.

We steadily improved as a ground crew and Johnny became chief. Before each takeoff, Beauchamp would tell us how much dust he needed for the next load. While he was gone we opened the bags and sat them beside the runway, which shortened his time on the ground.

To show his appreciation, he did a few stunts for us every day after the last flight. One evening just before dark, he must have decided that we deserved something special. After several rolls, he climbed high and made a steep dive, hurtling directly toward us. We tried to remain calm as the old plane screamed downward, but in the end we scattered like yard chickens. When he finally pulled up, the plane's wheel just cleared the chimney on Clemmon's house. Clemmon had been sitting on his front porch in a rocking chair. When we looked down to get his reaction, he was crawling through the front door on his hands and knees. The rocking chair was lying on its side and his Panama hat was in the front yard. After our hearts calmed down, we ran over to check on him, but he declined to come outdoors as long as the plane's motor was running.

"What did you think of it?" I said, through the screen door.

"That son-of-a-bitch is crazy," came the reply from inside the house's dark interior. We suspected that Clemmon's statement was a little bit true, but the air show was the most thrilling thing any of us had ever seen.

Beauchamp landed and we walked back to the field as he was tying down the plane. He took one look at our faces and broke into laughter. "Why did you boys run? Don't you have any faith in me?"

We all started to answer at once, talking excitedly about the plane diving toward us. He got in his truck and started the engine. "See you tomorrow," he said, still grinning.

A few days later there was more excitement. It happened as Beauchamp was about to go out with his second load of dust for the afternoon. Just before spinning the propeller to start the engine, he asked me to get him a pack of matches from the truck, which was parked close by.

I opened the truck door and searched the dashboard but found nothing. Then I leaned across the seat and looked in the glove box, but all I saw were receipts for aviation gas. The plane's engine started; it seemed a little louder than usual, though not enough to alarm me. I was still searching for matches when I heard Billy yell, "Terry, watch out!" When I raised my head and looked out the windshield, the plane was less than a truck length away and rolling toward me. Our pilot was hanging onto the side of the cockpit. I froze, staring at the spinning propeller unable to figure out what was happening. In two seconds the engine quit and the big blade stopped turning, coming to rest six feet from where I was sitting.

Beauchamp ran over to me; it was the only time I ever saw him look anything but cool. "Boy, are you okay? I thought you were a goner," he said nervously.

"I'm fine," I said calmly. I had been too mesmerized by the propeller to be scared.

After the plane departed with its load, Johnny told me what had happened. The engine had been hard to start on the previous flight, so this time Beauchamp opened the throttle a bit more. When the motor came to life, the aircraft lurched forward and its wing knocked him down. After it passed over him, he jumped up and grabbed the side of the cockpit. It took him a few seconds to find the switch and kill the engine; his quick reflexes had saved me.

Our time with Beauchamp ended before we were ready. One day he gave us the news we had been dreading. "Boys, we've killed all the bean beetles in this part of the county. I'm going to move the plane to another location. After this flight I won't be back."

"Can't we work for you at the new strip?" I asked.

"No, it's too far away, but I sure appreciate your help here. If you'll come back Saturday morning, I'll have a surprise for you."

For two days we tried to figure out his surprise but nothing we thought of seemed right. On Saturday the Bates boys and I went to the field at the appointed time and waited for the familiar truck. It was late. We were growing restless when a single winged plane appeared in the northeast sky. We gave it little thought until it circled and came in to land. As it taxied toward us we could see Beauchamp at the controls. He opened the cockpit door.

"Boys, I'm going to give you an airplane ride," he shouted. "Come over here Johnny, you're first." We looked at each other, surprised and a little afraid. Johnny hesitated. "Don't worry, I'll fly carefully—no stunts," Beauchamp said.

Johnny walked over and got in the front seat. As they rolled away, he looked at us as if it would be the last time he ever saw us. The flight lasted less than twenty minutes, and when they were back on the ground, I could see Johnny's big grin from far away.

Billy was the next to go up. While he was away I pumped his brother for information.

"Just wait and see for yourself," Johnny said. He kept smiling and looking at the plane in the distance.

When it came time for my flight, I was nervous but that disappeared when we lifted off. I watched everything shrink in size as we climbed out over Louie's farm. Beauchamp made a turn over the gut where we had found Milbert's old skiff, and for the first time I saw how the creek snaked back and forth on its way to the river. Over the Bates farm, I spotted the reflection from the gravel pit. He circled our house and pointed out the tiny figure of my mother hanging out clothes. She had no idea I was up in the plane.

When the flight was over, I knew I liked flying, but one thing had changed forever—the world around our neighborhood had gotten smaller. After seeing it from the air, none of my adventures seemed as wild as before.

* * *

When Beauchamp took off for the last time, most of the excitement of that summer went with him. Bobby and the Bates boys were often busy with chores at home, and I was left on my own to find something to do. On many of those mornings, I rode my bike to Champ to crab and fish. Mom let me keep enough money from my wages to buy a cheap rod and reel, and before leaving home, I always tied it on my bike along with the crab net. When I arrived at Champ, I started out crabbing, but when the tide was right, I took one peeler from my catch and went fishing for the perch and small rockfish that came into the harbor looking for food. I sat on the end of the county wharf and offered them pieces of peeler and a free lip piercing. If I caught any large enough, Mom cooked them for supper.

At the supper table, Dad always asked me what part of the peeler I had used to catch the biggest fish. He preferred the soft, new shell that was growing under the back of the crab. I liked to use the meat from inside the claws.

One afternoon I fished through most of the high tide without hooking any keepers. All the little perch had stolen my bait and my peeler was used up. I was about to quit when Sammy Mills walked down the wharf. He was a lifelong waterman about the age of my grandfather, and he made his living entirely from crabs and oysters. Not fond of shaving, he usually wore gray stubble and occasionally his face was red from something other than the sun. The proper members of our church, which he never attended, described men like him as rogues, but he was always nice to me.

"Little Noble, what are you catching?" Sammy said.

"Nothing, and I used up my bait."

He looked down at the remains of the female peeler lying in my basket. "You've still got some crab pussy there." He picked up the soft apron containing the reproductive parts and handed it to me. I had never heard that word used except to describe a cat.

"I've always thrown that part of the crab away," I said.

"Boy, there ain't no better bait than crab pussy, put it on your hook."

I took his suggestion, then made a long cast into the channel. He seemed satisfied and walked back toward the store. I had barely gotten the slack out of my line when a rockfish swallowed the bait and made a run across the creek. I fought it with my little rod and after an exciting battle, I dragged it on shore beside the wharf. At eighteen inches, it was the biggest fish I had ever caught on my own.

I picked up my catch and ran to the store porch where a half dozen watermen were sitting on the wooden benches, talking about a large school of stingrays that had migrated into the river. The men all acted impressed when I held the rockfish in front of them.

"I told you that was good bait," Sammy said. "You'll listen to me from now on I'll bet."

I was giving everyone a second chance to see my fish when a car drove up beside the store. I turned and saw my father getting out of our '54 Chevrolet. Court had adjourned early and he was coming to check on me.

"Look at this, Dad," I said holding up the fish.

"That's a good one, what did you catch him on?"

"Crab pussy," I said loudly, proud of my new word. Snickering broke out among the watermen. My father looked annoyed. The snickering turned to howls of laughter.

"Where did you learn that word?" Dad asked.

"From Sammy." I turned toward where he had been seated but he was not there. I saw the edge of his form disappearing around the corner of the store.

My father walked me over to the car and told me I should not use that word anymore. Laughter was still erupting on the porch and Dad frowned. He shouldn't have been surprised. It was not the only new word I would learn at the harbor.

* * *

Even though my father was the law on the river, he remained friends with most of the watermen. He had known the men at Champ since childhood, and his favorite was Bruce Bozman, an intelligent man with lively eyes that shone through his wire-rimmed spectacles. Bruce's ready smile and sense of humor made him fun to be around.

One day Bobby and I rode with my father on the *Somerset,* while he checked out the engines following some routine maintenance. Dad took the boat out to Fishing Island and the engines ran perfectly. On the way back he spotted Bruce crab scraping near Geanquakin Creek. He handed Bobby and me a pair of binoculars each.

"Keep an eye on him," he said pointing toward the boat. I could see Bruce bent over the washboard culling crabs. He was wearing his usual summer dress—white shirt, khaki pants and a straw hat with a green plastic visor.

Dad turned the *Somerset* toward Bruce and gunned the engines. The big boat began to plane the surface, bearing down on the smaller crab boat. For a full minute, the waterman appeared not to notice our approach and continued his work. Then he casually reached under the washboard, brought out a basket, and dumped its contents overboard.

"I knew it. Did you see him dump those oysters?" my father said with a chuckle. "He catches one or two with every pull of his scrapes. It's against the law but I know he keeps them. He pours them out around the stake where he ties up his boat. This winter when the weather is bad he can catch them again and make a little money right in the harbor."

"Well, you made him get rid of them today," Bobby said.

"Things aren't always what they seem. He poured them right in front of his scrape, which means he'll catch them all again. If I go over there now, he won't pull that scrape aboard until I leave. There's no way I can fine him unless I see the oysters in his boat."

My father turned the *Somerset* back toward Champ. He shook his head and grinned, satisfied that he had played his part in Bruce's game.

13. Dad is Shot

 IT WAS A SUNNY OCTOBER AFTERNOON AS THE TWO BOATS raced through the light chop near Deal Island. The rumble of their engines echoed off houses along the shore. The *Somerset* was in pursuit but my father wasn't on board; he was in the lead boat. Earlier in the week, the TFC had sent him another used vessel to put into service as a patrol boat in his territory. He was trying it out, comparing its speed to the *Somerset.* The new boat was only a little faster and he was disappointed.

Unbeknownst to Dad, his supervisor, the Chief Inspector, drove up to the harbor during the race. It was Friday and he had returned home from his job in Annapolis. He had procured the new boat, and he was furious when he saw my father putting it under such stress.

When Dad arrived at the dock, an argument started between the two men. My father insisted he needed to know the boat's speed and if it was reliable in a chase. His boss said it was hard to find boats at a reasonable price and he did not want that one ruined the first week in service. The argument grew more heated, and the Chief Inspector cursed my father while some of the officers under Dad's command stood within earshot. He was the only man that ever swore at him without paying for it physically. This time my father did an uncharacteristic thing—he walked away from a fight.

The next day Dad turned in his uniforms and pistol. By then the

Chief Inspector had cooled down and wanted him to stay on but my father declined.

The next few days were unpleasant at our house; my father seethed with anger and Mom worried about their financial situation. There were mortgage payments due on our house and the chicken house. They could not pay the bills with just the income from the chickens. She pleaded with him to ask for his job back. For days he refused, but at the end of the week he stuffed his pride in some dark corner and called the Chief Inspector. His boss allowed him to return to work but assigned him to the Potomac River again for the entire winter. It was disagreeable news, but my mother was happy to have the promise of a steady paycheck.

A week later, on the misty night of October 22, 1956, Dad and his mate were patrolling the Potomac River near Swann Point bar. Shortly after midnight, they shut down the *Somerset's* engines to listen for the sound of an illegal dredger. They heard the rumble of a large motor not far away. Dad restarted the patrol boat and moved toward the sound. In a few minutes he saw a flicker of light from the dredger's buoy. The watermen had marked a spot of plentiful oysters in the usual way, with an oil lantern covered by a bushel basket, floating on an anchored inner tube. It emitted just enough light for them to maintain their location over the oysters. My father knew that one or more boats would be working nearby.

Dad slipped the *Somerset* into neutral and waited. In less than a minute, a vessel passed in front of the lantern. He switched on his search light and was surprised to see the converted German patrol boat only a few yards away. It was the closest a TFC boat had ever been to the Virginia vessel. The light shocked the four oystermen on board, but their captain knew he could easily outrun the officers. There was one thing he had not considered—he had been running his 600-horsepower engine at idle speed, and when he gave it full throttle, it flooded and stalled.

Seeing his chance, Dad forced the *Somerset* up against the side of the dredger. His mate ran to the bow and began to lash the two boats together. The dredge boat captain picked up a hatchet and ran forward, taking several swings at the officer who retreated aboard the police boat. The waterman hacked through the lash rope, freeing his vessel. Dad's mate drew his revolver but did not fire.

My father stepped out of the cabin preparing to shoot the dredger's engine. As he was taking aim, the rifle went off prematurely and fell from his hand. Dad couldn't understand why it had gone off early and caused him to miss. In a few seconds the numbness in his arm and the blood dripping from his fingers gave him the answer—he had been shot.

The dredger managed to restart his boat and it quickly pulled away from the *Somerset.* Dad's mate, seeing what had happened, fired several shots at the fleeing vessel but only punched holes in the darkness.

My father's wound was in his right arm above the elbow. The bullet passed completely through his flesh and came to rest somewhere on the bottom of the river. Initially, he felt little pain and the blood loss was minimal. Using one arm, he ran the *Somerset* back to its Maryland port. An ambulance transported him to a hospital in Baltimore.

At home, Mom, Danny, and I slept peacefully through the night. The phone rang at 6:00 AM and my mother got up to answer it. A *Baltimore Sun* newspaper reporter was on the line.

"Mrs. Noble, can you tell me anything about your husband's shooting?" he said.

"I don't know what you're talking about, you must have made a mistake," Mom answered.

"Oh I'm sorry," the reporter stammered and hung up before Mom could ask any questions. Now fully awake and scared, my mother called the TFC chairman at his home in Crisfield.

"Yes, he's been shot, but he'll be fine," Dad's boss said. "I'm sending a car to take you to Baltimore." He went on to explain what he knew about the shooting.

Mom woke Danny and me and gave us a brief explanation of what happened. She told us to get dressed and that we were going to stay with our aunt and uncle for a few days. In the early morning light, she drove us to the Shockleys' house. Danny was still young and unaffected by the news but I worried about my father. It seemed impossible that he had been shot—I had always thought that he was indestructible. It was a relief when I remembered how often men were shot in the arm in cowboy movies, and were back to normal the next day.

In Washington, D.C., forty miles upriver from where my father was injured, I doubt if anyone heard about our problems. Their attention was on Hungary and the Middle East. In a little more than twenty-four hours, Russian tanks would roll into Budapest. In a week, Israel would invade Egypt and the Suez crisis would be underway. It was a week that changed our family and the world.

The day after the shooting, Maryland authorities charged the dredge boat captain with attempting to kill a TFC officer. Virginia State police arrested him but the court released him on bail. The conflict between the states had escalated to a point that Virginia refused to extradite him to Maryland for trial.

Dad and his mate were not sure if anyone on the dredge boat had fired a gun—they had not seen a flash. The doctors thought the bullet had entered from the back of his arm but they were not certain. If it were true, the shot could not have come from the boat they were trying to apprehend. To take the heat off themselves, the illegal dredger community at Colonial Beach floated the theory that Dad was shot by his mate. My father knew that was impossible, based on where his mate had been standing. He was convinced the shot was fired from another dredge boat working unseen in the darkness. He was aware that unless one of the watermen talked, the case would not be solved.

The bullet severed the median nerve in my father's arm, leaving him with a partially paralyzed hand. Doctors operated and reattached the nerve ends, hoping it would regenerate. He came home from the hospital with a leather and steel brace running the full length of his arm, which was to remain on for eight months.

My father asked to return to work with the brace but his boss said no. A few days later, word came that the Chief Inspector had promoted his brother-in-law to Dad's position. It was a restless time for my father, unsure of his future with the TFC and unable to do useful work in the chicken house.

Six months after the shooting, Virginia convicted the dredge boat captain of illegally dredging oysters and his boat was confiscated. No one was ever tried for attempting to kill my father.

After the incident, TFC officers got tougher with oystermen on the Potomac. Maryland acquired a PT boat from the Navy and its captain rammed and sank several Virginia boats. That caused many illegal dredgers to find another line of work, but the hard-core poachers continued to catch oysters.

Maryland and Virginia fought a legal battle in the Supreme Court over control of the river. In the end, an act of Congress formed the Bi-State Commission to regulate the waterway. It forced more cooperation between the states, but it did not end illegal oystering.

Three years after my father was shot, a Virginia boat tried to ram a TFC vessel. The officers opened fire, killing one oysterman and wounding another. After that action, illegal dredging all but disappeared on the Chesapeake. It marked an end to the violence over oysters that had been going on for nearly one hundred years.

14. Do Boat Motors Explode?

 THE BELLOWING SOUND COULD HAVE COME FROM A BULL but there were no cattle in Champ. The source of the noise was a mystery but it did not occupy my thoughts for long. I was poling toward the harbor, shirtless and barefoot, riding the incoming tide. It was a windless July day and I had been netting crabs all morning, near the mouth of St. Peter's Creek. I was eleven and, just the day before, I had passed my father's swimming test. He had given me permission to take a skiff down the creek as far as Crab Island. I was still not a strong swimmer, but I convinced him I could make it back to the boat if I fell overboard.

Another bellow rumbled down the creek and this time it sounded human. I continued poling and looked at the skiff bottom; as usual, it was covered with crabs, mud and eelgrass. I was planning to cull my catch and clean up the boat at the wharf. In my head I added up the value of all the soft crabs, peelers and Jimmies lying in view. It was a good haul and I would have extra money for the upcoming trip to Ocean City.

The sound came again, this time more of a roar, and I was close enough to make out some words. "BRING ME MY SKIFF!" Someone was obviously mad. A man was standing on the end of Mr. Albert's wharf waving his arms. Suddenly I had a sick feeling—it was Phil Ford and I had his skiff.

Earlier that morning I had come to the harbor planning to use Sigsbee's skiff, but someone had already borrowed it, which was common
practice in Champ. The only other skiff in sight was one I had never
seen before. It was freshly painted white with orange trim on the gunnels and it was a good size for dipnetting. Since it was too late for any
crabbers to be going out, I decided to use it.

I was loading my gear into the new vessel when Mr. Albert stepped
onto the store porch. "That's Phil Ford's brand new skiff." There was a
warning tone in his voice but I ignored it. I shoved off, in a hurry to
crab the last of the ebb tide.

Phil was a large, powerful man with heavy shoulders. His daughter
was in my class at school but I didn't know him well. He had a job on
land and seldom went out in his crab boat. It had been easy to convince myself he would not need his skiff that day.

"I WANT MY SKIFF NOW!" Phil yelled again. I tried to pole faster but my
arms had grown weak. I no longer saw the crabs, just the muddy mess
I had made of his new boat. My doom was getting closer with every
stroke of the pole and I saw no escape. Was Phil going to whip me or
throw me off the wharf into the creek? Either way, it would be embarrassing with the watermen watching from the porch. My mind was racing, looking for a way out, when I spotted Johnny Dize sitting on the
other crab wharf. He had his back to the creek and was culling through
a basket of peelers. Johnny was a gray-haired, distinguished looking
man who carried the collection plate at church on Sundays. I would
pass by him thirty yards before I got to where Phil was waiting. Suddenly, I had hope that he might save me.

I kept my eye on Johnny, looking for a sign or a suggestion but he
continued with his work, steadily tossing peelers into floats. I steered
close to the end of the wharf where he was sitting. The skiff almost
scraped the barnacle-covered pilings as I drifted by. My eyes fixed on
his back, hoping for a response, but it looked as if he was going to let
me pass without a word. At the last second he turned toward me with
a sly grin. "Fucked up this time didn't you?" he said.

I was stunned. Johnny was not going to help and he had used a
word no good Methodist should utter. He had been my last hope; I
poled toward Mr. Albert's wharf and whatever awaited me. I tied up at
the spot farthest from where Phil was standing and began to toss all

my crabs into a basket. The wharf creaked as the big man approached and when his shadow fell across the skiff, I did not look up.

"God almighty, what a mess," he said, looking at his boat. "Boy, I'm going to skin you, get it cleaned up right now."

"Yes sir," I said. I was relieved he was not going to kill me until his skiff was put right. Within a minute, all my crabs were in the basket except for a sook hiding under the deck. I reached for her in haste, and she clamped down on my hand with both claws. The pain was severe and I held her underwater to get her to release, but she did not let go immediately. Phil paced the wharf and the men on the porch laughed at the scene. My embarrassment was complete.

When the sook opened her claws and swam away, I removed my hand from the water and blood was dripping from two fingers. I ignored it and began to scoop out the mud and grass. When it was gone, I threw a few scoops of water into the bottom and began to scrub it with my tee shirt. In a short time the boat was spotless. I wiped off the last drop of blood and looked up at Phil to see what he was going to do. My hard work and the sight of my bleeding fingers must have cooled his anger.

"Boy, when I come to this creek to use my skiff, I want it to be here. I had plans to be down the river fishing by now," he said in a gruff voice.

"I'm sorry; I won't ever borrow it again." I said. I was ready to jump overboard and wade to shore if he tried to come after me. It was a surprise when he went on talking.

"If you want to use this skiff in the future, call me beforehand," he said. It was hard to believe I was getting off so lightly. I picked up my basket of crabs and headed to the store before he could change his mind.

From that day forward, whenever I saw Phil, he smiled and asked if I had been crabbing. We sort of became friends but I never had the nerve to borrow his skiff again. In fact, I never borrowed anyone's boat again without asking.

* * *

The brace remained on my father's arm for most of the summer and every few weeks he went to Baltimore to have it adjusted. He had come home from the hospital with his elbow in the flexed position and the doctors were slowly extending his arm. He was still not able to move his thumb, index and middle fingers. With the hot weather, a skin rash developed on his upper arm under the brace.

"This thing is driving me crazy," he said one afternoon, handing me his pocketknife. "Cut off some of this leather." He pulled the top of the device away from his skin.

"I might slice your arm."

"No, you can do it. Just be careful," he said confidently.

For the next half hour, I cut away the leather as he directed me. When I was finished he seemed pleased with the work. "Now maybe I can get some sleep." He headed for the sofa to take his afternoon nap.

Dad seemed lost without the job or a boat; when he wasn't napping, he could usually be found at the Corner Store or on the porch at Champ. With only one usable arm, he had a hard time completing even small chores in the chicken house. Mom handled the ventilation and kept the water troughs and feeders adjusted. She even did minor repairs, using some of her tools leftover from her time at the airplane factory. I took over the job of feeding the birds with a little help from Danny. I overheard Dad tell Mom that, for the first time in his life, he felt useless.

* * *

During the previous winter, Milbert and my father had sold their oyster boat. My uncle built a wide-beamed, square stern skiff to replace it. Dad bought a used outboard motor to power the new boat. The skiff was large enough for tonging oysters in the shallow water of their lease.

The Bates boys and I wanted to try out the new boat, but I was having trouble summoning the nerve to ask my father's permission. One afternoon at the harbor, after the three of us were bored with swimming, we approached my father on the store porch.

"Dad, can we take the boat down the creek just once?" I asked, in my most responsible tone. The porch was filled with watermen and I figured it would be harder for him to refuse in front of them.

"No, you boys don't know enough yet; you'll tear up something."

"Tom, don't be such a hard-ass," Bruce said. "Let the boys use the boat."

"Yeah, how are they going to learn if you don't turn them loose?" Sammy said. "Quit worrying about your old used motor."

My father laughed and I could see my plan was working better than I had hoped.

"Okay, you can use it but there are going to be rules," Dad said. "You have to buy the gas. You can't go out in the river and you can't go up the creek past Bruce's cove. There's a sunken boat up there, and if you hit it, you'll damage the motor." Bruce's house was on a small cove and the water got shallow past that point.

"Okay," I said eagerly. I would have agreed to any rules to get to use a powerboat, even a little one. The Bates boys and I started running down the wharf.

"Wait a minute," my father shouted. We stopped near the bait shack and he looked straight at me. "In the future, you can only use the boat if all three of you are here. I think Johnny and Billy are sensible enough to keep you from wrecking it."

"I'll be careful," I promised.

"Don't damage that motor or you'll be sorry," he said, pointing at me. We hurried to the skiff before he could come up with more rules.

Since my father owned the motor, I got to be captain first. I pulled away from the wharf with no problem and began to cruise slowly around the harbor, trying my best to look responsible. The men on the porch were surely watching. I was just getting the feel of the boat when my father waved for us to come to the wharf. I approached too fast and the skiff's gunnel bounced off a piling, causing him to wince.

"If you damage this boat you're going to pay for fixing it," he said. I had no doubt that he meant it. "That's enough time on the motor for today. You can use it again tomorrow."

The Bates boys and I arrived at the harbor early the next morning. We pooled our money and filled the little gas tank mounted on top of the motor. I headed for Crab Island, the southern boundary of the territory my father had outlined. I started out with the throttle at half speed, but with a little encouragement from Johnny, it was soon wide open. The boat was still slow, but full throttle was more exciting than half speed.

At Crab Island, Billy took the helm and ran back toward the wharf, following the shoreline in and out of every cove. When Johnny became captain, he steered in tight circles around every workboat stake in the harbor. We continued to take turns at the controls, attempting every maneuver we could imagine. When we ran out of ideas, we repeated everything with the motor in reverse. By then we were ready for something new.

"I dare you to go under the County Wharf," Johnny said, when I was at the helm. We had been under it before in Sigsbee's skiff; it was like passing through a dimly lit tunnel made up of pilings and beams. It would be a risky move under power but he had dared me.

I steered toward the wharf at full throttle, playing a game of chicken with my passengers. As we got close they began to yell for me to slow down, but I didn't cut the throttle until the last second. To avoid the beams, they lay backward until their upper bodies were level with the gunnels. I tried to do the same but my shoulders hit the motor. I slid sideways just before my head would have struck a beam. The tide was a bit higher than I had figured and the motor cleared the timber by less than an inch. Steering frantically from a prone position, I managed to miss the pilings and came out on the other side of the wharf.

"Dumbass, you almost cut our heads off," Billy said. I had to admit that it was a close call.

Happy that the boat was unharmed, we decided to play it safe and go fishing. On the way I stopped by Mr. Albert's wharf and filled the tank again with gas. Some of it spilled over the engine but I didn't worry about it; it had never caused a problem before. I headed for Crab Island Hole, the deepest spot in the channel, with Johnny and Billy sitting on the middle seat facing forward. About halfway there Johnny turned and looked back. His eyes grew large.

"The motor's on fire," he shouted. Thinking it was one of his jokes I refused to turn around. "I mean it. Look!" he yelled, pointing.

That time he sounded sincere and I spun around. Blue flames were covering the top of the engine. I shut off the motor but the fire kept going. For a few seconds we all watched in disbelief, and then Billy grabbed the bailing scoop and started throwing water on the flames. With each scoopful the fire died down, but it came up again as soon as the water ran off. Gas started flowing out of the vent hole in the tank cap and a blowtorch like flame erupted.

"It's going to blow up!" Johnny shouted. He dove overboard and Billy and I followed him. We swam away from the boat and treaded water, waiting for the explosion. A minute passed and nothing happened—the fire just kept burning. We swam back to the boat and splashed more water on the flames but they refused to go out. The paint on the motor was starting to bubble and I realized my father was going to kill me. As I listened to the motor sizzle, I had an even more horrible thought— what if the boat caught fire and burned up? Jesus, he would probably put me in reform school.

Fearing my father more than dying in an explosion, I pulled myself back into the boat. In desperation I removed my wet shirt and threw it over the motor. The blow torch sound fizzled out. I scooped more water onto the shirt and kept watching for flames to reappear. Mercifully, they did not.

Johnny and Billy climbed back aboard but we were all breathing too hard to talk. It was some time before I found the courage to uncover the motor. I lifted the shirt slowly, afraid the fire would return. The top of the engine was blackened, but the paint, which was not perfect before the fire, was mostly intact. The cool water must have caused the blisters to stick back to the metal. I scrubbed the whole engine vigorously with my shirt; the black soot washed off along with just a little paint.

It was ebb tide and we were drifting toward the river. To get back to the harbor we had to restart the motor, and Johnny stood ready with my wet shirt while I pulled the rope. It started easily in spite of having been drenched with water. There was no fire but we never took our eyes off the motor until we were back at the wharf.

I found some oil in the bait shack and wiped it over the engine. It evened out the color differences in the paint and put a nice shine on the surface. After I finished, it looked more used than before but it was hard to tell a fire had occurred. We all agreed there was no reason to mention such a minor incident to my father.

For the next two weeks, the Bates boys and I avoided Champ altogether, afraid to be there if my father noticed any difference in the motor. During most of that time, we worked for Milbert, hauling hay and cleaning out chicken houses. One day we picked tomatoes for Preston Lawrence. I had been sick the night before with an upset stomach and I still felt bad when it came time to go to the tomato field. It was my first time picking that crop and I was the youngest worker there. Besides the Bates brothers, Louie and two boys from Monie were the only other pickers. It was a hot, humid day and tomatoes were scarce; heavy rains in June had reduced the crop, requiring me to drag each basket some distance before it was full.

The rows were long and I soon fell behind the other boys. Even Billy, who was only a year older, was way ahead of me. When I started my second set of rows, they were half-finished with theirs. The sun climbed and by midmorning the temperature was over ninety. I was still feeling nauseated and wanted to quit, but I couldn't leave without completing my rows. Louie passed by me, returning from getting a drink of water.

"Master Noble, are you having a bad time?" he said.

"I don't eat tomatoes and I don't like picking them," I grumbled.

"It's just work. Like all of us, you have to get used to it."

"I can't finish these rows," I said.

"Sure you can. Just think about something that's fun, like fishing, and the time will pass easier." He bent over and started picking in my row and he kept at it until we caught up with Billy. "You can do it from here," he said, leaving to finish his rows. After he was gone I tried thinking about fishing, and it did make the job easier. It even helped me forget my stomachache. When the other boys reached the end of the field, I was not far behind. Once again, Louie had saved me when work seemed overwhelming. He had taught me to ignore physical discomfort, which was a valuable lesson. I picked tomatoes several times after that, and no one had to help me, but I never learned to like the job.

After two weeks of steady work, the Bates boys and I were ready for a trip to the creek. We started our day by taking a skiff out to the channel and using it as a diving platform. When we tired of swimming, we flipped the boat upside down, trapping air under it. All of us swam under water and came up in the air bubble, floating there with just our heads above the surface. It seemed like a secret spot that no one else could enter. Anyone watching from shore would have thought we had drowned.

The three of us stayed under the skiff a long time discussing girls. Johnny, who was nearly fifteen, was our teacher and he described in detail what some of the older couples in our school were doing. He was at a particularly good part when a man's voice penetrated our hideaway.

"Boys, you may not know it but everything you say can be heard through the bottom of that skiff."

We fell totally silent, too embarrassed to speak. A minute passed without a sound. Slowly we eased out from under the boat, surprised to find that it had drifted up beside a private dock. I peeped around the bow and saw Bruce walking toward his house. Even from the rear I could tell he was laughing. When he was out of sight, we righted the skiff and poled back to the wharf.

Mr. Albert greeted us. He said that Bruce had engine trouble and had come in early from crabbing. After lunch he would return to work on his boat. None of us wanted to face him, so we decided to go for a ride in the outboard skiff. Dad had not mentioned the damaged paint on the motor and it felt safe to take it out again.

This time I filled the gas tank carefully and there was no fire. As we cruised down the creek with the wind in our faces, our embarrassment began to disappear. It was great to be back in a powerboat but we longed to go some place new. Despite my father's warning, all of us wanted to explore the upper reaches of the creek. It wasn't long before I crossed his boundary and headed upstream. The tide was high and I thought it would be easy to avoid the wreck. As a precaution, I kept the motor at half speed until we were clear of the site.

It was exciting to be running the boat in new water and we followed the creek until it narrowed and became a gut. Along the way, I showed the Bates boys where the boats had gone ashore in the hurricane. Satisfied that now we knew as much about the creek as my father, I turned around and headed back to the harbor at full speed. I was certain we were well past the wreck when there was a clunking sound under the water and the motor tilted slightly upward. The engine picked up speed but the boat slowed down. Soon our forward motion stopped, and I tilted the motor enough to see the propeller—it was not turning.

A wave of panic swept over me. Desperately I shifted the motor in and out of gear, hoping the propeller would start to spin, but it never moved. I felt weak as my father's warnings flooded my mind.

"This is it, this time he'll really kill me," I said to no one in particular.

"Maybe we can fix it," Johnny said. For a moment that gave me hope, until I remembered he didn't know any more about outboard motors than I did.

I began poling back toward the wharf and Bruce walked out to meet us. What he had overheard no longer mattered. He examined the motor and checked the propeller's shear pin. It was designed to snap and protect the drive shaft, but someone had replaced it with a nail which remained unbroken. He decided we needed a mechanic.

The closest repair shop was at the Corner Store, three miles away. We tied the heavy motor onto the rear rack of my bicycle, and the weight flattened the rear tire, forcing the rim almost to the asphalt. I wasn't strong enough to ride it, so Johnny mounted up and began to pedal, but he went only a few feet before falling over. On his next attempt, Billy and I ran beside him, holding the bike upright and pushing hard. When we let go, the weight of the motor took over and the bike began to sway. It veered from one side of the road to the other with Johnny struggling for control. He fought valiantly and slowly straightened his course. The propeller protruding from the rear of the bicycle made it look like a scene from a cartoon.

At the cemetery, Johnny pulled into the funeral road for a rest and we stopped near my grandparents' graves. My Grandma Lena had died not long after the hurricane; she had always laughed at my antics and I wondered what she would have thought about this situation.

When we arrived at the store, the parking lot was empty, and I was relieved not to have to face the farmers and their wisecracks. We rode to the rear of the building and in through the open garage door.

Tom Reid, the mechanic, was working under the hood of a car, and he looked up as we rolled in.

"What did you tear up this time?" he said with a smile. Tom was a gentle man who repaired our bikes when we damaged them beyond our mechanical abilities.

"I hit something with Dad's motor and the propeller won't turn. He'll be home at four o'clock, and if he finds out I'm in big trouble."

"Maybe he won't have to find out," Tom said. "Let's have a look." His confident tone made me feel better.

Billy and I removed the motor from the bike, and Johnny sat down on the floor to catch his breath. Tom gave the engine a quick examination.

"I'm going to have to remove the cover from the drive shaft, but the bolts are corroded. If they twist off, it will be real trouble," he said.

"Do whatever it takes, I'll get the money to pay you."

Tom went to work, carefully heating each bolt with a torch before loosening it. The process was slow, and by two o'clock only half the bolts were out. At that point, Clarence Laird, one of the storeowners, came back to the shop and said he had to leave for an hour. Tom would have to cover the gas pumps and cash register.

For the next hour we watched in dismay as he was repeatedly called to the front. Precious time was wasting and the three of us paced the greasy garage floor. Not even the women on the parts company calendar could hold our interest for long. Finally, Mr. Laird returned and Tom got back to work. He managed to remove all the bolts without breaking a single one. When he lifted the cover over the drive shaft, the damage was less than he had expected. Only two interior shear pins were broken. He replaced them and in a half hour the repair was finished.

Tom carried the motor out behind the garage and mounted it on a rusty barrel full of oily water. When he started the engine and pulled the shift lever forward, the water churned vigorously until it almost came over the rim of the barrel. I had never seen a prettier sight.

"Good as new," Tom said. "Now, can you avoid tearing it up again?"

"We're never going to use it again," I said.

"Why?"

"The thing is jinxed; the fire should have been enough warning," Johnny said.

"What fire?" Tom asked.

"I'll tell you later, Dad is on his way home."

"Okay, if he stops by here I'll stall him," Tom said. He was a good friend and always ready to help us out of a jam.

He charged us two dollars and we pooled our money and paid him. We tied the motor on the bike and pumped up the tire. As we rode away, two farmers were staring out the store window with puzzled looks.

During the trip to Champ, I kept watching over my shoulder for my father's car but it never appeared. At the wharf we hurried to get the motor remounted onto the boat, and almost dropped it overboard in the process. Once it was in place, I furiously tightened the bolts and I had just finished when my father drove up.

Dad stopped on the porch to talk with Bruce and the other watermen. We sat on the dock and listened carefully—no one mentioned the motor. After a few minutes, he walked out to where we were sitting.

"Did you go fishing today?" he said.

"Just swimming and boat riding."

"You should go rock fishing at Crab Island."

"Maybe next week," I said, knowing I was never touching his jinxed motor again.

15. River Mud is Hard to Get Off

MY FATHER'S EXPRESSION WAS SOMBER AS HE CAME through the back door. He was returning from a meeting with his bosses at the TFC office in Annapolis. Mom had just put supper on the table for Danny and me.

"You're home early," she said, looking at him for an explanation.

"Yeah, it didn't take long," Dad answered. He carried his newspaper into the living room and sat down in his reading chair. I had never seen him refuse supper. Mom left her food and followed him and I listened closely from the kitchen.

"What happened?" she said quietly.

"They say my arm is too disabled to fire a pistol and I can't work in enforcement anymore," Dad said with a tone of disbelief. "The Chief Inspector won't let me have my supervisor position back or even give me a boat."

"I knew something like this would happen when he put his brother-in-law in your job."

The living room was silent for a few moments and then my mother spoke again. "What kind of job did he offer?"

"Pushing a broom around the office, with a reduction in pay." There was another silence. "For ten years I've worked night after night in the cold, risking my life, and now he wants to give me a job as janitor."

"He's just trying to make you quit; he's always resented you. What did you tell him?" she asked, seeming to fear the answer.

"I told him to go to hell." For a moment the fire came back to my father's voice.

"You mean you don't have a job."

"No Kathleen, I don't."

"How are we going to live?"

"I don't know. . . ."

My mother came back to the kitchen, sat down at the table, and picked at her food. Danny asked for more dumplings and she seemed not to hear him.

Dad sat alone for a long time, squeezing the rubber ball the doctors had given him to exercise his hand. The brace had been off for weeks and there had been no improvement. When he tried to make a fist, his thumb and forefinger refused to bend and he had no feeling in either of them. His middle finger curled halfway back to the palm and it had some sensation of touch. The other two digits operated normally. After a while my father dropped the ball in frustration. He had little else to say that evening. It was the beginning of an uncertain time for him and our family.

Late in September I went crabbing in St. Peter's Creek, hoping to catch a few end-of-summer Jimmies. I poled over the flats near the mouth of the creek, but there were few crabs of any size to be seen. After an hour I gave up and returned to the wharf.

Sammy came out of the store and walked down to where I was tying up the skiff. His hip boots were rolled down and his cap was cocked sideways. Being Saturday, his face was a deeper red than its usual weathered color. The top of a liquor bottle was sticking out of his right boot.

"Well little Noble, how was your crabbing?" he said.

"No good, just two Jimmies."

'That's poor—last week's cool spell moved them off into deeper water. They won't be back till spring."

"I guess I'm through for this year," I said, feeling sad that the season was over.

"You caught right smart crabs this summer. Made some money didn't you?"

"Yeah, I even saved some." I thought about the little pile of cash in my bureau drawer; it was my spending money. Mom was still putting my farm wages into my savings account.

"What are you going to do when you grow up?" he said.

No one had asked me that question for a while and I paused before answering. "I think I'll work on the water. I like crabbing more than anything."

"What about oystering? You've got to do that in the winter and it's mighty cold work. You'd probably freeze your little thing off out there," he said with a chuckle.

"I can take the cold," I said defiantly. His comment had embarrassed me.

"Hah, I bet you can, too. Well, working on the water ain't bad. Soon as you're old enough to leave school, come and join us."

It was the first time a man had ever asked me to join his group and it felt good. I responded without hesitation. "I'll do that."

Sammy seemed pleased with my answer. He pulled out his bottle and took a long swallow. "I guess you're a bit young for this," he said, looking at the container. "Won't be long though. Come and see me when you're ready to go to work. I'll take you on as mate."

"It's a deal," I said. He swayed down the wharf toward his boat.

I gathered up my net and two crabs and headed for the store. Bruce was sitting there on the porch, alone. He had overheard my conversation with Sammy and his usual smile was missing.

"Boy, don't get too much of this river mud on you—it's too hard to get off."

"What do you mean?"

"I mean working the water isn't such a good way to make a living anymore, and you don't want to get stuck here. Oysters are scarce in this river and crabs are good only a few weeks a year." His words surprised me; I had never heard him talk that way before.

"Why are you still doing it?" I asked.

"Because I'm too old to do anything else, but you've got your whole life ahead. Don't get hung up on the water." He was more serious than I had ever seen him.

"My grandfather makes out okay," I said.

"Yeah, but he's like me—doesn't have much." I had never thought of my grandfather as not being well off.

"He's got a boat and a house," I argued.

"But he'd have a hard time getting them the way things are now."

"I still like crabbing," I said.

He shook his head and his smile returned. "Christ, you're as hard-headed as your old man. Think about what I've said."

I was glad to have the conversation over. On the bike ride home I thought about Bruce's comments, but my mind was unchanged. I still wanted to be a waterman.

A week later my father and Milbert decided to inspect the oysters on their leased ground. Dad hoped that some of them would be large enough to sell and they would give him a small income for the fall. He had a lawyer working with the state, trying to get back the retirement money that had been deducted from his salary. In those days, Maryland kept the money unless an employee worked to retirement age. If he received any payment, the check would not arrive for months. There was also talk of a small settlement for his disability but that, too, required a legal fight. He had to find immediate cash to support our family; the income from one chicken house would not be enough.

When my father asked me to go with him to the oyster ground, I was hesitant. Even though Tom Reid was a good mechanic, the motor had not been tested propelling the heavy skiff. If it broke down, I figured it would be best if I weren't around. Besides, there was little challenge in tonging, because oysters just lay on the bottom waiting to be raked up. There was none of the excitement of chasing a fleeing crab. I was about to tell my father no when I saw him pick up his fishing rod. That meant he was going to troll for rockfish on the way to Geanquakin Creek. I grabbed my rod and followed him to the car.

When we arrived at the harbor, Bruce was at the end of Mr. Albert's wharf, filling his boat's tank with gasoline. Milbert walked over to say hello while Dad went into the store for a new anchor rope.

I loaded the oyster tongs into our skiff and waited, hoping the motor was going to work. Bruce and Milbert engaged in a long conversation and several times they looked my way. I had the feeling they were talking about me, but I was too far away to hear. As they parted, my uncle nodded and looked at me one more time.

On the way to the oyster ground the motor ran perfectly. Dad and I trolled yellow bucktails close to the marsh bank, and near Green

Point two rockfish hit the lures almost simultaneously. When the fish were on board, Dad and I compared our catch. This time mine was bigger and I bragged about my superior fishing ability, even though there was little skill involved in trolling. We saved the rock for Sunday dinner; Mom would bake them with potatoes and onions topped with fresh bacon drippings, one of my favorite meals.

My father's arm was still too weak to operate tongs, so Milbert caught the oysters. Dad was pleased that many of them were large enough to sell. He selected a few of the bigger ones and shucked them on the boat seat. As he examined their flesh, a look of concern came to his face. He quickly opened several more before putting down his shucking knife.

"Milbert, they've got green gill," he said in disgust.

My uncle stopped work and leaned over the line of oysters on the half-shell. Dad pointed out a green coloration on the outer fringe of each one.

"What causes it?" Milbert asked.

"Either an algae or high copper content in the water. The state biologist isn't sure."

"Will they die from it?"

"I don't think so. But one thing is certain—nobody will buy them looking like this."

"Maybe they will clear up later in the winter," my uncle offered.

"Maybe," Dad said with doubt in his voice. "But there will be no money out of them before then. We might as well go home." He threw the oysters overboard and went back to the motor, looking beaten down as he struggled to pull the starter rope with his injured arm.

* * *

One afternoon a few days later, I rode to the Shockleys' farm after school. Milbert and my cousin Harry were transferring corn from a wagon to the corn house. I watched as the last yellow ears tumbled from the wagon and into the conveyor. Through cracks in the siding boards, I saw that the building was almost full; my uncle's crop had been good. A loud clatter erupted as the conveyor began to run empty, and Harry shut down the motor, producing instant quiet.

"Howdy Captain, we were just talking about you," my uncle said. As a sign of respect, men in the community were often addressed as captain, even if they did not have a boat. Milbert sometimes applied the title to the boys who worked for him and we felt special when he did.

"Why were you talking about me?"

"We think you need something to do, like raising pigs," Harry said. My oldest cousin was a big man in his thirties with a crew cut. He loved farming, especially buying and selling livestock, and my parents said he was shrewd with a dollar. Harry had never left the Eastern Shore and he had no desire to go anywhere else.

"Why would I raise pigs?" I said.

"Because they'll make you more money than crabbing and not just in the summer. Farming is a good way of life and you're not likely to drown," he said.

I sometimes helped Bobby with his pigs but I had never considered owning any. They were a lot of work—it seemed better just to harvest what the Bay produced.

"You could use the land behind your father's chicken house for pens," Milbert said. "Harry has a litter of pigs now and he could sell you two gilts." I knew that gilts were young female pigs. "I've got plenty of corn that you could feed them," he continued. "I'll sell it to you cheap."

"I'm not sure if I want pigs."

"Just think about it," Harry said.

That night after I went to bed, I lay awake considering what the Shockleys had said. I trusted them completely but their suggestion seemed complicated. Sleep shut down my mind before I could make a decision.

The next evening at supper, my father brought the subject up again. It was the first time he had spoken to me since our trip to the oyster ground.

"Terry, I've been talking to Milbert and Harry and they think you ought to get in the pig business." He paused to take in a fork full of macaroni and cheese. "They say you could make good money, maybe you should try it."

"I'm saving to buy a .410 shotgun and I'm still twelve dollars short. I don't want to spend my money on pigs."

"We'll take the money from your savings account," he said.

"What about for their house and the wire for the pen?"

"Same thing," he said. My mother frowned at the thought of emptying my account.

"Okay, I'll do it." If all the men I trusted believed I should become a farmer, I felt obliged to try it.

On Saturday Dad and I took Milbert's truck to the sawmill to buy lumber for the pig house. It was a noisy place with air smelling like turpentine from the fresh cut pine. The sawyer took my order and I watched as he turned round logs into boards. When it came time to load the lumber, its heavy weight surprised me. The boards were green and full of sap and I struggled to get them onto the truck. Pine resin stuck to my hands and clothes. Right then, I ruled out ever working in a sawmill.

Shortly after we arrived home with the lumber, Milbert came by to help with the construction and Dad brought down my grandfather's tools from the attic. They were seldom used; he had always made it plain that he did not want to be a carpenter like his father.

"You'd better get to work," Dad said. "It's your pig house and you have to build it."

"I don't know how."

"We'll help you," Milbert said. He pulled out a drawing from Howard Anderson, the local high school agriculture teacher. My father guided me as I measured and marked the boards. When my arm tired from operating the handsaw, my uncle relieved me. I pounded most of the nails by myself; Mr. Pusey's gifts and my boat building had given me all the experience I needed.

By late afternoon we had completed a sturdy A-frame pig house. I was proud of what we had accomplished and I knew I could build another one without help when the pigs required it.

In less than a week, Harry delivered my two little gilts, each weighing a little over 20 pounds. They were typical of the Yorkshire breed—all white, with erect ears and long bodies. He held them up by their back legs so I could count their nipples. Each of them had fourteen, which was important, because their mother had delivered that many piglets and they might too.

I had everything ready for the gilts' arrival; there were troughs with food and water outside the house. Inside, deep straw bedding covered the floor. When Harry released them, instead of consuming feed they began to root up the grass. Their pink noses quickly turned over the sod and in a short time the enclosure appeared tilled. They were interesting animals, and I sat on the fence watching them until it was almost dark.

The next morning Mom called me out of bed early so I could care for my pigs before school. It was October and cold air had settled in overnight. A heavy frost covered the grass as I shuffled across the yard half asleep. I saw no reason to get up early unless I was going out on a boat; doubts were already creeping into my mind about raising pigs.

When I reached the pen, I quickly woke up—the gilts were gone. I felt a wave of panic; my father and the Shockleys were going to be so disappointed in me. What had I done wrong? I ran around the chicken house and through my uncle's field looking for the lost animals, but they had disappeared.

I went back to the pen and looked for a hole in the fence where they could have escaped, but there was none. How had they vanished? They were too large for a fox to have taken. In desperation, I said aloud, "Where are you?" A soft grunt came from under the straw bedding. A snout and two eyes poked out through the yellow stems, quickly followed by another set. In a second, the two pigs burst out of the straw and ran toward me, squealing for breakfast. I felt foolish, realizing they had buried themselves to avoid the cold. It was my first lesson about how clever they could be.

When the pigs were fed and watered, I headed back to the house for my breakfast, relieved that they had not disappeared. I was already beginning to like having them around.

* * *

My twelfth birthday arrived a few weeks later and I was not expecting much, maybe a pair of gloves or a large pack of BBs. My father had just sold a flock of chickens, but he said money was scarce and the family would not have anything extra to spend for a while. I was in the living room reading when he came home from town. The sounds of a box being unpacked drew me toward the kitchen. When I walked in, he was holding the .410 shotgun that I had looked at so often in Warwick's Hardware. For a moment I was confused; I could not possibly be getting that.

"We took the money from your bureau," he said.

"But I was still ten dollars short."

"Your mother and I made up the difference. It's time you had a shotgun."

Nothing could have made me happier. The Bates boys already had .22 rifles and they were regularly killing squirrels. A shotgun was better, because I could also hunt quail and ducks. I got to hold my present for only a minute before my father went into a long safety lecture. It was similar to the one he gave with my BB gun.

"Never point this gun at anyone, even when it is unloaded."

"Never bring it into the house loaded."

"Never take it out around any other children; you can only use it alone."

"Never shoot anything that you don't plan to eat."

"Keep it clean and well oiled."

"Do you accept what I've said?"

"Yes sir."

"If you break any of these rules, I will take the gun away for a year."

I knew he meant it and it would be 365 days, not 364. If I even asked to get it back early, he would extend the ban to eighteen months. I may have gone beyond his boundary with the outboard, but I would never have considered bending one of these rules.

"Let's go outside and shoot it," he said.

My father set a can on a fence post by our side yard and I took careful aim before firing. When the pellets hit the can, it thrilled me to see it fly backwards into my uncle's pasture. "This is easy," I said.

"Okay, try a moving target." He tossed a can into the air with his injured arm. It was an awkward throw and the can did not move fast, but when I fired, it was a clean miss. "Your grandmother can shoot that well." He threw two more and I missed them.

"These shells must not be any good," I said.

"Right. If you can't hit these slow moving targets how will you ever kill a quail or a duck?"

"Throw some more," I said, trying to sound confident. I was frustrated and his teasing didn't help. He obliged and I missed another two before scratching one can with a single pellet.

"Any meat you kill will cost so much in shells we couldn't afford to eat it," he said. He was starting to make me mad.

My parents at a nightclub in Norfolk, VA, shortly after they were married.

Dad and me a few months after he got home from the war.

My grandfather, Captain Willie Thomas, and grandmother Ruth.

Dad's father (left) as a young man.

Dumping a crab scrape bag onto the washboard. The crabs are in the ball of eel grass which hasn't yet come aboard. Photo courtesy of Larry Chowning, *Harvesting the Chesapeake,* Tidewater Publishers.

A typical crab scraping boat. Ours was larger and it had a cabin at the bow with a cook stove. Photo courtesy of Larry Chowning, *Harvesting the Chesapeake,* Tidewater Publishers.

Dipping soft crabs from a shedding float. The harvest from several floats rests in the wooden box on the skiff. Soft crabs were removed from the water within two hours after backing out of their old shells to prevent them from becoming hard. Photograph by A. Aubrey Bodine. Copyright © Jennifer B. Bodine. Courtesy of AAubreyBodine. com.

Tongers harvesting oysters.

My father's patrol boat, the *Somerset*.

Dad at the helm of the *Somerset*. He was proud of his boat and I loved being on board with him. He never wore his pistol in the summertime.

Tongers taking up seed oysters on the St Mary's River.

Barge loaded with oyster shells about to be planted on the river bottom, as a place for young oysters (spat) to attach and grow.

Planting oyster shells by washing them off a barge.

FBI photograph from one of my father's early cases. He surprised an illegal oyster dredger and the man cut the rope leading to his dredge. Dad dragged the river bottom until he found the device. He asked the FBI to match the rope from the dredge (left) with the piece still attached to the boat.

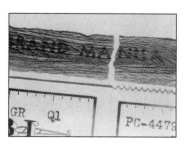

Inset: Microscopic photo of the paper strip inside the dredgers rope. It was a perfect match and Dad won the case.

Chesapeake Bay skipjack, a legal oyster dredge boat. Photograph by A. Aubrey Bodine. Copyright © Jennifer B. Bodine. Courtesy of AAubreyBodine. com.

Damage to a patrol boat after it was rammed intentionally by an illegal dredger.

Working the dredge aboard a skipjack. It has just been emptied and is about to go back into the water. Photograph by A. Aubrey Bodine. Copyright © Jennifer B. Bodine. Courtesy of AAubreyBodine. com.

Me, about the time my
father was shot.

Howard Anderson, my favorite
teacher and mentor. Without
him my life may have turned
out very differently. Photo
courtesy of William and
Shirley Anderson.

My senior yearbook photo.

Dad in his oyster boat, heading out
St Peters Creek for a waterfowl hunt.

"Let's see you do it." I handed him the gun and it took him a while to get his middle finger placed on the trigger.

"I haven't fired a gun since I was shot." He practiced bringing the stock up to his shoulder.

"No excuses," I said. We changed positions and I began to throw cans. I tossed them hard, some high, some low, trying to make him miss. Even with his injured arm, he hit five in a row.

"Someday, maybe you'll be as good as your old man," he said, handing the gun back to me.

I let his taunt go unanswered, but I made up my mind that someday I would outshoot him. My feeling of competition with him was growing.

16. Hurting My Best Friend

ALMOST EVERY FALL AFTERNOON I HUNTED SQUIRRELS until dark. Cindy, the Chesapeake pup, had grown up and she became my hunting partner. Even though she was not bred for it, she became a first-rate squirrel dog and learned to roam ahead of me in the woods, finding the animals and barking at the tree until I arrived.

With my new gun and Cindy, I began to overtake the Bates boys in total squirrels killed. It was a major competition and we kept the animals' tails for proof. I salted mine and stashed them in my bureau drawer under some clothes I seldom wore. When Mom discovered the hairy, gray pile, I moved them to the attic. She was willing to cook the meat for me but she could not tolerate my trophies in the house.

Cindy became best friend to Danny and me. She escorted us to the bus in the morning and waited by the road for our return in the afternoon. When I walked out the door with my shotgun, she ran circles in the yard, excited about going hunting. She learned to find rabbits as well as squirrels, sniffing in every hiding place until one flushed from cover. Her speed was remarkable and she occasionally caught a rabbit before it could fully accelerate out of its set.

One Saturday afternoon, we went hunting in the yard of the old plantation house on Preston's farm. It was not far from where I had picked strawberries and tomatoes. No one lived in the old structure; one of its doors was missing and the fireplace mantels and most of its heart pine floors had been removed. Pine trees and honeysuckle vines were overtaking the yard. Rabbits liked it there and one or two were always hidden in the vines. They usually flushed out of range and disappeared in the myrtle bushes along the marsh edge.

On that day, as I made my way through the little pines, Cindy was ahead and off to my right nosing at some honeysuckle. Suddenly a rabbit broke out of a clump of grass just in front of me and ran straight away toward the marsh. I threw the gun to my shoulder and concentrated on the bobbing, white tail. Just as I pulled the trigger, I sensed that something else was coming into my narrowed field of vision.

My eyes blinked with the blast, and when they opened, the rabbit was tumbling over dead. To my surprise, Cindy was only three feet away, spinning around and biting at her left front leg. She let out a squeal of pain. My heart split with the sound and the realization that I had shot her.

By the time I got to her side, she was standing still with her paw in the air, whimpering. Blood was seeping into the hair from multiple holes in her leg. I rubbed her head and said, "I'm sorry" over and over. I felt an awful sickness and I just wanted it to be a bad dream.

My cousin Harry's farm was only a quarter mile away but Cindy was too heavy to carry that far. I tried to leave her and go for help but she insisted on following me. She hopped along slowly on her uninjured front leg, and every few steps she tried to put the other foot down, but the pain caused her to cry out.

As we neared my cousin's house, she appeared to be getting weaker. Harry saw us approaching and drove his pickup out into the field. I hurriedly explained what had happened and he helped me load her onto the truck seat.

"I didn't mean to do it," I said. "It was an accident."

"Don't worry—everybody knows how much you love that dog."

Harry drove fast to our house and I carried Cindy from his truck to our back porch. My father walked out of the kitchen to meet me. I explained the accident, desperately wanting him to tell me it would be okay, but that didn't happen.

"After all I taught you about gun safety, I can't believe you did this. You disappoint me more every day." He examined Cindy's leg and his expression grew more serious. "I'll call a vet," he said and headed for the phone. I knew her condition must be bad; only once before had he taken a dog for medical care.

Mom brought out a blanket and placed it in the corner. I gently laid Cindy on it and in a few minutes she went into a deep sleep.

"I can't get a vet," my father said coming back into the porch. "The one in Pocomoke is not answering his phone and the guy in Salisbury just left to treat a sick horse. He won't be back for hours. It looks like she will have to make it on her own."

For the rest of the afternoon, I sat by Cindy's side. She would not take any food or water. Only once did she acknowledge my presence, with a single weak thump of her tail on the porch floor. I was angry that we could not find a vet and frustrated that I did not know how to help her.

After supper Mom brought out pieces of scrapple and placed them in front of Cindy's nose. Scrapple, a mixture of pork, corn meal and spices baked in a loaf, was my favorite breakfast food, and sick dogs often ate it when they would eat nothing else. In our community, dogs that refused scrapple were considered poor candidates for survival. The smell of the meat caused Cindy to open her eyes a little, but she made no effort to eat.

I stayed by her side all evening and her breathing continued to get slower. Midway through the *Lawrence Welk Show*, Dad came out to check on her. There was a wet spot on the blanket from my tears and I quickly folded it over so he would not see the stain. "How's she doing?" he said.

"Hardly breathing," I said, trying to hold my voice steady.

He bent down to take a closer look and his expression became grim. When he went back inside, I heard him tell Mom in a low voice, "She may not make it."

At bedtime my parents insisted that I go to my room. It was a long time before I fell asleep—the accident played over a hundred times in my mind and I could get no relief from the guilt. Finally, exhaustion took over and I drifted off.

On Sunday morning, I awoke early and immediately went to the porch, afraid of what I might find. Cindy appeared to be the same as when I had left the night before. I lifted her head, holding the water bowl to her mouth, and she took two feeble laps with her eyes closed. Relieved that she had at least made it through the night, I curled up beside her and fell asleep until I heard my family getting ready for church.

We attended both services that Sunday and I listened closely to the sermon, hoping to find something to ease my mind. Nothing the preacher said seemed to help. When it came time to pray, I pleaded with God to spare Cindy.

We arrived home a few minutes after noon and I was the first to the porch door. What I saw amazed me—Cindy was standing up. I opened the door and she walked stiffly toward me, wagging her tail. As I rubbed her head the life returned to her eyes. I ran to the refrigerator and got the scrapple, and this time she passed the test, swallowing it in big gulps. I felt the greatest relief of my life. For the first time I thought one of my prayers had been answered.

Our whole family stood quietly and watched Cindy eat. My father broke the silence. "Terry, I'm not going to punish you for this. Nothing I could do would hurt you as much as what you've already been through. I think you've learned your lesson." I stared at the floor, not wanting to meet his eyes.

"You left your gun outdoors last night," he continued. "You better bring it inside and oil it."

"I don't want it anymore. I'm through with hunting."

"No, you're not through. You'll want to go again and so will Cindy once she's recovered."

My father was right. Within two weeks, my love of the woods and squirrel hunting overcame the guilt I was feeling. One afternoon I picked up the shotgun and stepped out the back door. Cindy, who seemed fully recovered, saw the gun and began to race around the yard in glee. I walked up the road toward the Bates's farm and she took her spot in the lead, obviously happy to be hunting again.

I never forgot the lesson of the accident. After that, I never pulled the trigger without first determining where my dog was standing. Some rabbits got away because of my hesitation but that didn't matter.

In a few months, the shot pellets in Cindy's leg worked their way out of the muscle and became trapped under her skin. They were lodged just beneath the surface and everyone in the neighborhood came by to feel them. Most of the kids squirmed when they felt the pellets but it never seemed to bother Cindy.

* * *

The winter was uneventful. I took care of my pigs and they grew steadily. Somehow, my parents found enough money to see us through until warm weather, even though the oysters on the lease continued to have green gill.

In the spring my father received a small settlement from the state for his injury. With that money and another loan he started building a second, larger chicken house. His financial situation was still uncertain and he decided to do most of the construction himself. His hand had slightly improved and he could awkwardly hold a hammer. I helped after school and on weekends. The job went on into the summer.

Toward the end of the project, my gilts were reaching breeding age. Bobby promised to let me use his boar to father the first litters. When they came into heat, Dad helped me haul them to the Shockleys' farm and I watched with interest as the animals mated. It would be four months before they gave birth and two months after that before I could sell their pigs. My savings account was empty and I took any job to get money to buy pig feed. When I was out of money, Milbert gave me corn on credit. For the first time I knew what it was like to be in debt.

* * *

I had always thought of Dad as my protector. Knowing that he was on my side gave me a warm, comfortable feeling. I was sure he had the power to solve all of life's problems, no matter how large they seemed to me. Now I was sensing some change in his attitude—nothing that my barely thirteen-year-old brain could formulate into words, but I had a vague uneasiness. Danny was older and spending even more time with him, but that was not all of it. One thing I was sure of—the closeness that had once existed between me and my father had diminished.

Just how far the bonds were stretched was revealed one day as I was standing on the road in front of our house. I was talking to the Bates boys about girls, and Danny was upset that I was ignoring him. He pedaled his bike toward me with a determined look. It was the third time in two minutes that he had attempted to run into me. As he approached, I grabbed the handlebars and the bike stopped suddenly. To my surprise he lurched forward, falling onto the asphalt and scraping his arm. He immediately began to cry.

When I reached down to help him, he rose up and hit me hard

under the ribs. For a moment I lost my breath. I gasped for air, amazed at how much force he mustered with that skinny little arm. When he saw that I was hurting, he immediately switched from crying to laughing. As usual his laughter cooled my anger and prevented me from retaliating. We had been through dozens of similar fights, and even though I was older, he always managed to hold his own with some tricky move. We knew when things were even and as far as we were concerned the fight was over.

I was just getting my wind back when the front door of our house opened.

"Terry, come here, I want to talk to you," my father said from the steps. He sounded mad. When I walked inside he was as angry as I had ever seen him.

"I saw you throw Danny off his bike. You're mistreating him and I'm not going to put up with it."

"But he tried to run into me . . ."

"That's no excuse; you're bigger than he is." His eyes had grown dark and I knew better than to say anything else. "From now on I'll be watching the two of you and I'll be on Danny's side. If you mistreat him in any way, you'll be sorry. Do you understand?"

"Yes sir." I left the room wondering why he was so angry over a minor scuffle. Money was short and he had been on edge, but he had never talked like that before. It hurt to hear that the man I had wanted so much to please was on someone else's side.

After that day my father seemed to grow even closer to Danny, and he became more critical of my behavior. Soon my brother was noticing it too. One Sunday we decided to ask for permission to play softball on a neighboring farm. Mom never approved of us participating in sports on the Sabbath, so we knew it was useless to ask her. I was about to approach my father when Danny stopped me.

"Let me ask Dad. He likes me the best," he said.

It was a surprise to hear him say what I had been thinking. There was a divide growing between my father and me, and I didn't know why, or how to stop it. The warm feeling between us was cooling and being replaced with wariness, as we sized each other up. For the first time, the air had the whiff of impending combat. I may have to be tamed but I wouldn't make it easy for him.

If there was one point in time that I could say was the dividing line between childhood and my teenage years, this was it.

* * *

Later that summer a new family moved into our neighborhood, which was a rare event. They came from Baltimore and one of the kids, a black-haired boy named Vincent, was about Johnny's age. He was friendly and the Bates boys and I soon began to include him in our group. Some days he worked with us on my uncle's farm; he had a good attitude, but the dirt and the physical labor came as a shock to him. Nothing about life in the city had prepared him for hours of shoveling chicken manure.

Although he knew little about farming, Vincent had a lot to teach us. He talked about gangs and what boys in the city did for excitement. Once, he mentioned getting into trouble with the police but he never gave us details. It all sounded wild and far away.

By then Johnny had his driver's license and he was spending less time with Billy and me. Vincent's uncle gave him an old Buick, and he and Johnny began to tinker with the engine in the evenings. They often test drove the car past our house, always with the accelerator to the floor. The engine had some major defect and I could hear it backfiring through the carburetor as they went by. They never corrected the problem, but they became good friends, and Billy and I were left out.

* * *

The start of my eighth grade brought major surprises—many of my classmates looked different. Some of the girls had grown taller than me and they had curves I had never noticed before. Two boys who had always done poorly in sports had developed body hair and they could now run faster than the rest of us. Vincent, who was almost two years older, was placed in some of our classes, which made him the biggest and strongest one in the grade. Our social order was shaken up and it would be a while before it was sorted out.

With the seafood industry declining, farming became the county's biggest business, and the school board thought we should learn something about it. Every eighth grade boy took an agriculture class for one hour each day, while the girls had home economics. The ag teacher, Howard Anderson, was a powerfully-built man with a warm, confident manner. He reminded me of John Wayne. The entire male student body, even those who thought agriculture was a waste of time, respected him.

During his thirty years at the school, Mr. Anderson had taught most of the county's young farmers and a number of his students had gone on to college and professional careers. There were lawyers, businessmen, teachers, engineers, and veterinarians who had followed his agriculture curriculum. One of "Andy's boys," as the ag students were known, went into politics and became Maryland's Secretary of State.

In addition to his teaching job, Mr. Anderson operated four farms, raising vegetables, grain, and purebred Angus cattle. He used the farms as laboratories for teaching students. During my seventh grade ancient history class, I often looked out the window and saw him leaving school with a group of students in the back of his pick-up truck. They were headed for one of his farms to learn some new agricultural practice. Whatever they were going to do, I figured it was better than what I was doing. It wasn't that I disliked those dead Egyptians—I even carved a Sphinx from a bar of soap for extra credit—but I needed more action and agriculture class seemed to offer it.

The largest annual production at the school was the Princess Anne Livestock Show. Held every October, it was a major fall event for the county, second only to the Crisfield Crab Derby. The show was funded and managed by Andy's boys, all of them members of the Future Farmers of America (FFA). There were two days of farm animal exhibitions, with ribbons and substantial prize money awarded. A livestock show queen was crowned—a bigger honor for a girl than being selected prom queen.

Planning for the show began as soon as the FFA members returned to school in the fall. The boys designed the program booklet and sold ad space to raise prize money. Trophies, ribbons and food for the concession stand all had to be ordered. During the week before the show, most of Andy's boys were excused from class to set up tents, prepare show rings, and build animal pens. I was still too young to be an FFA member, but I watched it all with great interest and anticipation.

A few days before the show, Mr. Anderson stopped me as I was leaving agriculture class. "Mr. Noble, I hear you're in the pig business," he said, in his slow gentlemanly manner.

"I have two gilts but they haven't had pigs yet." I was surprised that he knew about my animals.

"When are they due?"

"In a few weeks."

"Good, let me know when they're born. I'll come by your house, and maybe I can help you with them." He seemed pleased to have another boy with a livestock project. I was about to leave but he had something else to say. "We need two students to be ring boys for the show. Would you like to be one of them?"

"What will I have to do?"

"Shovel up the manure from the show ring and keep the sawdust raked level. I'll have to get you excused from classes for a day. Could you handle that?"

"Absolutely," I said enthusiastically, honored to have been chosen.

Friday, the first day of the show, was devoted entirely to dairy animals. Trucks hauling Holstein, Guernsey, and Jersey cattle began arriving early. Most of the cows were not milked that morning to make their udders appear large for the judge. Milk dripped from their teats as they were led to their waiting area.

When the show got underway, I was nervous and afraid that I would enter the ring at the wrong time and spook the cattle, or offend the judge. I worked carefully, trying to fit into the flow as the animals moved in and out of the arena. Once the judge frowned at me when I accidentally banged my shovel on the wheelbarrow while he was talking.

By afternoon I relaxed and concentrated on keeping the sawdust in perfect order. Between groups of animals I was often in the ring alone. Things went well until some upperclassmen were excused from school for an hour to see the show. Two of the town boys, who thought agriculture was a joke, began making wisecracks as I worked. "Hey pooper scooper, you missed some over here" and "Why don't you put a cork in those cows?" were their favorites. I was embarrassed but said nothing. They were having a good time until I "accidentally" spilled manure through the fence onto their shoes. The crowd laughed and they threatened to whip me, but I stayed in the ring where I was safe. Eventually they gave up and went back to class. When the show was over,

Mr. Anderson said I did an excellent job, which made me feel proud, and that was all that mattered.

* * *

Although things were changing rapidly in my life, Dad was still struggling to find a way to provide for our family. One afternoon he and Mom were talking in the living room as Danny and I came in from the school bus.

"Are you sure you want a boat?" Mom said.

"We can't make it on just the chicken house money; we need some other source of income," he said.

I dropped my books on the kitchen table and listened. Danny cut the remainder of a coconut cake into two pieces and took the larger slice. He was breaking Dad's rule—if one of us divided any food, the other got first choice of the portions. He tried to shield his plate, but I pinched off enough of his slice to make my portion a good bit larger than his. It was a game we had been playing or years.

"No one on Deal Island seems to be making much money on the water," Mom said.

"Maybe, but I know places where the state planted shells that no one has ever tonged. Those shells should be loaded with new oysters."

"Why don't you get a job at Wayne Pump?" Wayne was a gasoline pump factory in Salisbury where a few men in the community worked.

"I can't stand to work indoors all day. I'm not going to spend my life in a factory," he said. "Besides, I've already picked out a boat in Mt. Vernon. She's in good shape—I've run an ice pick down her bottom and there's no rotten wood."

"So you've already decided to buy it?"

"Yes,"

"Why did you even bother to tell me?" Mom said sarcastically.

My mother may not have been happy about the new boat but I was excited. Dad said he planned to pick up the vessel on Saturday and he was going to take Danny and me with him on the long run from Mt. Vernon to Champ.

Saturday arrived clear and cold with only a light wind. We were scheduled to leave at noon, but at the last minute Mom decided the weather was too harsh for Danny to go. Dad turned to me.

"Terry, it's going to be a long, cold trip but you can come along if you like."

"I'll go," I said. Dad and I had not done anything together since Danny's bike incident and I wanted to be with him.

My father purchased a V-bottom boat, known locally as a bateau, and it had been built for crab scraping. At 31 feet, with a wide beam and settling boards on the rear, it was perfect for working in shallow water; it was also easy to rig for tonging. The previous owner had recently installed a four-cylinder jeep engine, which connected to the propeller shaft by a simple forward and reverse gear box. Like most crab boats of that time, it was not built for speed.

We left Mt. Vernon harbor and cruised down the Wicomico River at five miles per hour. My father pointed out the landmarks, showing me the entrances to Monie Bay and the Nanticoke River. For the first time I saw the Dames Quarter shoreline from the water. Dad stood behind the engine box, steering with just his leg on the tiller handle. I stood beside him near the exhaust pipe, letting its heat keep me warm.

At Deal Island, we ran under the bridge and through the Thorofare to the Manokin. Near Fishing Creek, hundreds of canvasback ducks took off from the water. Dad said he had seen thousands there when he first began work on the police boat. The sound from the hundreds of pairs of wings was loud and I tried to imagine thousands taking flight.

Sunlight was growing scarce as we turned into St. Peter's Creek. I looked at my father, standing at the helm in the fading light, and he seemed happier than at any time in the past two years. I was glad he had a boat again and that I had been along on the first trip.

17. A Wrong Gets Righted

"ONE OF YOUR GILTS IS PILING UP STRAW IN THE CORNER of her house," my father said, as I came in from hunting. That meant she was making a bed in which to farrow (give birth). I dropped my squirrels by the back door and ran out to her pen. When I arrived she was standing in her house, rearranging the straw. She was restless, unable to be satisfied with the bed she had created. After rooting up the pile with her snout, she switched to pawing it with a front foot. The food I placed in her trough did nothing to distract her.

I climbed into the pen carefully, aware that some females had attacked people who got too close during farrowing. The gilt paid no attention to me until I began to scratch behind her ears; then she stopped pawing and began to relax. I took a risk and ran my hand along her nipples to mimic the nuzzling of pigs. She grunted softly and lay down on her side in nursing position. When she was settled, I pulled on a front nipple and two streams of milk squirted out, landing on the straw six feet away. It would not be long before the first pig arrived. Helping Bobby with his animals had removed many of the unknowns from what I was about to face.

To my surprise, an hour passed and there were still no pigs. It was growing dark and the temperature was dropping. I turned on the infrared heat lamp that I had rigged up in the corner of the A-frame. The light reflecting off the straw instantly gave the house a warm glow.

Soon I felt the heat from the bulb. It would warm the pigs and draw them away from their mother when they weren't nursing. Sows, the name for gilts after they give birth, often lie on their pigs and crush them. It was difficult for a four hundred pound female to lie down with ten babies wandering between her legs.

Mr. Anderson told me the heat lamp would help more of my pigs survive. He said weaning larger litters was the key to making money. According to him I could save another two pigs per litter if I wiped the mucous from each newborn's nose, dried the pig off and helped it to start nursing. With that information, I resolved to be with my females every time they farrowed. Each pig born would sell for ten dollars if it lived to eight weeks. Saving a pig was a lot easier than working ten hours to make the same money.

The gilt began to breath deeper and she went into a stupor, appearing not to notice me. Occasionally her muscles tensed and she drew a back foot up to her belly as if feeling pain. I began worrying that she might be having trouble and I would have to call a vet. Suddenly her tail began rotating in circles, hitting the straw with a swishing sound. Within seconds, a pig squirted out into the world.

The newborn lay still, covered in yellow mucous and appearing lifeless. It was depressing to think that my first pig was dead. Then its whole body jerked in a convulsive effort to breath. I picked up the baby in an old towel and carefully wiped its nose and mouth. It made two more gasps for air. I gave its whole body a vigorous rub down and it began to squirm. Within half a minute it was breathing regularly.

When I laid the pig in the straw beside its mother, it gave a tiny squeal and she answered with three soft grunts. It began to struggle to an upright position. Five minutes later the baby was on its feet, stumbling around, occasionally stepping on the foot-long navel cord it was dragging. Its spunk and determination were impressive. I placed the pig in front of a nipple and squirted milk into its mouth. Immediately the little animal became excited and tried to grasp the milk source, but it kept slipping away. It repeatedly attacked the nipple until it learned to hold on and then it nursed continuously for about a minute. With a little food in its stomach, the newborn let go and moved up the udder, sampling other nipples along the way. At the front one, it settled down and began to drink, instinctively recognizing that it had found the best milk producer.

In a short time, the gilt's tail swished again and another pig appeared. This one was stronger and it was soon on its feet looking for food. When it bumped into the first-born, it began pushing, trying to take over the front nipple. That didn't work, so number two used its sharp milk teeth to bite the first pig on its lip. The nipple owner held on but began to squeal from pain. The attacker began to squeal, frustrated at not getting its way.

Hearing the noise and thinking that something might be harming her pigs, the gilt became agitated and began to grunt loudly. I hastily moved the combatants to different nipples but they went back to the same one and began to fight again. The gilt jumped to her feet and began a sharp grunting that sounded like barking. For a moment I thought she might attack me, but after sniffing her pigs and finding them unharmed, she calmed down. She turned her attention to rearranging the straw and I moved the pigs to keep her from stepping on them. When she was satisfied with the shape of her farrowing bed she lay down again.

The number two pig found the other front nipple, which had been covered with straw, and it began to nurse quietly. For a while there was no fighting but the peace did not last long. Two other pigs were born in quick succession and the squealing started again. This time the gilt grunted but she did not stand up, accepting that her offspring were okay.

Outside in the darkness, I heard footsteps and Danny's voice.

"Mom sent you a sandwich and some pie," he said. "I'm leaving it here in the lunch box." He did not come over to look at the pigs. I heard him running back toward the house and wondered why he had left so quickly. After I washed my hands and opened the food container, I saw the reason—he had eaten all the meringue off my slice of lemon pie.

For two more hours I stayed with the gilt until she finished farrowing. Mostly I just lay in the straw and waited for her tail to switch. No one had told me about this early warning system but it was handy and reliable. When a pig arrived, I wiped it off and placed it with the others. Once, I fell asleep and awoke with a newborn trying to nurse on my ear.

In the end, the gilt had eleven live pigs, a good start for my livestock enterprise. Walking toward our house in the cold darkness, I felt tired but satisfied. Homework would have to wait until morning. Thankfully, my father had skinned my squirrels.

* * *

Johnny hung out at Vincent's house almost every evening after supper and they became best friends. Billy said they sat in Vincent's room and talked about cars and girls. I wanted to be part of their group but they thought I was too young. I had never even seen Vincent's room.

One evening my mother sent me to deliver a pie to Vincent's family; she often baked extra ones and gave them away. Johnny had a date that night and Vincent must have been bored because he invited me upstairs. When I entered his room, I was shocked—it was much larger than the one I shared with Danny. He had a full-size bed and a vanity dresser with a mirror on the back. More comic books than I had ever seen were stacked in piles on the floor. The walls were decorated with Baltimore team pennants. None of the other kids in the neighborhood had a room so luxurious.

After I looked around, Vincent put a stack of comic books on the dresser and invited me to sit down and read. I picked out a Superman and began to leaf through it. My back was to Vincent, but I heard him walking around the room. Suddenly he stopped and let out a laugh, like a crazy person in a movie. I looked in the mirror and saw him standing behind me with his .22 caliber rifle pointed at my head.

"I always wanted to do this to someone," he said in an insane sounding voice. The look on his face convinced me that he was going to shoot but I was too scared to move.

When the rifle went off, I felt an impact on the back of my head. Surprisingly, there was no pain but my heart almost stopped. So this is what it's like to be shot? I wondered why I was still conscious. I touched the back of my head but could not feel any blood.

Vincent fell over on the bed in fits of laughter. "It was a blank," he said, when he could find enough breath to talk. My mind felt numb and I could hardly understand what he was saying.

"The bullet hit the back of my head," I muttered.

"It was just the blast from the blank, you moron!" He went into another spasm of laughter and it began to sink in that I was not really shot. I stood up, glad to be alive.

"That's what I used," he said. He showed me a stubby, blank cartridge. "I did the same thing to Johnny." Vincent went on trying to make conversation, but I didn't feel like talking. As I left, he said he was sorry but I was not in the mood for forgiveness.

On the way home, my feeling of relief turned to anger. Every boy in the community owned a gun but none of us would have even considered doing what Vincent had just done.

I never told anyone about that night. He and I remained outwardly friendly, but I never trusted him again. Secretly, I hoped he would somehow be paid back for his actions.

* * *

Mr. Anderson began our eighth grade agriculture class by teaching us the proper words to use when describing livestock.

"Farm animals are divided into *species* and those species are divided into *breeds*. Each breed has certain *characteristics*, such as color or *conformation* that identify it. The word *kind* should not be used when describing animals. You can use kind when talking about cars or chocolate bars, but in this class, when you describe animals, you will use the word breed."

He went on to teach us that Angus cows were more protective mothers than docile Hereford cows. We learned that Holsteins produced more milk than Guernseys, but that the latter gave more butterfat. He told us that Yorkshire sows had larger litters, but Duroc pigs grew faster and had more muscle.

When we had mastered the breeds and their characteristics, Mr. Anderson moved on to the names for different age and sex groups. He instructed us that a young female bovine was called a heifer and one that had already calved was known as a cow. We found out that a castrated bovine was a steer and a castrated pig was a barrow.

Most of the cattle and pig terms I already knew, but I had no experience with sheep. For some reason, I found it difficult to remember that a young male sheep was a ram-lamb and a neutered male was a wether. Someone in the class came up with a question that always gave me the right answer. It went, "Did you hear about the ram that rammed a ram-lamb and turned him into a wether?"

After finishing with the names for ages and sexes, we turned to anatomy. Mr. Anderson insisted we use teat, udder, or mammary gland when talking about the milk producing parts of a female body. He said there was a three-letter word in common use, but it was unscientific. We also learned the correct names for the male and female sex organs. Mr. Anderson ran an orderly class but during this time there was a lot of snickering and whispering. He ignored it and went on with his lecture. I think he knew he had everyone's full attention.

The next subject was carcass quality and cuts of meat. For days our teacher talked about how livestock-raising practices affected the quality of the meat we ate. He told us that if pigs were fed only peanuts, their fat was so soft it dripped on the floor when they were hanging in the cold locker. He discussed "marbling," the spread of fat throughout the muscle tissue, which improved the flavor of a steak and made it more tender. Feeding a steer grain for ninety days greatly increased this desirable characteristic.

Vincent, who had no interest in cuts of meat or agriculture, began to disrupt the class. Because of his size and age, many of the boys looked up to him. Our textbook had drawings of carcasses and sides of meat hanging on hooks and he decided to make additions to those illustrations. On some he drew large male sex organs; on others, he penciled in human looking breasts. The other boys copied his work and soon the carcasses in most books were well hung.

One afternoon Vincent was disturbing the class at a new level. I was sitting three desks back and I could see the boys around him grinning and talking. As usual, Mr.Anderson was walking up and down the aisles as he lectured, seemingly unaware of the disruption.

"The dressing percentage is determined by dividing the weight of the carcass on the rail by the weight of the live animal," he said, as he passed my desk. I was looking down at my textbook when he went by.

Suddenly, I heard a loud "POP" and looked up in time to see Mr. Anderson's arm in a follow-through position, like a handball player. Vincent was sitting on the floor looking stunned. I realized that he had been slapped completely out of his desk.

"Offal is the term for entrails and other waste products for the carcass," Mr. Anderson said, continuing up the aisle as though nothing had happened.

Vincent crawled back into his desk, looking like a dog trying to sneak in the back door without being seen. The side of his face was turning red. Except for our teacher, the room was totally silent, even though we were all biting our lips to keep from laughing. When Mr. Anderson reached the front of the room, he turned and addressed us in a serious tone.

"Now Vincent, perhaps that will help you concentrate on the subject at hand," he said. "For the rest of you, I'll suggest there shouldn't be any drawings in your text books."

In a moment the sound of erasers in action filled the room.

All my anger at Vincent for shooting at me disappeared. Seeing him sitting on the floor and crawling back into his desk wiped it away. All I could do was laugh inside.

From that day on, the behavior of the students in agriculture class was nearly perfect and Vincent set a shining example. He had lost his power over us younger boys; after the slap we viewed him in a different light. Mr. Anderson had shown us real power in action.

18. Boys On Strike

 I SHIVERED AS I HUDDLED BESIDE THE BOAT'S RUSTY exhaust pipe in a futile attempt to stay warm. The faint pink glow in the eastern sky reminded me it would be a long time before I felt the sun's warmth. I already regretted leaving my extra sweatshirt at home. My father and I were heading down the Manokin River to tong oysters. He was taking me along as culling mate. I had another day off from school because of a broken furnace and he didn't want me to waste it.

"Go into the cabin and build a fire in the stove," he said as we were approaching Cormal Point. "If you get her hot, we'll have a cup of coffee before we go to work."

"Mom doesn't let me drink coffee," I reminded him.

"Well, she's not here, so get to it if you want to get warm."

It was no warmer inside the cabin than outdoors but at least the air was still. Using a flashlight, I stuffed the miniature stove full of newspaper and small sticks. With the touch of my match the paper flared and for a few seconds my face and hands were warm. Those flames quickly died but their descendants were already licking at the edges of the kindling. In a minute I added larger pieces of wood, and the stove began to "tick" as it expanded from the heat.

My father opened the cabin door and ducked inside. "Sparks were coming out the stack, so I figured you had a fire going."

"Who's steering?" I said.

"She's steering herself for a while. This boat will hold a pretty true course with no one at the tiller." Reaching under the bow deck, he pulled out a wooden box. From it, he retrieved a dented old coffee pot with no innards, a bag of coffee and a partially frozen jug of water. After filling the pot, he threw two handfuls of coffee directly into the water. "Keep it centered over the fire. The wind is starting to blow and it's going to get rougher."

Dad went back to the helm and I felt the boat turn as he brought her back on course. Light was now filtering through the cabin's portholes. The seas picked up as he predicted, and the coffee pot began to slide. A rail around the stovetop prevented it from flying off, but to get the water to boil I had to hold it over the hottest part.

The smell of coffee brought my father back to the cabin. He poured out two cups of the dark liquid and added liberal quantities of sugar and condensed milk. After a few sips of that sweet, milky warmth, I decided his coffee was okay except for the crunchy texture.

I followed my father back to the helm, carefully balancing my coffee as the boat pitched. The sun was just sneaking a look over the waterfront community of Rumbley. As I drained my cup I began to feel good. The cold air had lost some of its bite and the morning seemed to hold promise. We were headed to a spot where, years earlier, my father had seen the state plant oyster shells but no one had ever tonged.

After a short run, Dad slowed the engine.

"I have to locate my marks for this spot," he said, gazing toward Crisfield. As I had often seen him do before, he was using landmarks to pinpoint a location on the river bottom. He maneuvered the boat while keeping an eye on a church steeple in Crisfield. When it moved in front of a particular tall tree in the woods behind it, he turned and steered along an imaginary line running through those marks. At the same time he kept watch on a black buoy that was barely visible to the west. When it came in line with the southern tip of Deal Island, he cut the engine.

"Drop the anchor," he said. I tossed over the grapnel and played out what I thought was enough rope.

"How's that?" I asked.

"Not enough, it won't hold the bottom. Give her twenty more feet." I did as I was told and tied the line off to the bow cleat.

My father had begun the oyster season hand tonging in Holland Straits, partnering with another waterman from Champ. Oysters on the leased ground still had green gill and they were starting to die off. Each morning Dad and his partner made the two-hour trip down the river and across Tangier Sound. Their catch was enough to make it worthwhile but my father's arm proved too weak for a full day of hand tonging.

Recently, he had outfitted the boat with "patent" tongs. They were large steel rakes with short metal shafts that were raised and lowered with a rope attached to a winch. The winch was powered by a noisy gasoline engine. Dad had installed a mast at the front corner of the boat's cockpit and near its top was a boom with a pulley. The rope ran from the tongs, through the pulley and down to the winch.

"Watch out for the tongs, they're dangerous," Dad said as he began work. "The way the boat is rocking, they'll swing a lot. If you're head gets caved in out here, it's a long way to the doctor." He raised the heavy rakes from the culling board and they immediately began to sway. He pushed them out over the water and dropped them to the bottom. In a few seconds he brought them back above the surface, grabbed them with his good hand and pulled them back over the culling board. The operation required precise timing; if he made a mistake the boat could be damaged or we might be injured.

When my father emptied the tongs, there were a lot of shells and only a few live oysters. He frowned as he looked through the muddy pile. Coming across a clump of four live ones attached together, he held them up for me to see.

"Let me show you how to cull." Using a notched stick, he measured the length of each oyster. "This one is under three inches and it has to be thrown back." He took out a small hammer made for culling and knocked the small one loose. "Don't keep any undersized oysters. I don't want the men who used to work for me to arrest me."

"Here's a good one," I said. I picked up what I thought was a healthy oyster. Dad tapped it with the hammer.

"Hear that hollow sound? It's dead." He pried it open and showed me the foul looking mud inside. "The buyers get upset if you put many of those in the catch."

He went back to operating the tongs; I put on heavy rubber gloves and began to cull, trying to concentrate on my work. Often I was distracted by the marine life coming aboard with the shells. There were tiny oyster crabs less than an inch long, bright red bloodworms and several kinds of sponges. Once, my father grabbed the tongs to keep them from hitting me.

"Pay attention," he shouted above the roar of the winch motor.

"I will," I vowed.

We worked for hours, but each dump of the tongs produced the same result—plenty of shells but few oysters. Dad moved the boat several times but the result was the same.

"For some reason, there wasn't a good strike of spat on these shells," he said. He shut off the winch motor and we took a break. Our fried hot dog sandwiches tasted good after the cold morning's work.

In the early afternoon my father gave up on his secret spot and decided to return to Champ. I pulled the anchor, thinking how tonging was less fun than crabbing. It did not change my mind about wanting to be a waterman. I was sure that once I got my own boat, I could find more oysters than my father.

When we arrived back at the harbor, there was only one buyer on the county wharf. He was a pear-shaped man with a stubby cigar continually hanging from his lips. The bed of his rusty, blue pickup was half-full of oysters. As I tied up to a wharf piling, he made an announcement.

"Tom, the price of oysters has dropped. I'm only paying four dollars a bushel today."

"Jesus Christ, we only caught four bushels. Sixteen dollars minus the cost of the gas for a days work; do you think that's fair?"

"My hands are tied. The shucking house cut the price it pays me. Do you want to sell or not?" The man took a puff from his cigar as he waited for Dad's answer.

"I guess so," my father said in resignation. It was a long trip by boat or truck to another buyer.

At the end of the wharf was a wooden boom used for lifting oysters. The buyer swung it over our boat and began to play out the rope, lowering the steel, bushel-measuring tub into the cockpit. When it came to rest on the deck, I began to shovel oysters into it.

"If he's only paying four dollars a bushel, don't give him even one extra," Dad said.

I filled the tub level with the rim and stepped back. The buyer looked down at me, expecting more. It was customary to add at least another shovelful, rounding the pile and making a "good" bushel. I glanced at my father but he just smiled and said nothing. After an awkward pause, the man pulled the rope and the tub moved upward. The pulleys creaked under their load and he grunted from his effort.

As I was filling the tub a second time, the buyer decided to strike up a conversation.

"Tom, did you know I buy oysters from Captain Willie?"

"No I didn't."

"Well, I do, and he's quite a guy. Captain Willie always fills the tub up plenty and then he lifts it from the bottom of his boat to higher than his head. I can't get the slack out of the rope until it's seven feet above his deck."

"Is that right," my father said coolly.

"Yeah, it takes a lot of work off me. Hard to believe he lifts the tub so high. You can see the muscles bulging under his shirt and he's going on seventy."

"Captain Willie is tough," Dad said. "All those years of hand tonging will keep a man in shape."

I listened carefully to the conversation, proud that someone thought highly of my grandfather. When the tub was full, just to the rim, I tried lifting it, but barely got it above my waist. Dad was sitting on the engine box, watching.

"Don't strain yourself for four dollars a bushel," he said.

* * *

As Christmas neared, I had two litters of pigs old enough to sell. Between them, my gilts had weaned eighteen. I decided to keep two of the females as additional breeding stock and to sell the remaining sixteen. The farmer who bought them would feed them grain for four months, until they reached market weight.

My sows were already pregnant again and they would farrow their second litters in the spring. For the next fall, I was planning on four litters, two from the original sows and two from the new gilts.

Mr. Anderson came out to see my operation as promised. He made several good suggestions about how to improve my houses and he started me on a bookkeeping system. Together we calculated that I would soon show a nice profit. The money from the first litters had paid for most of my start-up expenses. I was beginning to get used to the responsibility of caring for pigs seven days a week. Many things about the business were enjoyable, like watching sows have their pigs and figuring how much money I would make when they were sold.

The poultry industry was expanding and more of our neighbors were building chicken houses. Cleaning out those houses between flocks became a major source of spending money for the Bates brothers and me. After they were clean, we usually got the job of spreading truckloads of wood shavings used as bedding for the next flock.

Cleaning out and putting down shavings were the only two jobs for which my father paid me. All the other chicken house work and lawn mowing were considered dues I paid for being part of the family. I quit asking for an allowance, tired of hearing about how he allowed me to eat at his table.

When I began working for other farmers, my father seemed concerned that I might not do a good job for them. One day he gave me advice while we were filling chick water jars. It was a chore I disliked and I was in a hurry to finish.

"You know, any job worth doing is worth doing right," he said. "Take pride in your work. Always do the kind of job you'd want somebody to do for you, if you were paying them."

I screwed the lid back on a jar and promised that I would always do good work for our neighbors. He wasn't satisfied.

"Work hard. Give the man a good hour's labor for an hour's pay. If you do more than he expects, you will always have a job."

I thought about his comments as I carried some full jars back to the chicks. On my return to the faucet with more empties, I began to complain about a farmer who was doing his own chicken house clean-out and not hiring us. My father frowned and shook his head.

"Terry, nobody owes you a job just because you say you want one. If your work won't make the man some money, he doesn't need you."

That was a new concept to me and I never forgot it. Looking back on that conversation, I realized it contained all I needed to know about being a good employee. But my education about bosses was just beginning.

One evening I received a call from a woman who needed our crew to spread shavings in her chicken house. She wanted the work done the next day after school, but that was Friday and Johnny had a date. He really liked the girl and did not want to be late. The job usually took more than three hours, but we decided it could be done faster if we worked at absolute top speed.

None of us particularly liked working for this woman; most of the other farmers gave us a dollar an hour, but she paid only sixty cents, and she kept time to the minute. Since she was a member of the church, my father insisted we do the job for whatever she paid. When we arrived at the chicken house, the lady was waiting in her car. She was overweight and struggled to get out the door. Since I knew her best, I was made spokesman.

"Instead of working by the hour, we'll do the job for a total of six dollars, just like the last time," I proposed. Aware of what other farmers were paying, she appeared happy that we had not asked for more.

"That sounds fine to me," she said with a smile.

The lady drove away and we began spreading shavings, working faster than we ever had in our lives. Billy and I were shoveling so rapidly our breaths came in gasps. Johnny was working just as hard, running as he pushed our wheelbarrow full of shavings to the far end of the house. In ninety minutes we had the job completed. All of us were sweating and panting as if we had been playing soccer. Just as we were loading our tools in the Bates family pickup, our employer returned.

"Finished already," she said, walking up to inspect our work.

"We worked really hard; Johnny has to go out tonight," I said.

Her eyes narrowed as she calculated how much we had made per hour. "Just a minute," she said, returning to her car. She came back with a roll of bills and handed each of us a dollar. "Boys, I can't pay you six dollars, you didn't work long enough. I'm giving you sixty cents per hour plus a dime tip. Thanks for doing the job on Friday afternoon."

I was too shocked to say anything. The woman got in her car and drove away, leaving us standing beside the chicken house wondering what to do.

"She agreed to a price of six dollars," Billy said, in disbelief.

"We really didn't make but thirty cents an hour," Johnny said.

"Let's shovel up the shavings and put them back in a pile," I suggested. I was mad and wanted to get even, somehow. The others liked the idea until Johnny remembered his date.

Unsure how to respond, we climbed in the truck and headed home. Johnny drove slowly and we tried to come up with a way to get our money. Every plan we thought of was discarded because it would upset our parents. We made a pact never to work for the woman again, no matter what my father said.

At home I told my parents how we had been treated and that I was going to inform everyone in church. My father cut me off.

"She's an important woman in this community and you're not going to say anything. Some people have a hard time letting go of their money. You've just learned that valuable lesson."

His tone said I would regret pursuing the matter. I went to my room angrier than ever. I had learned that people didn't always practice what they said "Amen" to in church on Sunday.

A week later Sigsbee called and asked us to spread shavings in his chicken house. I told him I would discuss the job with the Bates boys. Sigsbee was a fine person, but he paid only seventy-five cents per hour, and we were still mad about our treatment on the previous job. There were stories on television about coal miners on strike and we decided to follow their example. I gave Sigsbee his answer while we were standing in the churchyard after Sunday services.

"We're not going to work for you unless we get a dollar an hour," I said, defiantly. He looked surprised and a half frown came to his face.

"I think I'll get someone else to do the job."

"That's fine with us," I said. My bluff had been called but I did not want the money badly enough to give in. His chicks were scheduled for delivery in four days, which did not give him much time to find someone else. I didn't mention the strike to my family and for two days we heard nothing from Sigsbee. On the afternoon of the third day, my father was waiting in the yard when I got off the school bus. He was not happy.

"What's this I hear about you refusing to work for Sigsbee?"

"He doesn't pay enough and we're on strike."

"Strike, my ass. Have you forgotten how much he's done for this family and how many times you've borrowed his skiff?" I suddenly saw the situation in a different light and began to feel guilty for my actions.

"He wasn't using his skiff," I said weakly.

My father looked at me as if I was from outer space. "I tell you what's going to happen," he said. "You are going to spread Sigsbee's shavings for whatever he pays. I can't make the Bates boys work, but if they don't help, you are going to do the entire job yourself—even if you have to take off from school."

Reluctantly, I called Johnny and Billy and they agreed to help me. They were true friends and I could always count on them. We worked late in the evening to get the job done. When it was finished, Sigsbee paid us a dollar an hour.

"Boys, is that good enough?' he said.

"Yes sir," I answered.

"You're not going to strike again?"

"No sir."

"Good. I'll call you the next time I have work." His smile returned and I was glad there were no hard feelings.

The lady who had underpaid us called several times that year, asking us to do her work, but I always said we were busy. If my father was aware of the situation, he never mentioned it. The Bates boys and I whooped in delight when we found out that the man she hired to level shavings charged her twice what she had agreed to pay us.

* * *

Many of my other life lessons came from the men at the Corner Store. One Saturday Bobby and I took a break from grinding corn and went there for a snack. Nearly a dozen farmers and watermen were sitting on wooden soda bottle cases, talking about a man who had just pulled away from the gas pumps.

"He wouldn't work in a pie factory," Scoot was saying as we walked in.

"Hell no, he's too lazy to scratch fire off himself," a short, wiry waterman added.

"If his wife didn't work, he'd starve to death," Preston said.

Bobby and I made our way to the soda cooler; we had heard similar discussions before. The store was a place where boys could learn what the men in the community thought was proper behavior. It was as important as the church in helping me decide how to live my life. The confusing part occurred when the men professed one thing at church but acted differently at the store.

Bobby and I were just finishing our Grapette sodas when one of my classmates walked through the door. Her name was Page and she came in to pick up a quart of milk for her mother, who was waiting in the car. She lived on a farm not far away and we were becoming friends. Her body had developed more than any girl in our class, and it was hard not to notice it in her shorts and white sleeveless blouse. She waved at me as she walked from the milk cooler to the register, and I smiled back.

The men were silent while Page was in the store, but as soon as the door closed behind her, a married member of the church spoke up.

"Whew, that girl is growing up fast. That body of hers could make a man forget all his teachings," he said, with a lecherous grin. Most of the other men laughed and voiced their agreement. I was surprised and disgusted by his comment. How could he talk like that if he believed in the Ten Commandments? What right did he have to be looking at her anyway? He was almost old enough to be her grandfather.

Maybe I was a little jealous about Page. After she left I sat on the soda cooler for a long time thinking about how she looked. I was still gazing out the store window when a faded green pickup rolled slowly into the parking lot. The driver was sitting in the middle of the seat, steering as though he was sighting down the hood ornament. It had to be Tommy Toots; no one else drove like that. When strangers saw him coming down the road, they must have thought, "Okay, I see the passenger, now where is the driver?"

Tommy was a skinny, middle-aged bachelor with an Ichabod Crane look. Toots wasn't his real last name, but he talked so loudly and with such a brogue, it sometimes sounded like he was tooting a horn. People called him Tommy or Toots depending on how loud he was that day. Not only did he have extra volume, but he leaned in close to a person's face when talking and his eyes bugged out as he tried to make a point. The effect was unforgettable.

Toots lived in a worn-out house on the edge of the Oriole marsh. He owned a small tractor and farmed low-lying patches of land that no one else would touch. When he was not farming, he worked on the water in a small boat. Even with those two sources of income, he sometimes ran out of money and had to do physical labor for anyone who would hire him. Determined to be self-sufficient, he never took money from state welfare.

Tommy sometimes got into trouble with the law on both land and water. He received a number of traffic tickets, but none was for speeding—he never exceeded twenty-five miles an hour. TFC officers arrested him several times for minor violations like crabbing without a license, but he never paid the fines up-front, always insisting on a trial where he could proclaim his innocence. His behavior drove some of the judges crazy and when he went to trial, the courtroom was usually packed with spectators. After one raucous appearance the judge called the TFC officer to the bench.

"In the future, no matter what he does, he can't deplete the oyster and crab populations enough to justify bringing him into my court." From that day on, he got a free pass whenever he worked on the water.

As Tommy approached the door I wondered what was on his mind.

"Hello, Toots, what have you been up to?" Scoot said.

"By God, I just drove from Salisbury and people were really friendly. They were waving and blowing their horns—I never saw anything like it."

"What road did you drive on?" Clarence Laird, Jr. asked. He owned the store in partnership with his brother.

"Route 13, same as always," Tommy said.

"The two new lanes of Route 13 are now open for traffic. The old lanes are one way going north. You were driving the wrong way, that's why people were waving."

Tommy paused, trying to understand what he had just heard. The rest of us pictured him happily going the wrong way toward the other frantic motorists. Clarence explained what he had done wrong and how he could avoid the mistake in the future. He was obviously grateful.

"Thank ye Junior, thank ye," he said. "By Jesus, I could have been killed."

After talk of his driving subsided, Tommy selected a coconut pie from the snack case and sat down beside me.

"Man, this pie crust is tough," he said. I looked at his pie and saw that his bite included a piece of the cardboard tray. He was chewing hard but I stopped him before he could swallow. When I pointed out his error, he thanked me for half a minute.

The conversation among the men lagged and some of them left the store. Milbert came over to speak to Tommy.

"How are you getting along?" my uncle asked.

"I'll tell you the truth, Milburn, things are kind of hard. I didn't catch many oysters and there ain't no crabs yet." He sounded worried.

"If you're short of money, I need some trees cut down along the edge of my pasture. How's your saw working?" Tommy owned an antique chain saw that he struggled to keep operating.

"Oh, she's running good, Milburn."

"In that case, come by Monday morning and I'll put you to work."

"By God, I'll be there Milburn, thank ye."

Probably my uncle had planned to cut the trees himself, but he offered the job to Tommy to help him out. It would give him immediate cash and firewood for next winter. My uncle was not alone in his charity—many people in the community helped Toots survive. Women took him home-cooked meals, aware that his food usually came from a can. The men helped him keep his truck and tractor running. He appreciated it all and everyone received a "Thank ye." It was usually loud enough to count as two.

As I was leaving the store, I thought of what my father had once said. "If Tommy had been born in the city, he may have wound up in an institution, but in the country he can live as a free man."

Maybe Oriole wasn't a bad place to live even if some of its residents did forget their "teachings."

19. A Shark Up Close

IN MAY THE FIRST BIG RUN OF PEELERS ARRIVED AND MY father scraped on the river, catching more than a thousand on good days. For a few weeks he was happy with his income, and his attitude at home improved. He even found fewer reasons to criticize my behavior. But the number of peelers soon tapered off, and by the time I was out of school and free to go crabbing, the catch was down to a few hundred a day.

It was disappointing to have missed the big run, but I was glad to be working on the water. I was strong enough to pull the scrapes a few times each day and my father was pleased to have the help. His arm was stronger but the work was still not easy for him. As the days went on, a friendly rivalry developed between Bruce and us over the number of peelers caught. With his experience on the river, there was usually no contest—when the crabs moved, he always seemed to find them before we did.

Those days on the boat were the best my father and I had together for a long time. The fights that developed between us at home were quickly forgotten on the river, and we worked together for weeks without a cross word. I was disappointed when the catch dropped even more, barely covering the fuel bill, and my father decided his time would be better spent on chicken house maintenance.

For weeks after that the boat lay idle, swinging at her stake with each change of the tide. I asked my father to let me take her out alone, but he was hesitant. Since my early childhood he had been teaching me about the weather and tides, and how to be safe on a boat, but he had given me only one swimming lesson. Dad seemed to believe it was up to the boys to teach each other, and that's how I learned. He still had doubts about my ability.

"You don't swim well enough to be on the river by yourself," he said.

"I'm better than you think. What do I have to do to prove it?" He thought for a moment before answering.

"You have to swim across the creek and back at high tide. Then you have to tread water for fifteen minutes."

"I can do that," I said, not sure if it was true.

The next afternoon my father stood on the county wharf, while I attempted to pass his test. I nervously pushed off. "Don't make me have to jump in and save you," he yelled. There was no doubt he could do it, even with his bad arm; he had all the life-saving badges from his days with the TFC.

I set off at a fast pace, determined that he would not have to rescue me. By the time I crossed the creek and returned, a distance of 150 yards, I was already tired. My father kept a close eye on his watch as I swam back out to the channel to tread water. When he called time, I paddled to a piling and held on, gasping for air.

"Not bad, but you're still not ready to take the boat out," he said.

I was too short of breath to argue, but I was mad that I had passed his test and he had changed the rules. A few days later, I went on a fishing trip with Danny and my father. As we headed across the river to a creek known for big rockfish, my father asked me to repair a hole in one of the scrape bags. I squatted on the washboard and began to lace up the tear with cotton twine. The boat was running full speed, and I was concentrating on tying good knots, so the repair would hold. Suddenly I felt a push in my back, and in an instant I was under water.

I came to the surface confused. Everything had happened so fast. Who or what had pushed me? I looked toward the boat and it was still going away at full speed. My father was at the helm looking forward as though nothing had happened. Danny was staring back at me with an expression of surprise.

I treaded water and waited for the boat to turn back but it kept moving steadily away. Fear rose up in me and I struggled to force it back into that dark hole where it normally resided. I thought over my options and there was no choice but to start swimming toward the nearest shore. It was only a few hundred yards away but it looked farther.

After a minute of the most serious paddling of my life, I paused and glanced toward the boat again—it was on its way back to me. As it drew closer, my father stared into my eyes. Danny was beside him, sporting a wide grin.

"Who pushed me?" I yelled.

"Nobody, you fell overboard," Dad said. "You won't be much of a waterman if your balance is that bad." A slight upward curl at the corners of his mouth gave him away. A guilty smile always forced itself to his lips when he tried to lie.

"You did it," I said. My fear came back as anger and my father broke into a full grin.

"I wanted to see how you would react if you fell overboard unexpectedly. You handled it well."

I swam to the stern and climbed on to the settling boards with a strong desire to throw the old man in the water, but I was not big enough, yet.

"Now, can I take the boat out by myself?"

"I'll think about it." It was the first time he had said anything besides no, which encouraged me, but my initial voyage as captain was still a ways off.

* * *

We didn't catch a big rockfish that day, but I still had the desire to land one I could brag about. Sigsbee and my father had caught stripers weighing nearly twenty pounds but I had never brought in anything over five. I needed a fishing partner but the Bates boys were both working with their father that summer. He was a carpenter and they were building a house in Salisbury. I settled on Richard Tyler, a sandy-haired kid who lived halfway between our house and the Corner Store. He was more than a year younger than I was, but he was the next oldest boy in the neighborhood. Even at thirteen he had a dry sense of humor and a flair for exaggeration. Bobby and I had begun calling him Salty because he delighted in telling tall tales.

When I asked Richard to go along on my fishing trip, I knew that getting permission from his mother would be a problem. She was a worrier, always afraid that he would somehow be injured. He seldom got far from home without her coming to check on him. I told Mrs. Tyler that I was experienced on the water and that nothing could go wrong. We must have caught her at a weak moment because she said yes.

I still did not have Dad's okay to use the bateau and the outboard motor was being repaired, so Richard and I used a small skiff that Sigsbee had recently built for my father. We poled out to the river shore and anchored against the bank. With a high tide and an overcast sky, it looked like a good day for fishing.

We tied on our usual rig—two 2/o hooks and a three-ounce lead sinker. I removed the outer shell from a peeler and cut the crab into four pieces with my pocketknife. We baited our hooks and walked along the marsh edge, searching for a bald spot offshore where there was no eelgrass. Keeping the bait free of grass made it more visible to the fish. Each of us found a good spot and we settled down to some serious fishing. After half an hour we had landed only one small rock and two eels. The second eel twisted Richard's line until it resembled a slimy bird's nest.

"Why did he have to do that? I was going to turn him loose," he said in exasperation. I laughed as he continued to grumble and tried to untangle the mess. Finally he gave up, cut off the snarled line and tied on a new rig. He had just finished his repair, when there was a huge splash near the bank on the other side of the creek mouth.

"Did you see that?" I said.

"It had to be a big rock. I'll bet it's over twenty pounds," he said.

"Let's go get him," I said. Richard was already climbing into the skiff. We talked in whispers as we poled toward the fish, discussing his size and how to catch him. Richard soon had his weight up to forty pounds, even though a rockfish that big had never been caught in the river. Drawing close to the spot, we slowed down and moved quietly, careful not to let our poles scrape the gunnel. Slipping along in barely four feet of water, we felt like true hunters of the sea.

The skiff was almost to the shore, when the water suddenly began to boil under the bow where Richard was standing. The force of it threw his end of the boat sideways and he fought to keep his balance. We both watched, dumbstruck, as a stream of churning water moved off to our left. When it had progressed two skiff lengths, a large dorsal fin, perhaps fourteen inches high, broke the surface. Neither of us had seen a shark up close before, but we recognized it instantly. The big fish stayed on the surface only a few seconds before submerging. As it went under, it appeared to be turning back toward us.

Richard and I had been standing frozen with our mouths open, but that suddenly changed. Without saying a word, we both jammed our poles into the bottom, and shoved with the strength of those about to be eaten. The skiff jumped forward and came to rest with half its length on the marsh bank. Richard scrambled over the side and I was right behind him. Our legs tangled and we fell near the water's edge. We hardly touched the mud before we were up and running. Neither of us stopped until we were twenty yards deep in the needle reeds. Only there did it feel safe. I stared at the water, looking for some sign of the predator but the surface was calm.

"I'm walking home!" Richard said. It was a mile to the harbor through mud and across guts, but I considered the idea, too.

As we began to calm down, I remembered the picture on my bedroom wall of my father in the South Pacific standing beside his shark. My desire to catch a bigger one overcame my fear, and I decided to go fishing. Carefully, I approached the skiff and retrieved my rod. Putting a whole crab on each hook, I cast to where I had last seen the shark and checked the drag on my reel. I waited nervously but nothing happened. I moved down the shore and cast again—still nothing. Richard joined me and we worked the entire shoreline without a bite. After half an hour we decided the shark might have gone to deeper water.

Our courage returned but not to the point where we would get back into the boat. We walked on the shore pulling it with a rope for a long distance, until we came to a soft spot in the marsh where we had to climb aboard. Our adrenaline was high and we poled hard toward the harbor all the time looking back, afraid we would see that fin coming up behind us. At the wharf we told several watermen about our encounter but they looked skeptical.

During the bike ride home, Richard and I talked constantly about our narrow escape. When we pulled into our yard, Dad was just coming out of the chicken house. He listened to our story but I could tell he thought we were exaggerating.

"It was probably just a nurse shark, but not as big as you think," he said. "They're not man-eaters but they come in the river sometimes to feed on soft crabs."

"I don't care if it was a nurse shark or a doctor shark, it was big and it was after us," Richard said. I understood what he meant. We had poled a skiff on top of a big shark and we had a story to tell. No one was going to diminish it.

When Richard's mother found out, she declared he would never go anywhere with me again. Fortunately, his father had taken an interest in fishing and I knew he would not be banned from the water for life.

One evening a week later, I went fishing with my father and Danny about a mile downriver from where we had seen the shark. My father had just purchased a larger outboard motor for Milbert's boat and we used it. We anchored on the edge of a bar where the bottom dropped off abruptly into a small channel. The bar was sandy and almost without vegetation, but the channel was lush with eelgrass and marine life. We sometimes netted crabs there when the tide was at its lowest. Even then, the water was five feet deep, but it was clear enough to see doublers hiding in the grass. At that depth, they were hard to catch because of refraction and the resistance of the water on our nets, but we brought in enough to make it worthwhile.

A short time after we started fishing, a boat approached that my father did not recognize. He hated being crowded on his fishing spot, especially by strangers. Anyone within a half mile was too close for him. He stood up and was about to wave the boat away when we recognized Richard and his father on board. His father had been building a new skiff and they were taking it out for its maiden voyage. The Tylers anchored close by, and for a while we caught small rockfish and speckled trout as fast as we could bait our hooks.

Abruptly, the fish quit biting. We were all facing the channel where our baits were lying on the bottom but some inner sense made me turn and look back over the bar. There, silhouetted against the light colored sand, was the shark. It was less than thirty feet away, cruising slowly, with its dorsal fin and tail out of the water. There was at least six feet between them. I alerted the others and everyone turned and watched in awe. Richard and I were more comfortable than during our first encounter because we were in larger boats. When the shark disappeared in the distance, Dad broke the silence.

"You boys were right, that is a big one. And it may not be a nurse shark. I think we should try to catch him."

The next morning my father drove to Ocean City and purchased large hooks of the type used for marlin fishing. When he returned home, we rigged four lines from a spool of heavy trotline cord. Each had a stout wire leader and three plastic jugs which served as a float. After they were complete I went to the chicken house to catch birds for bait.

Early in the afternoon, Dad, Richard and I took the boat back to the spot where we had seen the shark. We set our lines along the channel's edge, baiting each one with a whole chicken that we let bleed into the water. To further entice our quarry, Dad ladled out the fish guts from the previous night's catch.

"If he comes back this way, we'll get him," he said.

It was a scorching hot day, and as we waited in the blazing sun, I was nervous. The thought of having that big shark next to our little boat was unsettling. Richard was uncharacteristically quiet, and he stared constantly at the floats. My father loaded the rifle he had brought along to kill the big fish. I sat quietly and wondered what the next hours would bring.

In fact, they brought nothing. Throughout the rest of the day we watched floats that barely moved, except to swing with the tide. Richard and I grew bored and we took naps on the hard wooden boat seats. Our rest ended when the green-head horse flies came off the marsh and found us. Unable to sleep, we netted a doubler that swam by on the surface, and used the peeler as bait to fish for rock. We soon learned that nothing was biting but the flies.

By the time the sun set behind Deal Island, the excitement of shark fishing had disappeared. The day had seemed so long and dull that I never wanted to try it again.

A week later, my father went dip-netting for crabs on the flats near the mouth of Broad Creek. Shortly after arriving he saw a large fin cutting through the water heading his way. The depth was only two feet and he watched the shark swim up beside his skiff. At first Dad was alarmed, but he quickly realized he and the shark were there for the same thing—soft crabs.

For nearly an hour the two of them crabbed side by side. Sometimes the shark came so close that Dad bumped it with his net to move it out of his way. Eventually the animal muddied the water and my father could no longer see the bottom, so he had to quit crabbing.

During supper I listened with fascination as he told the story. To my surprise he said that he had developed a fondness for the shark and no longer wanted to catch it. I assured him it wasn't the man-eater that had been after Richard and me.

20. Clever Young Veterinarian

 WITH THE END OF SUMMER MY FATHER RETURNED TO tonging, trying to supplement his income from the chicken houses. Each day when the weather permitted, he rose two hours before dawn and made the trip down the river. He tried his luck on different oyster bars, hoping to find a spot where the shellfish were still plentiful. But it was the same as the year before—too few oysters anywhere to justify the long, cold day on the water. The seed oysters planted on the lease should have been at their best that fall, but they were dying and he realized that he might never make any money from them.

By early December, my father was discouraged and one evening he made an announcement to Danny and me.

"Boys, I've taken a job at Wayne Pump, working on the four to midnight shift. That means I won't be around as much and you'll have to do more in the chicken houses," he said in a defeated tone. His statement came as a surprise; in our small house I usually overheard my parents making decisions.

Dad's first paycheck came in just before Christmas and my mother was happy to have a regular income again. For a while his job seemed to be nothing but good for our family, but it caused unexpected changes. Danny and I never saw him except on weekends. During the week, he was sleeping when we left for school and when we returned, he had already gone to work. There were no more family discussions at the supper table because Dad ate at 3:00 PM. Five days a week he was a distant presence, not really involved in my life.

When the weekend came, my father was not in good humor after running a metal press for forty hours. He tried to make up for his absence from my life by being especially strict, as though he was afraid that I was getting out of control. None of the jobs I had completed during the week was good enough for him. The jobs I did on the weekend were never fast enough. I had my own ideas about how to organize my chores but they never matched his plans.

* * *

Late one Saturday afternoon, I was getting ready for a movie date with a girl in my class. Other than the monthly school dance, meeting a girl at the Arcade Theater in Princess Anne was the only option for a boy without a driver's license. Johnny had agreed to drop me off in town on his way to pick up his girlfriend. Another neighbor was going to drive me home after the movie. I was getting dressed when my father knocked on the door of my room.

"Terry, I want you to feed the chickens in number two house this evening," he said.

"I can't, I'm leaving for town in an hour. They don't need feeding until tomorrow." Oriole Methodism permitted feeding animals on Sunday.

"I don't care what your plans are, I want them fed tonight." I was about to continue my protest, when Mom announced that supper was ready and he went to get his meal. I ran out to the chicken house and walked through it quickly, checking the feed level. I moved fast and the birds scattered in front of me, raising a cloud of feather dust. There was obviously enough food remaining in the feeders to supply them until the next morning.

When I returned to the house, my father had finished eating and he was downing the last of his coffee.

"I checked the feed and it will last until tomorrow." I said. "I'll get up early and feed them before church."

"I told you I want them fed this evening. If I hear any more argument, you won't go to town for another month."

I recognized my father's end of discussion statement and it was impossible to negotiate after that. If I pressed the issue, he would take away one of my existing privileges. I had no choice but to cancel the date but I knew it would not always be that way. Someday I would control my own life without anyone telling me what to do. I made decisions every day about how to care for my pigs, and they were doing fine, but that didn't seem to matter. My father's rule at home was still absolute and I never challenged him head on. At school it was a different story. I tested the authority of my teachers every year, until I pushed them past their level of tolerance.

* * *

I fired my clothespin gun and the yellow kernel of corn bounced off Mitch Robertson's head. It skittered up the aisle between the rows of desks. Mitch was a good-looking black-haired boy and we often competed for the attention of girls. Our music teacher did not see my shot; he appeared to be in a trance, standing beside the record player. Mr. Walz was a nice, middle-aged man but his classroom was always out of control. His new record from the Broadway show, *The Music Man,* was on the turntable. "Seventy Six Trombones" was blaring from the speaker. It had sounded good the first four times, but this was the fifth.

I had assembled my little corn gun the night before, copying one a senior boy showed me on the bus. It was made from half of a spring type clothespin that I modified and jammed into a clip-on style clothespin. The spring could be set under tension and when triggered, it would fire a projectile with much more force than a peashooter.

I reloaded and took another shot at Mitch. He ducked and the corn hit Page on the back of her head. She turned around and slapped him. The teacher was still unaware of anything but the music. I looked to see if the boys behind me had appreciated my shooting. They were in fits of laughter about Mitch being slapped. That's when I noticed a face looking through the little window in the classroom door. I recognized the principal's bald head shining through the glass. He wiggled his finger, signaling that I should come out into the hall.

C. N. Baughn had been principal ever since my father was in high school. He was a tall, slender man who tolerated little nonsense but the students considered him fair.

"Mr. Noble, come with me," he said, as I stepped out of the classroom. He started toward his office at a fast pace and I followed a few steps behind. I wasn't worried about the outcome; it was my third trip to the office and the school year was only two months old. The previous incidents had resulted in my writing sentences for days. My last punishment had been to write five hundred times, "I will not fly aeroplanes in class." Mr. Baughn had chosen aeroplanes because it had one more letter than the usual spelling. Even with three pencils taped together, it had taken a while to finish. This time I figured it might be a thousand sentences.

When we entered the office, the principal closed the door behind him, something he had never done before. He sat behind his big, oak desk and I stood in front of it. The room had a strong smell of mimeograph fluids; some teachers had recently prepared a handout on the old hand-cranked machine. He stared at me for a long time before speaking and I tried to look unconcerned.

"Mr. Noble, I've been trying to get your attention, but nothing seems to work," he said. "You've written hundreds of sentences with apparently no effect. Maybe your penmanship has improved but your behavior hasn't."

At that point I was feeling good about the situation, thinking I had him confused.

"You're grades are good but your teachers tell me you could do much more. They say you act up in class, wasting everyone's time. What do you think I should do about it?"

"I don't know," I said casually. Immediately, I knew I had made a mistake; my carefree attitude seemed to inspire him.

"Well, I have a plan." He sprang to his feet and went to the little closet in the corner of the room where he fumbled around on the top shelf. "Here it is," he said almost gleefully. When he turned toward me, he had what appeared to be a shiny board in his hand. In a second, I realized I was looking at the famous paddle that all the students had heard about but few had seen. It was a thick piece of hardwood with a handle carved on one end and holes drilled up the middle.

My casual attitude disappeared and for the first time I felt a little concerned. I worked to buoy my spirits. I'm fourteen. I'm tough. How bad could it be?

Mr. Baughn pulled a straight back wooden chair into the center of the floor.

"Mr. Noble, bend over the back of that chair and put your hands on the seat." I did as he asked, using all the cool I could summon. "Now bring your toes up against the chair legs," he said.

As soon as my feet were in position, the first blow came without warning. There was no time to prepare or brace myself. The force of the paddle was stunning; if the chair had not been there, I would have stumbled forward. A little sound escaped from my lips that was part cry and part moan. Instantly, I regretted it, not wanting him to know how much it hurt. When the next two blows came I was ready and managed to stay silent. He stopped after the third swing.

"I'm just getting warmed up here but I'm going to quit for now," he said. "Stand up." I straightened up, stiffly, really glad that he was not swinging a fourth time.

"Now if your behavior doesn't improve, next time I'm going to show you how long I can go with this paddle. Do you understand?"

"Yes sir," I mumbled.

"Okay, go back to class."

I walked down the hall rubbing my backside, shocked at how much it still hurt.

When I entered the classroom, the music was still playing. The teacher was unaware that I had left the room or returned.

"What happened?" Mitch asked, as I passed his desk.

"I got paddled." His eyes lit up at my answer.

"Did it hurt?" he asked eagerly.

"No, it wasn't bad," I said, lowering myself gingerly into the desk. I knew if I could stay tough, I had a real badge of honor to wear; none of the other boys had been paddled.

My backside was sore for a few days, but I managed to hide from my father the fact that I had been whipped.

Mr. Baughn never had to discipline me again. My behavior was not perfect, but after that I never seriously disrupted a class and my grades improved. I harbored no hard feelings against the principal, figuring I got what I deserved. One thing that bothered me was the knowing little smile he gave me whenever our paths crossed. It told me he knew that he had gotten my attention.

* * *

It was a sunny Saturday in April, but a cool north wind had forced Bobby and me to the south side of his father's barn. We were sitting on tomato baskets, warming ourselves in the spring sun, while we waited for the new veterinarian who was already an hour late. He had been called because we both had sick animals. One of Bobby's sows had farrowed three days earlier and she was off her feed. I had a six-week-old pig with a swelling on its back leg.

Of the two cases, Bobby's sow was the most serious. She was producing very little milk and her pigs were hungry. She spent a lot of time lying on her belly as though it was painful when they nursed. The babies lined up along her side, nudging with their noses and squealing. When she did roll over in nursing position, they did not stay at her nipples for long. They soon wandered off toward the heat lamp, crying as they went. It was obvious that something had to be done quickly or they would starve.

Neither of us had met the new vet and he was a bit of a mystery. We knew his name was Leroy Johnson and that he had passed through Mr. Anderson's agriculture program years earlier. He had recently started a practice in the town of Pocomoke, located about a half hour to our south.

Bobby and I were dozing in the warm sun when the sound of a car on the farm lane brought us back to consciousness. Looking up, we saw a strange little white vehicle slide around the turn in front of the Shockleys' house. It straightened up and then accelerated toward the barn. When it slid to a stop in front of us, a vigorous young man with a crew cut and a broad grin hopped out. He was wearing aviator sunglasses, a white tee shirt and kaki pants.

"Are you Dr. Johnson?" Bobby asked.

"You're looking at him." Before we could complain about his late arrival, he went on the offensive. "Why are you lounging around? I've got work to do. Where is the sick sow?" he shot out in rapid-fire order.

"Down at the farrowing house," Bobby said, pointing toward the building.

"Well, let's get going, I don't have all day," the vet said.

Bobby and I started toward the farrowing house at a fast walk. Dr. Johnson folded himself back into his little car and sped past us.

"Why were you late?" I shouted in the open window as he went by.

"Uncooperative cow . . ." was all that we could make out of his answer.

When we arrived at the sow barn, the doctor had already found the sick animal and was taking her temperature. In a moment, he removed the thermometer.

"She's got a two degree fever and her mammary glands are hot and hard. It's got to be mastitis." He vaulted over the wall around the sow's pen and headed for his car. We followed, hustling to keep up.

For a few moments he dug through the cases of medication that were stacked where his passenger seat should have been. He emerged with a bottle of pink fluid bearing no label. Stepping to the front of his car, he opened the hood. To our amazement there was no motor, only veterinary equipment.

"What kind of car is this?" I asked.

"Haven't you ever seen a Volkswagen? I bought it when I was in the Air Force." He retrieved a syringe and needle from a black leather bag.

"Where's the motor?" Bobby said.

"In the trunk—where did you think it would be?"

My cousin and I looked at each other, not sure if we should believe such a radical statement. Something about the doctor's grin said he was not above tricking his clients, even ones he had just met. While we contemplated the thought of a rear-engine car, he gave the sow a shot and she lay quietly, too sick to protest. He handed the syringe and bottle of pink liquid to Bobby.

"Give her five cc's a day for three days. Feed the pigs on cows' milk for forty-eight hours and they should be okay."

"What is this pink medicine?" Bobby asked.

"Don't worry about it, just use it," the vet said. He vaulted over the fence again and went back to his car. Once his gear was stowed, he opened the trunk and we stared at the little motor in amazement.

"Whose lawnmower did you steal that from?" I asked.

"Its power will surprise you. Do you want to drive it?"

"Why not," I said confidently. I lowered my body into the driver's seat and tried to back the car away from the farrowing house but it would not go into reverse; each time I let out the clutch, the transmission was in neutral or high gear. I looked over at the owner for help, but he was leaning against the building shaking his head as if he couldn't believe my ineptness. Bobby decided to end my embarrassment and he got behind the wheel, but his efforts were no more successful than mine were. Finally the vet called a halt to the humiliation.

"Okay, that's enough. I sure thought you boys in this part of the country at least knew how to drive. What a disappointment," he said, shaking his head again. Bobby got out and the doctor slid into the driver's seat. He quickly backed up the car and turned it around, too fast for us to see how he got it in reverse. "Am I supposed to examine one of your pigs?" he said to me.

"Yes, the biggest one in my last litter."

"Well, get in and show me the way."

"Okay, but where do I sit?"

My driver moved some bottles of medication and then patted a cardboard box marked IV Fluids. I sat down on the box and closed the door. Immediately the car lurched forward and I rolled into the jumble of supplies in the rear of the vehicle. I struggled to pull myself forward and reached an upright position just as we careened around the turn in front of the Shockleys' house. Desperately, I clung to the window crank trying to maintain my balance.

"I know you can't drive but I thought you could at least sit up," the doctor said with a chuckle.

The trip to my house did not take long. As we pulled in the driveway, Mom was returning from the clothesline carrying a basket of freshly dried sheets. She looked puzzled as the strange car approached, but her expression changed to a frown as our dust cloud reached her laundry.

We stopped at my pigpens and I carried the sick animal, kicking and squealing, to the car. The pig had a swelling the size of a small orange on its right hip, and after feeling the lump for a moment, the doctor decided it was an abscess. He retrieved a scalpel from his black bag and prepared to lance it. I leaned over for a good look.

"Not so close," he said. "Sometimes these things are under pressure."

I leaned back and he stabbed the blade into the swelling. A stream of pus shot out four feet.

"Hah! Glad you listened to me, aren't you?" He was obviously pleased with his work.

"Yeah, but you'd better take a look at your car," I said. He turned to see pus cascading down the windshield and on to the fender.

"Aaah, look at that. Boy this is going to cost you. How much money do you have?"

"Whatever it costs, it was worth it," I said, shaking with laughter.

"You think it's funny? Wait until you see my bill. Hold that pig still so I can finish my work." He flushed the wound with antiseptic and then gave an injection of the pink medicine.

"Give him one cc per day," he said, handing me the syringe. "Do you have any questions before you get a bucket of water and wash my car?"

"Yes, two questions. First, what is this pink fluid?"

"Like I told your buddy, don't worry about it, just use it." I realized that I was looking at a secret formula and would never get an answer.

"Okay, how do you put your car in reverse?"

"Oh that's easy, just push the shift lever down toward the floor before moving it to reverse." It was good to have one mystery solved. I drew a bucket of water and helped him wash the foul liquid off his car. When we were finished, I asked how much his work was going to cost me.

"Three dollars will cover it," he said.

"Is that all?" I said, astonished.

"You're one of Andy's boys, aren't you?"

"Yeah."

"Well, three dollars is enough."

The doctor packed up his gear and in a few moments his car raced out the driveway. His visit reminded me of a covey of quail flushing: there was a lot of fast action and a minute after he was gone, I wondered if he had ever really been there. One thing was sure—time spent around him would not be dull.

In twenty-four hours Bobby's sow began eating, and in two days she was giving milk again. All her offspring survived. My pig healed quickly, and when I sold him, the scar from the incision was hardly visible. The pink medicine was to become legendary among livestock producers in the area.

21. Flaming Rats

I TRIED TO ACT CASUAL AS I BROUGHT THE BATEAU INTO the harbor, but my pride must have been showing. At thirty-one feet long, it was a big step up from the outboard skiff. I was returning from my first day of crab scraping alone. I had finally passed my father's swimming test and he had given me permission to use the boat. My catch was not large that day, but I felt grown up as I approached the crab wharf. Bruce had just finished selling his crabs and was pulling away from the dock. He looked at me with a smile and shook his head because I had not taken his advice to avoid working on the water.

I eased the boat up to the wharf and the gunnel barely kissed the pilings. "Not bad for a know-nothing kid," Johnny Dize said. "But you'd better not be bringing me any trash crabs." Johnny was the man who didn't help me when Phil Ford was about to kill me for borrowing his skiff. He was still the crab grader and his word was law.

"My number one and number two Jimmies are in separate baskets and they're measured perfectly," I said. "My peelers are all good and there's not a snot among them. I didn't catch many soft crabs but they're all soft—no papershells."

"We'll see about that," Johnny said, as I sat my baskets on the wharf. He quickly looked at my soft crabs and they met his approval. Next he picked through my baskets of Jimmies, measuring the smallest. All of the number ones were at least six inches across their shell. All the number twos measured five or more inches. "They're okay," he said, sounding disappointed.

Johnny opened my peeler basket and began sorting. Peelers were graded by the color of a line on the inside margin of their back fin. The rank crabs, those closest to shedding, had a dark red line. The green peelers, which may not shed for two weeks, had a white line. In the middle were pink sign crabs. Johnny's boss recognized two grades—rank and green—and he paid more for the former. Johnny could make extra money for his boss by grading more pink sign crabs as green. After he had tossed a crab into a float with a hundred others, there was no way to get it back and protest.

I stood behind Johnny as he worked, trying to put pressure on him to grade more crabs as rank. Once, I groaned as he called a peeler green. He looked at the next one and said, "snot," and threw it back in the creek, meaning I would get nothing for it. After that lesson I remained quiet.

There was always minor tension between watermen and seafood buyers, but generally the people were fair and the system worked. I liked everyone involved in the business, even Johnny.

I crab scraped many days that summer and sometimes the catch was good, but often it was not. When crabs were scarce, Milbert and Harry found new jobs for me on their farms. They hired me to drive a tractor to help them cultivate corn and soybeans. I liked being on a tractor anytime, especially if I could go fast, but cultivating small soybean plants was boring. It required a speed of one or two miles per hour, and it was necessary to stare constantly at the row to keep from damaging the crop. After eight hours of it, all I saw were little soybean leaves when I closed my eyes at night.

Part of my work with the Shockleys' tractors involved cultivating my own corn. My father's job had given him the confidence to buy ten acres across from Louie Reid's farm, where he planned to build a third poultry house. The land was known as the Ross place and Charlie Ross's abandoned house was still standing. I wasn't thrilled about the prospect of feeding more chickens, but I could use most of the property for growing corn, so I didn't complain.

Corn was the single biggest expense in producing pigs. My sows were weaning large litters and the income was more than I had expected, but I hated to write the checks for the yellow grain. In the spring, Milbert and Harry had volunteered to plant corn for me at no charge. All I had to provide was gas, seed, and fertilizer. It was a generous offer and I felt lucky to have relatives like them. After my crop broke through the ground, I watched with pleasure as the little green plants grew. When they were six inches high, I carefully drove the cultivator through them for the first time. It wasn't as exciting as crabbing but there was a good feeling in tilling the land.

* * *

Late in the summer, my father decided to reshingle the roof on our house. Damage repair from Hurricane Hazel and a series of other storms had left it with multiple patches, none of them quite matching the original color. Dad hired Willis Henry, our closest neighbor, to help with the work. He lived directly across the road from us in a bungalow similar to ours.

Willis was a short man about my parents' age, and he had a reputation in the community for being difficult to work with. His wife had left him and he spent his spare time building furniture in his garage. Often people were enticed into his house to view his latest creation. I was once trapped there for an hour, listening to endless details about sanding, staining and finishing. After that experience, I generally avoided him.

We started the roof work early on a steamy August morning. By 8:00 AM, a lone cicada was already tuning up in our beech tree, a warning of the heat to come. After the scaffold was set up, Dad and Willis began nailing the asphalt shingles to the roof and I was given the job of keeping them supplied. I carried the heavy bundles of shingles up a ladder and deposited them on the scaffold.

At first they worked slowly and I had no trouble meeting their needs, but as they moved up the roof their progress sped up. After two hours I was struggling to deliver enough shingles. The heat and heavy lifting were tiring me out, and on one trip up the ladder my legs trembled a little. Willis took notice.

"Boy, aren't you strong enough to carry a few shingles?" he said.

"Don't worry about me," I said, dropping a bundle at his feet.

"Damn, I don't think he's tough enough for the job, Tom."

The smirk on his face annoyed me and I wanted to wipe it off for him. Maybe he thought he was being funny but it wasn't a joke to me.

"He's pretty strong for his age," Dad said. "I think he can handle it."

I appreciated my father's vote of confidence but I was not sure it was warranted. After he said it, I tried to push myself harder, but there was not much more to give. By then, they were working on hanging scaffolding, which was just a narrow board nailed to the roof. When they moved up to the second one and I had to carry the bundles higher, I began to fall behind.

"Boy, we need shingles," Willis said. "If you can't do the job we'll get someone else."

"You take care of your work and I'll do mine," I replied. The heat was rising in me and it was not all from the sun. My father said nothing, but I could tell he was watching me closely. For a while I channeled my anger into lifting shingles and it helped.

As the men moved farther up the steep roof, I had another problem—it was a long way to the ground and I was uncomfortable walking on the narrow scaffolding. I moved cautiously and Willis could not let it pass.

"If you're scared at this height, what would you do on a really tall roof? You'd probably wet your pants." I was hot, tired and a little afraid and he had pushed me to my limit.

"You have a big mouth," I said.

Willis was surprised but he quickly recovered. "I'm man enough to back it up." He drew himself up as though he was ready to prove it.

I had a strong desire to tackle him and throw him off the roof, but I knew if we struggled, I might be the one to go. My father was silent but there was a half smile on his lips. Unsure of what to do, I swallowed my pride and went back to work.

When lunchtime came, Willis went to his house to eat, and Dad and I headed for our kitchen. On the way he had some advice.

"Terry, you'll have to learn to handle men like Willis. He does have a big mouth. As I see it, there are three ways to deal with him. You can totally ignore him, you can laugh at him, or you can whip his ass. When he was growing up, most of the boys whipped him at least once. I straightened him out years ago."

As we ate lunch, I thought about my father's comments. For the time being, I had to choose the first option, but at fourteen it was hard to ignore someone who made fun of my strength and bravery. In a few years, I planned to choose his third method of dealing with Willis. I didn't know that an opportunity to pay him back would come along sooner.

* * *

Like all summers, the one of 1960 ended too soon. Suddenly, the start of school was only a week away and I still had to buy clothes. That year I had enough money to pay for them myself, which gave me more say in what I would be wearing.

A few days before classes began, Mom drove me to Salisbury to shop in the department stores, and under her watchful eye I picked out a basic back-to-school wardrobe. The clothes we bought were okay, but nothing was really cool.

On the way home, my mother stopped in Princess Anne to buy groceries. With some money left, I walked down the street to the men's clothing store. Jim Tilghman, the proprietor, was a likable fast-talker who could convince shoppers they looked good in anything in his store. Jim often had a better selection of clothes for teenagers than the shops in Salisbury. He seemed connected with what the kids were wearing in the cities.

On that afternoon the store was busy, and I browsed while Jim waited on customers. Eventually, he came my way with his usual big smile. "You look like a man on a mission. What do you need today?"

"Some pants for school."

He led me to a table where he had just laid out a new shipment. After searching through the pile, he selected a pair of pants like I had never seen before. They were brown with a wild pattern and the legs were extremely narrow with no cuffs.

"This is what they're wearing in Philadelphia, you should try them on," he said, exuding confidence.

I had doubts, but at Jim's urging I carried them to the fitting room. The pants legs were so tight that I could barely pull them on; I had to wiggle my feet to get them through. When I walked out to the mirror, Jim was waiting for me.

"Man, they look good on you! I think that's the coolest pair of pants I've ever seen," he said.

I turned toward the mirror and immediately realized that he was right. "I'll take them."

"You made a good choice," he said reassuringly.

In the next ten minutes, I picked out a bright, lime-green shirt and a half-inch wide belt to go with the pants. I may not have had much shopping experience, but I knew the outfit was coming together. The only thing missing were new shoes.

"You're almost fifteen and you have a need to be seen," Jim said, as he handed me the bag of clothes. I thanked him and left the store.

On the way back to the car, I looked in the window of the A&P and Mom was still shopping. I decided to run a block to the new shoe store. I was not sure what kind of shoes I wanted but they had to make a statement. A pair of cream-colored loafers in the store window caught my attention; they were completely smooth in the front except for a strap with a buckle. The manager said that was the only pair he had in that style and, luckily, they were my size. He seemed particularly pleased when he placed them in the bag.

During the drive home, I did not mention my purchases to Mom. At the house I tucked them away in the bottom drawer of my dresser. They were no ordinary school clothes and I was saving them for a special occasion.

I chose the first Friday night dance of the school year to wear them. I was in the tenth grade and all the girls in my class would be there. With my sharp, new clothes, it promised to be a good night. There was only one problem—my father was supposed to work that evening, but he had taken some time off and was at home. I was afraid he might not appreciate my new pants.

After feeding the chickens and pigs, I showered and then dressed quietly in my room, until I heard my father leave the house for his evening inspection of the chickens. I gave him time to reach the first building before I slipped out the door. I was surprised to see him coming back across the yard toward the house; a water trough had broken and he was returning to get a tool to fix it. I tried to ignore him and began walking out the driveway.

"What are you wearing?" he said, with a tone of amazement.

"Some new clothes I bought."

"Oh good, I was afraid you had stolen them from a clown."

"I bought them at Jim Tilghman's store," I said defensively.

"He sold you something like that? I'll get your money back tomorrow."

"I like these clothes," I said, raising my voice.

"Well you're not leaving here with them on," he said, in a louder voice.

The screen door opened and my mother appeared on the back steps. "Thomas, the kids are wearing a lot of different things these days. I think you ought to let him go," she said.

"What if someone we know sees him? We'll be the laughing stock of the community."

"It will be all right," she said calmly. "Don't you remember some of the things you wore when we were dating?"

"Nothing like that," he said, pointing at me. Then he paused, thinking over what she had said and he seemed to soften a little. "I still don't think he should go dressed like that."

"It will be fine," Mom assured him. I could see that she had saved me, and I headed up the road at a fast walk, not looking back. I was on my way to meet Billy; he had recently gotten his license and was driving me to town.

When I arrived at the school, Mitch and Jack Northam were standing on the steps. Jack, one of my other friends, was a tall, good-looking boy who was working hard at being smooth with girls and he was way ahead of the rest of us.

"Jesus, Noble, with that green shirt and those skinny leg pants, you look like a lime Popsicle," Jack said.

"These are the classiest pants you've ever seen," I said, trying to keep my confidence up.

"They are pretty neat," he admitted.

"Where did you get those fairy shoes?" Mitch asked.

"You just wish you had a pair."

"Not a chance, I wouldn't be caught dead in those things."

That ended their smart remarks and I thought I had gotten off easy. We stood outside for a while discussing which girls had already shown up for the dance. A group of Deal Island boys was hanging out on the other side of the steps. They kept glaring at us like they were looking for a fight. I wasn't surprised; it often seemed as if the entire island was populated by the sons of *Popeye*. Deal Island boys had a strict Methodist upbringing and when they became teenagers, many of them rebelled. They usually came to Princess Anne looking for beer, girls and a fight. Dad said when they got older they usually found religion again and some became preachers.

The group must have decided they were more interested in dancing than fighting, because they walked up the steps and through the big white doors. Just before going in, they turned and gave us another mean look. We scowled back at them.

"Damn honkers," Mitch said, as they went in. Deal Islanders were often called honkers because of their brogue. When a number of them were tonging on an oyster bar and yelling between boats, some people thought they sounded like geese.

We were still discussing what to do about the Island boys when a car drove up. Page got out of the passenger side and came up the steps. We all said hello and she looked me up and down with a smile; I wasn't sure what it meant. When she went in the school we followed, just to watch her walk.

The lights in the auditorium were dim as we circled the room checking out the girls. Each grade had an unofficial area where the students hung out. We moved quickly past the seniors; we had no chance with those girls and if we dallied in their area the boys would yell out embarrassing put-downs.

My evening improved when the three of us reached the tenth grade area, and sat down with our classmates. Several of the girls complimented my pants and shoes. No one seemed to like my shirt—maybe it was the light. I was on the floor for every slow dance that night, taking a turn with most of the girls in my class who interested me. When the DJ played "Twilight Time" by the Platters, I held Page tight and she put her head on my shoulder. Later in the evening, during a ladies choice, a junior class girl asked me to dance. "Nice shoes," she said as we started toward the floor. I knew that Mitch liked her and the fact that he was watching made it especially sweet.

When the dance was over, I walked uptown for a soda with a group of my classmates. On the way, Mitch said, "I think I'll get a pair of those shoes."

* * *

With the start of school, students in my class were faced with choosing a curriculum to follow for the next three years. Most of the teachers believed I should be in the college prep program, but I preferred agriculture. I had never given higher education much thought; no one in my family had ever been to college. It seemed likely that I would be a waterman or a farmer, but I loved science.

As often happened, Mr. Anderson solved my problem. He convinced the school administrators to let me take the college prep program and substitute agriculture class for typing and French. Skipping French seemed like no great loss; the teacher, Mrs. Richards, was not one of my favorites. She was a large, pretentious woman who wore tons of makeup and a beret. The thought of sitting in her class listening to hours of language tapes did not appeal to me.

Agriculture, however, did appeal to me. My ninth grade year in Mr. Anderson's class had been one of the best experiences of my life. Each day I looked forward to walking out to the ag-shop. It was a brick building, separate from the main school. Mr. Anderson talked about crops and livestock, but he also held long discussions on markets, politics, current events, sports and history. Each week we studied the *Drovers Journal*, which reported on grain and livestock markets. Each day we read the *Baltimore Sun* and learned how government was affecting our lives. Using its business section, Mr. Anderson taught us about stocks, and the bulls and bears. On Monday mornings during football season, we reviewed the performance of the Baltimore Colts. No matter what the topic, he drew a lesson from it that would help us make decisions in later life.

I became a member of the FFA, the most active club in the school, and purchased one of their blue corduroy jackets with the gold emblem on the back. None of the other clubs had anything like it and girls were always asking if they could wear it. Each year the FFA put on the Livestock Show, the Sweetheart Dance, and the Father and Son Banquet. For each event Mr. Anderson chose a boy to be Master of Ceremonies and coached him in public speaking. It was something I wanted to try.

In addition to local events, Mr. Anderson took his students to regional, state and national FFA meetings. There were trips to livestock shows in Baltimore and Harrisburg, Pennsylvania. He accompanied us to every event, often to the detriment of his farming operation. He always had time for "his boys." He was there to instruct us, and to prod us to do more than we thought we could. When it came time for me to select a curriculum, agriculture had to be part of it.

* * *

In late September, Harry was ready to begin harvesting my corn and I needed a substantial corn crib. Mr. Anderson came up with a design for an inexpensive, pole and wire structure with a metal roof and concrete floor. It was larger than anything I had ever built, so my father helped me with the construction. In spite of several arguments, we completed it in just over a week.

Harry started filling it right away and it was soon packed to the roof with golden ears. It was a satisfying feeling not having to buy any more corn, but my enjoyment was short-lived. With the first cold snap, rats left the fields and migrated to the crib. They dug burrows under the floor, and when they were hungry, they went upstairs for all they could eat. I trapped some of them but the survivors soon grew wise, and with Cindy around, I was afraid to put out poison. My corn was being devoured and there seemed to be nothing I could do about it.

One sunny fall afternoon, as I was getting feed for the pigs, Bobby drove up in his blue and white '57 Ford. He was then nineteen, handsome and a hit with the girls. I rarely saw him anymore except when we were doing farm work. He wanted to know how many pigs I had for sale; our buyer was coming the next week and Bobby was making the arrangements. As we talked, he noticed the rat burrows.

"Man, you're raising more rats than pigs," he said.

"I know—I've been trapping but there seems to be more of them every day."

"You'd better do something or you'll lose half your corn."

His prediction startled me; I had no idea they could eat that much. I brought up an idea that I had been considering. "What about gasoline? I'm thinking about pouring some in their holes and lighting it."

My cousin's eyes widened and a smile came to his face. Everyone hated rats and a chance to eliminate some was always gratifying. "That'll work," he said. "Why don't we do it now? Do you have any gas?"

"Are you sure it will be okay?" My cousin was older and I respected his judgment.

"Absolutely. It's got a concrete floor and it can't catch fire. What could go wrong?"

Satisfied with the logic of his argument, I went to my father's shed and came back with a can of gasoline and matches. I walked around the corncrib pouring a little of the fuel into each of a dozen burrows.

"That's not enough," Bobby said. "Give 'em plenty of it."

I retraced my steps, and poured more into each hole, until he was satisfied there was enough gasoline under the floor to do the job. I stepped back and tossed a lighted match to the nearest burrow. For two seconds nothing happened—then there was a loud WHUMMP sound. The ground shook and fire shot out three feet from all the burrows. Bobby and I staggered backward. The pile of corn seemed to rise into the air; several ears fell out of the open door at the top of the crib. At the sound of the explosion, thirteen thousand chickens stopped clucking. The force of the blast was stunning but we quickly recovered.

"See, I told you it would be alright," Bobby said.

At that instant two flaming rats, looking like demons from hell, raced out from under the concrete. We watched in disbelief as they ran into the tall dry grass beside number two chicken house, leaving trails of flame behind them. We sprinted after them, urged on by visions of facing my father standing next to smoldering ruins.

Before we caught up with the rats, the gas on their fur burned out and they disappeared into the grass. They left behind a growing fire, nearly a third the length of the chicken house. Flames were already licking at the plywood siding. Bobby and I stomped the grass and beat the fire with our shirts until we were exhausted. Mercifully, we put it out before the building ignited.

"Great idea you had," he said, as we tried to catch our breath. I was too tired to debate whose fault it was.

I didn't tell my father about the fire, knowing the more time that lapsed between a screwup and its discovery, the less grief that came my way. He spotted the burned grass a week later and came over to the pigpens to ask me about it. I explained how it happened, expecting a long lecture, but he just looked at me with an expression that said, "What kind of idiot am I raising?"

Actually, the fire was a great rat control method; there was not another one in the corn that year. There was one problem—when the crib was finally empty, I discovered that the concrete floor was cracked like a jigsaw puzzle. It was still usable, and in my diary of experiences I put that one down as educational.

22. My Biggest Decision

MR. ANDERSON HAD JUST FINISHED HIS LECTURE ON SOIL testing and I was at the rear of a line of students leaving the agriculture shop.

"Mr. Noble, may I see you for a minute?" he said. I walked toward his desk and he was wearing a little smile, as though he was hiding a secret. "How would you like to be in the newspaper?"

"What do you mean?"

"I think the *Salisbury Times* farm editor would do a story on you." It sounded intriguing but I thought he must be mistaken.

"Why would he write about me?"

"Because your swine operation is performing so well," he said. "Don't you realize that you are selling far more pigs per litter than the national average and that your profit per sow is very high?"

My bank account was growing nicely but I was unaware of the national averages.

"What would I have to do for the newspaper?" I asked.

"The editor will come to the school and interview you, and then we'll pay a visit to your operation." He must have noticed my concern about being interviewed. "Don't worry, I'll help you," he said reassuringly.

The day before I was to meet with the newspaperman, our agriculture class reviewed my farming records. Mr. Anderson compared my results to the industry averages and the results were better than I expected. I was weaning an average of 10.25 pigs per litter, three more than the typical farmer. My teacher said that even though my operation was small, the numbers were still impressive. After we calculated the value of my animals, buildings and corn, I felt rich.

On the morning of the interview, I met with Mr. Anderson in the ag-shop.

"Are you ready for this, Mr. Noble?"

"Sure, if all I have to do is answer his questions."

"Maybe I had better give you some new words to use. They will impress the editor and portray you in a good light."

"Okay," I said, not sure why I needed new words. I knew more about my operation than anyone else did and I thought that was all that mattered.

"Sometime during the interview, you need to use *prolific* when describing your sows. It means they produce a large number of pigs." He wrote it on the blackboard and I committed it to memory.

"And tell him about how you give the sows extra feed after weaning. That *stimulates ovulation*, which means release of eggs from the ovaries. You know about ovaries from our anatomy discussions, right?"

"Yes, sir."

"One more thing," he said, pulling a paper from his pocket. "This is a summary of all the calculations we did yesterday. Give it to him at the end of the interview or he'll never get the numbers right."

As we sat and waited for the newspaperman, I was surprised that my teacher was asking me to use bigger words to impress him. The concept was new to me; none of the men I had grown up with would ever try to impress anyone. Their philosophy was, 'If you don't like me the way I am, the hell with you.' In our community if you tried to present yourself as better than you actually were, you were considered phony. Bragging in any way was ridiculed. If someone was paid a compliment, he had to immediately make a negative comment about himself or be considered indirectly boasting.

The same held true for property. If I told a waterman, "You have a nice looking boat," he would respond with something like "Yeah, she's okay, but she throws a lot of water on you even in a small sea, and there's rotten wood up near her bow." I came from that background and I was being asked to show off. I was not sure if I could do it.

The newspaperman picked us up at the school, and then drove uptown for a cup of coffee. He was tall, with dark-rimmed glasses and a bookish appearance. He parked on Main Street and we did the interview in his car. I sat on the front seat and Mr. Anderson sat in the back. After ten minutes of questioning, the editor seemed unimpressed and a little bored. I decided that I had better take Mr. Anderson's advice.

"What is the main reason your pig operation is so profitable?" the editor asked.

"It's because my sows are so prolific."

He paused and looked straight into my eyes. I felt panicked; maybe he knew it was not my word and he was going to challenge me.

"That's good, very good," he said. He began to scribble on his note pad and I glanced at Mr. Anderson. He appeared to be battling to suppress a smile. Our eyes met for a second and then he turned and looked out the window.

"Is there anything special you do to get bigger litters?" the editor asked.

"I feed my sows all they will eat between weaning and the next breeding. That stimulates ovulation."

"Excellent, excellent," he said. There was more vigorous note taking. In the back seat, Mr. Anderson shifted position and lightly cleared his throat. I was starting to enjoy myself. I dropped a few more words like estrus and gestation and they were well received.

The interview seemed to end too soon. After it was over, we drove out to look at my operation. The newspaperman seemed to like what he saw and he took pictures of me holding two fat pigs. He promised the article would be in the next edition.

When the paper came out, my picture and the story covered the entire front page of the farm section. The picture he selected wasn't very good—my eyes were almost closed. I noticed "prolific" and "stimulate ovulation" were featured prominently in the article. My mother and aunt Hilda bought extra copies and they said it was flattering. After my father read it, he looked up from his chair and said, "Don't get too full of yourself, it's only the farm section."

It was only a small article in a small paper, but it taught me valuable lessons about preparing for meetings and being sure of what I wanted to say. It was also my first indication that style sometimes triumphs over substance, and it left me feeling a little disgusted.

* * *

A few weeks later, during English literature class, I received a note from the principal's office. It said "See Mr. Anderson immediately." Mr. Leckey, our English teacher was discussing *David Copperfield* in way too much detail. I was happy to leave class but I worried about the urgency of the note.

Mr. Anderson was lecturing to his eighth grade agriculture class, and after I knocked on the door he came out into the hall.

"I got a call from Leroy Johnson," he said. "He has to do a cesarean section on a gilt at Jack King's farm this afternoon. No one is available to help him and he asked if you could go along as his assistant."

The request surprised me. To that point, I had only helped Dr. Johnson with minor procedures on my own pigs and I was honored that he had asked for me.

"How do I get out of school?" I asked.

"I'll write you an excuse—it's a special field trip." He looked at his watch. "Leroy will pick you up at the ag-shop in twenty minutes."

I went to the shop and waited. It was an hour before the Volkswagen slid to a stop beside the building.

"Hurry up. We're late. Let's go," the doctor said. He spoke as though it was my fault that he was behind schedule. He was wearing his usual wide grin and aviator glasses.

"Dr. Johnson, you need to get a watch," I said.

"Watches make me nervous. And call me Leroy, everyone else does."

I stood by the car while he arranged the medicine boxes into what he thought was an acceptable seat. As soon as I was in the car, he spun out the gravel driveway and I held on like a dog on ice.

Jack King's pig operation was on a farm just over a mile past my house. He was a tenant farmer on what used to be an old tobacco plantation. The eighteenth century manor house was still standing on the shore of the Manokin River. The pig barns were located some distance away, so the smell would not reach the "big" house.

Once inside the farrowing barn, we quickly located the gilt in her stall. She was of the Hampshire breed, all black except for a white belt around her shoulders. The female looked exhausted from her long, unproductive labor, and she was lying quietly on her side, breathing deeply. One back foot was drawn up toward her abdomen to ease her pain.

Leroy washed his arm with disinfectant soap and lay down behind the gilt, slipping his hand inside her. When he was halfway up his forearm, he stopped.

"Jack is right, she'll never get a pig through that little pelvic opening." He removed his arm from the animal and stood up. "Follow me," he said, leading the way to his car. Once there, he loaded my arms with supplies for the upcoming surgery. I looked closely at everything, trying to figure out how it would be used.

Back inside the building, he took the supplies and handed me a wire snare used for restraining large pigs.

"Slip this over her nose, and hold her head still while I inject the anesthetic." He was already filling his syringe.

When I caught the gilt by her snout she stood up, but there was little fight in her. She remained calm as he slipped the needle into her ear vein and began to inject. In a few seconds she collapsed to the floor. I had never seen an animal put under anesthesia before and I was amazed at how fast the drug acted.

"I gave her a light dose of barbiturate," he said. "If I put her too deep, the pigs will come out totally anesthetized and won't survive. If she starts to wake up before I'm finished, you may have to hold her down." At first I thought he was joking but his expression told me differently. I realized why he invited me to come along. "Someday we'll have better anesthesia, but for now this is the best we can do."

I sat down beside the gilt's head and Leroy scrubbed and shaved her flank. There was no joking now—he was all business. His hands moved quickly, like a man with little time to spare. After disinfecting her skin with iodine, he injected a line of local anesthetic where the incision would be. While it was taking effect, he organized his instruments and supplies for the surgery.

In a short time, he picked up a scalpel and made a foot long incision with one easy stroke. At first I was shocked by the size of the wound, but the feeling quickly turned to fascination. I watched closely as he separated the muscle layers and gently entered the abdomen. His hands searched through the abdominal contents and came up with a pink tube about four inches in diameter.

"That's one horn of the uterus," he said. In a moment, he found a lump in the tube and made a small cut over it. A baby pig's head appeared in the opening. He extracted the newborn and laid it on its mother's chest.

"Boy, you're loafing," he said, handing me a towel. "Rub him down, he's barely alive."

I picked up the pig and began a vigorous massage. It was semi-conscious and its breathing was shallow. In a few seconds, the doctor produced another pig and my work doubled.

While I took care of those newborns, he searched down each uterine horn looking for more. Eventually he removed eight pigs. Two of them were dead but the other six were struggling to live. The anesthesia had its effect; none of the babies could stand, and when I placed them under the heat lamp, they only wiggled around and emitted faint squeals.

I stared at Dr. Johnson's hands as he began to close the incision. With deft motions, he sutured the innermost lining of the abdomen. Then he moved on to the muscle, using larger sutures. By the time he got to the skin, the gilt was beginning to move her legs. I lay across her shoulders in case she tried to get up.

"You can relax, we're home free," he said. "I can zipper her up fast from this point." In a little over a minute, what had been a gaping wound was put neatly back together. With the operation over he turned his attention to the newborn pigs.

"They'll be over the anesthesia in an hour or so. Jack will be home by then and he'll make sure they get a teat." He rose stiffly to his feet. The entire surgery had been performed kneeling on a concrete floor. He looked down at the gilt which was beginning to tremble.

"Is she cold?" I asked.

"No, they do that when they're coming out of anesthesia."

We picked up the equipment and carried it back to the car.

"What did you think of the operation?" he said.

"It was the neatest thing I've ever seen."

He laughed heartily. "It wasn't that good. Barn floor surgery is not my best work."

On the drive back to my house, I peppered him with questions about what I had witnessed. For once, he gave me serious answers. As he pulled into the driveway I asked, "How long did you go to college to become a vet?"

"Eight years."

I was stunned—eight years seemed like an eternity. My respect for him was growing. It was getting dark and through the kitchen window I could see Mom preparing supper. I thought he might like to eat with us.

"Are you finished with work for the day?"

"Finished with work? Do you think this is a government job? I still have to hold evening office hours for dogs and cats."

I wondered how he could do it all; I was tired from just watching the surgery. When I started to get out of the car he stopped me.

"How much do I owe you for your assistance?" he said.

"How much is in your wallet?"

"Two dollars."

"My bill is a hundred dollars but you can owe me."

He laughed again and then in a serious tone he said, "I really appreciate your help."

I climbed out of the car and the gravel flew as he rushed out our driveway.

During the next few days I thought often about the cesarean. I saw Jack at the Corner Store and he told me the gilt and her pigs were doing fine.

On Sunday I went with Mom on her weekly visit to my grandparents. It had been several months since I had seen them. When we arrived, Grandpa was out in the yard, enjoying the beautiful spring day. He greeted me in his usual jovial manner.

"Hi, T, you haven't been around much. Girls keeping you busy?"

"A little," I said, blushing.

"I thought so. Come on, let's sit out here in the swing until dinner is ready." He led the way to the old maple tree. "Ruth got home late from church. Must have been some serious preaching today. I reckon her soul feels better."

For a while we sat quietly, enjoying the breeze. Then he launched into one of his favorite topics: how the rabbits were raiding his garden and eating his cabbage plants. I volunteered to shoot them but it was obvious he did not want them hurt. When I suggested catching them in live traps and moving them somewhere else, he liked the idea. Immediately, he knew whose yard he wanted them released in.

When the rabbit discussion was finished, I asked him something that had been on my mind. "I've been wondering what I should do after high school. What do you think about being a waterman?"

"Well, it's alright for Ruth and me, because the boat and house are paid for. We don't spend much, so we can get by when the Bay doesn't give much." He turned and looked at me straight on. "But if I was a young man, I don't believe I'd follow the water. There are too many slack times."

His answer confused me; I thought he would try to convince me to follow in his footsteps. Instead, he agreed with Bruce.

"Oh, I could have made better money on the water," he went on. "My brother, Edwin, wanted me to go in with him up on the Delaware Bay, leasing oyster ground and buying large boats to work it. I was too afraid to borrow the money." He looked off toward the garden and seemed to be thinking about what might have been. "You've seen how well Edwin has done. He always comes here with a new Chrysler and fine clothes. He wasn't afraid to go into debt."

I had never seen my grandfather so serious and I didn't know what to say.

"T, your life is ahead of you. If you ever see an opportunity to make money, don't be afraid to borrow some to get started."

It was obvious he thought it was important advice, and I decided never to forget it. In a few moments he returned to his lighthearted self.

"Aaah, it would be a waste for me to have money. I'd still want to go out on my boat every day, and Ruth would give most of it to the church, anyway. He let out his booming laugh and slapped me on the knee. "Let's go inside and see if dinner is ready. There ought to be a chicken wing we can split between us."

As I followed him to the house, I noticed how strong his shoulders looked. Edwin always appeared soft and frail compared to him. My grandfather never seemed to have a worry but his brother often complained about his business. I was unsure who had the best of things.

For the next week, my mind kept going back to the pig surgery and the conversation with my grandfather. The question of what to do after graduation seemed pressing for the first time. My thoughts came together one evening while my family was watching Jack Benny on television. "I'm going to college to become a veterinarian," I announced during a commercial.

For a few moments no one spoke. My father looked at me with curiosity.

"What made you decide that?" he asked.

"Seeing Leroy do the cesarean."

"Can you tolerate going to school for that many years?" Mom asked.

"You always said you thought you could do anything that anyone else could do," I answered. "I believe if other people can go to college for eight years, I can too."

My father shifted position in his chair and he seemed to be bothered about something. After a minute he spoke. "You've done a good job with the pigs, and you'd probably be a good veterinarian," he said, solemnly. "But we don't have the money to pay for college. You'll have to do it on your own."

The idea of college was so new, I had given no thought to its cost. But my father had no reason to be concerned; I would never have considered asking my parents to pay for it. Like most boys in the community, I had gotten the message that I should be on my own after eighteen and no longer a burden to my family.

"Don't worry—I'll get the money," I said, without a clue where to start.

The next day I sat in church thinking about how to raise the funds for college. I didn't think God would care that my mind was on financial matters; the preacher was always looking for money and urging the congregation to give more. After finding out that part of the offering went to pay his salary, I was seeing things in a different light.

On Monday morning before classes started I went to see Mr. Anderson. He was in the ag-shop, sitting at his desk reading the *Drovers Journal.* When I told him my decision about college, he broke into a broad smile.

"Mr. Noble, I believe you'll make something out of yourself yet."

"Maybe, if I can find the money to pay for it. I'm thinking about expanding my pig operation."

He nodded in approval. "You're on the right track. How many sows can you handle?"

"Probably twelve. How much college will that pay for?"

He thought for a moment and then went to the blackboard.

"It's over two years before you go off to school. Let's look at the numbers."

He laid out the cost for a year at the University of Maryland. The pre-vet program was there and it was the most logical route for getting into vet school. We calculated how many pigs I could sell from twelve sows and what the profit would be.

"If hog prices stay up, you might have enough to pay for three or four years of college," he said. "But you know that hog prices cycle, with a low occurring about every four years. You could get caught on the down side."

I knew about the low end of the price cycle, when farmers overproduced and lost money, but I was optimistic.

"I still think pigs are my best hope."

"I agree. Over the years, they've made a lot of money for farmers. In the Midwest they're still called mortgage lifters. I once made enough from thirty market hogs to buy a new pickup truck."

We ended the discussion by deciding that I should keep female pigs from my current litters to increase the sow herd. It would be nearly a year before their pigs would be old enough to sell, so I had no time to waste.

With the expansion of my herd, I needed more corn and a way to grow it. One day a used tractor and most of the implements required to produce corn were advertised in the local paper. On the following Saturday, I went to look at it and the Shockleys came along to advise me. When we arrived at the farm, I was disappointed by the look of the equipment. The tractor was a 1940s Oliver brand that started with a hand crank. The other items were nearly as old but they were well-maintained. The price for all of it was almost exactly the amount in my bank account. Milbert and Harry thought it was a good buy, and even though I liked things modern, I took a deep breath and wrote the check.

After I purchased the equipment, I began to look for more land to raise my crop. A few years earlier, two middle-aged women moved from the city to a property in Champ and they bought some of the highest land in that low-lying village. These ladies did not attend church and they met with disapproval from a few people in the community. Their bright lipstick and flashy clothes raised suspicion about what they may have been in their earlier life. They drove a long, blue Lincoln and one of them smoked little cigars. Sometimes they stopped at the Corner Store to talk to the men. To some, it was all evidence that they were dangerous but they were always nice to me. One day at the Champ store the redhead sat down beside me on the porch bench. "I hear you're looking for land. We'll let you farm ours rent free, just to keep it from growing up in pine trees." It was a generous offer and I accepted immediately.

Within a week I was plowing their property, and each time I worked there they invited me in for iced tea. Their house was nearly engulfed by vegetation, and it was like walking into a cave—privet hedge and locust trees had taken over most of the yard, and multiflora roses covered one end of the structure. Someone had cut a hole in the greenery to allow light to the kitchen window. We sat at their table and had long conversations, mostly about my life. They seemed glad to have some company and I could tell they were pleased to be helping me raise money for college. They may have been questionable characters to some people, but I thought they were great.

23. Revenge is Sweet

THE SOUND OF DISTANT MUSIC FORCED ITS WAY INTO MY sleeping brain. As I became more awake, I recognized Frank Sinatra's voice singing "Come Fly with Me." My parents were talking in their bedroom at the other end of the hall.

"Oh no, it's Willis's clock radio again," my mother said, in a sleepy voice.

"It's 4:00 AM and it's turned up full blast," Dad said. "How can he sleep through that?"

"I told him yesterday that it was too loud and that he was waking up the whole neighborhood," Mom said.

We were in a July heat wave. It was a muggy night and the windows in every house were wide open. It was the third morning Willis had awakened us with his radio. He was working at a construction site near Ocean City and he had to get up early to make the long drive. To beat the heat, he was sleeping on the floor of his entrance hallway, catching the breeze that came through his front screen door. Only the screen wire and a hundred feet separated the radio from my parents' bedroom window.

On the previous two mornings it was thirty minutes before Willis turned down the music. My father had gotten home from the factory at midnight and he was not going to tolerate it again.

"Turn the damn thing off," he yelled from the bedroom window.

187

"It's no use, he can't hear you above the music," Mom said.

"If he didn't drink so much at night, he wouldn't have so much trouble waking up," Dad said.

From my darkened bedroom, I made a halfhearted suggestion. "Maybe we should throw one of my big firecrackers in his front yard." To my surprise, Dad seemed to like the idea.

"Have you got any handy?"

"Yeah, in my bureau drawer."

The firecracker I had in mind was the type game wardens gave to farmers to scare deer out of their fields. They were powerful little bombs, stronger than anything we could buy at the fireworks stand. The Bates farm was overrun with deer and Mr. Bates got the firecrackers by the boxful. Over the years Johnny, Billy and I appropriated at least half of them for other uses. We blew up everything in the neighborhood that was considered disposable. When we discovered they would explode under water, it was a short time before we bundled three together and dropped them into Crab Island Hole. The blast brought perch and small rockfish to the surface and we caught them in landing nets. It was fun for a day but we decided that maybe it was not sporting.

The music continued to fill the house and my father had had enough.

"Get your firecracker and let's wake him up." He got out of bed and started toward my room. Remembering how Willis had treated me on the roofing job, I picked up two crackers. As we walked through our darkened house, I twisted the fuses together.

Outside, a retreating moon gave plenty of light for our mission. We crossed the yard wearing nothing but our underwear, and the dew on the grass felt cool to my bare feet. In the moonlight, my father's legs looked as white as a buckram's belly. I was working hard at getting a tan and I thought he needed some time in the sun.

We stopped in the middle of the road and the asphalt was still warm from the previous day's sun. I held the firecrackers and my father struck a match. When it flared I could see that he was grinning. The radio was still blaring when the fuse began to spark.

"Throw them in his yard up close to the house," Dad said.

I don't know if it was the dim light or a twinge of revenge in my arm, but the firecrackers landed on top of Willis's front steps. All that separated them from his head was a few feet and the metal panel on the bottom of his screen door.

Dad and I retreated to the shadow of our beech tree as the fuses burned. When the explosion came, it rocked the pre-dawn stillness. The noise reverberated between the houses and echoed off the woods. By the time it subsided, the radio had already been turned off.

For five minutes there was no sign of life in the house. I knew Willis was not hurt and I laughed, thinking about him lying there trying to figure out what had happened. Finally, a light came on deep in the house's interior. I suspected he might be having an early bathroom call.

"I believe that got his attention," Dad said. "Let's go back to bed."

I lay awake until Willis left for work. In the morning light we could see a blackened area on his top step. Although he gave me dirty looks for weeks, he never mentioned the explosion. More importantly, the radio never came on again.

* * *

The bateau got little use that summer; I was busy farming and my father was working at the factory. I only crab scraped when I needed fish bait or my mother wanted crabs for meals. I used the outboard skiff for fishing trips because it used less fuel. Mostly the big boat stayed tied to her stake and we went aboard once a week to pump out the bilge.

My father began to talk about selling the boat, saying it made no sense to keep it. I argued against it, knowing there was a chance I might still be a waterman. He put off making the decision, seemingly troubled by the thought of being without a large boat.

* * *

The beginning of my junior year brought change to my life at a pace I had never experienced. It started on the first day when our American History teacher seated me in front of Karen Wasser, an attractive girl with a way of moving that caught every male's attention. She had been dating an older boy from another school and I didn't know her well. Finding her next to me, and looking better than ever, was intriguing.

As I sat down, she gave me a faint smile. Until then talking to girls had never been much of a problem, but this time things were different. Everything I thought of seemed dumb and I sat through the entire hour without saying a word. As class was ending, the pressure began to build. I had to say something and I wanted it to be clever, but that didn't happen. She stood up and prepared to leave.

"I think history will be fun," I blurted out.

A quizzical smile came to her face. "Are you kidding?" She gathered up her books and put them in a neat stack. "See you tomorrow."

She left the room and I watched until she disappeared from view. Her long black hair shimmered as she walked. I noticed that Mitch followed her out the door.

The next day, I got to history class early and worked on an opening line. When Karen sat down at her desk, I said the amazingly clever, "I hope you're smart enough to help me through this class."

"Not likely." She laughed and told me that she wasn't a great student. As our conversation went on, I noticed that she laughed a lot and that talking to her was easy. Too soon, our teacher began her lecture on the Boston Tea Party. I turned around and pretended to pay attention, but my mind was not on the Revolution.

Over the next few weeks, I looked for opportunities to talk to Karen outside of class, and I maneuvered to be close to her before school and at lunchtime. She always seemed happy to be with me, but too often Mitch was hanging around. One night I called her to ask a history question, even though I already knew the answer. We talked for a long time and after that I called her regularly. She never mentioned her boyfriend or what she did on the weekends. The only thing that kept me from asking her out was lack of a driver's license. It would be a month before I could take the test, and I decided to wait.

* * *

Soccer was the fall sport for most Eastern Shore schools and practice started as soon as students returned in the fall. I went out for the team and made it as a fullback. The coach was our physical education teacher, Bill Pump, a slender, athletic man who had been a college track star. I was not a starter but he put me in for almost half of every game.

In our league, soccer was a rough sport, where hard collisions and knockdowns were regular occurrences, and there were plenty of bruises. Penalties were not called unless fouls were blatant. Our game allowed us to show our toughness, and I loved every minute I spent on the field.

Parents never attended our matches, although there was no rule against it. It would have been uncomfortable to have them on the sidelines. The sport was for our coach and us. It was about testing ourselves against boys from other schools. If parents had been watching, it would have diminished the game.

* * *

Shortly after the school year began, the junior class faculty advisors called a meeting and brought us all together in one room. They reminded us that it was our year to put on the Junior-Senior Prom. We were told that the election of class officers had to be soon, and we should be thinking about candidates. The people elected would lead the effort to raise money and make the dance a reality. Most of us had been together as a class for ten years and there was no need for a long campaign. Nomination of candidates and the election were set for the following week.

In the days leading up to the vote, Sally Adams, the attractive, dark-haired daughter of a farmer and one of the smartest girls in the class, was talked about as the best candidate for president. We were friends and I knew she would do a great job because no one would work harder. In the past, if a teacher assigned a two-page report for us to write, she usually submitted ten.

On election day, when the time for nominations was almost over, only three names were on the blackboard - Sally and two other girls. Mitch did not like the all female slate, and at the last minute he nominated me. After several ballots, I was declared class president and Sally was named vice president. It was flattering to be chosen. At the time I gave little thought to the work involved. After all, the prom was seven months away.

* * *

My responsibilities at home continued as usual. There was no end to the chicken feed—it just kept coming. Every week, large tank trucks pulled into our driveway delivering feed to the tall metal bins attached to the chicken houses. The truck engines roared as they powered the large blowers forcing the feed through a pipe and into a bin. I never liked the sound; all it said to me was, "Here's another six tons for you to lift."

When I was not working in the chicken houses, I was busy with my pigs or in a field picking corn. My one-row picker was slow, but like every farmer, I felt proud as I watched the ears tumble into the wagon. The crop was good and the crib that I built the previous year was soon full. The rats didn't return; maybe the survivors had warned the others about the treatment they could expect.

During the summer, I had constructed a farrowing house behind number one chicken house. With multiple stalls and a concrete floor, it was a big improvement over the A-frame houses. In the future, it would be the place where all my sows gave birth. Except for during far-rowing time, I began to keep the females at the Ross place, a quarter mile away from our house.

When the corncrib was filled up, I began to store the extra grain in the abandoned Ross house. I shoveled ears from the wagon into the old kitchen, and by the time I finished harvesting, the room was nearly full. The house provided a dry storage place near the sows' pasture, which made feeding them easy. Later in the winter, a two-legged rat would find my grain pile and have to be dealt with.

* * *

The day after my driver's test I decided to ask Karen out. It was noon before I could talk to her alone. She was sitting at her desk in home-room.

"Did you get your license?" she said as I sat down beside her.

"No problem. I screwed up one hand signal but the officer was look-ing at his clipboard." She was wearing a pink sweater and I couldn't help but notice how good she looked.

"I hope I'm so lucky." She went on questioning me about the test and I was happy that she was interested. Eventually I ran out of things to say. It was time to ask her out, but the words hung in my throat. What if she said no? An awkward silence surrounded us and Karen leafed through her history book. I was just about to speak when Mitch walked up.

"Hi," he said to Karen.

"Hello Mitch," she said, with a sweet smile.

"Noble, haven't you got some important prom work to do?" he said.

"No, and why don't you get lost?"

"Okay, but if you don't ask her out, I will." As he walked away, he flipped the back of Karen's hair. It did not seem to upset her.

Mitch's comment had raised the tension and forced my hand. Karen sat sideways in her desk and looked at a chart of the periodic table.

"Would you like to go to a movie on Saturday night?" I said. I kept my voice low so she had the option of pretending not to hear me.

"Sure, I'd love to go." She turned toward me with a smile and I felt a wave of relief, the kind that only a teenage boy knows when he is not shot down.

"I'd better give you directions to my house. It's kind of remote." It turned out that she lived on a farm in the southeastern part of the county. It was a long way from my house but that didn't matter. She had said yes.

On Saturday I washed and waxed the car. My father started asking questions as I was about to leave for my date. He was annoyed when he found out where Karen lived.

"You're going to drive my car way out there? Can't you find a girl closer to town?"

"I'm buying the gas." I said.

"Are you going to pay for the wear on the tires from those winding roads?"

"I'll level some shavings for no pay." I thought that would satisfy him but it was not enough.

"If you continue to date this girl, there's going to be a rule—you can't drive to her house more than once a week."

I didn't argue. It was only the first date and I just wanted to be on my way. I began to ease out the back door.

"Be home by eleven, not a minute later . . . and don't you race that car," was the last I heard.

I drove toward Karen's house, trying to remember her complicated directions. On my side of the county, there were rivers running east and west, dividing the land into necks and providing guidance. On her side, there was just a maze of interconnecting roads, most of them built on old Indian trails. I made a wrong turn at the fourth crossroad and arrived twenty minutes late. She was gracious, saying that everyone got lost on the way to her house. Her parents introduced themselves and asked me a few questions. They were nice and I started to relax.

We drove to the Wicomico Theatre in Salisbury. It was built on the edge of the river, right at the foot of a drawbridge. A Rock Hudson/

Doris Day movie was playing and the line stretched across the bridge. Luckily, the span did not have to be opened before the show started.

After the movie, I drove to the Oaks Drive-In Restaurant, a hangout for teenagers from all over the lower Eastern Shore. I backed into a space and we ordered cheeseburgers and milkshakes. There was a constant stream of cars circling the building, all carrying people our age. Some had engines so large that we heard their rumble long before they appeared. While we were waiting, two of the fast cars pulled on to Route 13 with tires squealing. They were headed off to drag race and other cars with spectators followed, but their departure did not slow the parade. A station wagon rolled by with four girls inside. A boy standing in a group next to us yelled out to them, "Come around again . . . I think I love you." The girls giggled and promised to come back.

As Karen and I ate our food, I found out more about her. Just before the school year started, she had broken up with her long-time boyfriend. He was off at college and she vowed never to go steady again. I felt a twinge of disappointment. I had never wanted to go steady with a girl before, but I didn't like having it ruled out.

We talked for a long time before I drove her home and parked in her driveway. I was in no hurry for the evening to end.

"Thanks for a great time," she said.

"I'll walk you to the door."

"There's no need, I promise nothing will devour me in the yard," she said, laughing. Suddenly, I realized how much I liked her laugh.

On the way home I drove fast; it was already after eleven and I had missed my father's curfew. With luck he would be sound asleep and would not hear me come in. If not, I would just have to deal with him in the morning. It had been a good night and he was not going to spoil it.

24. You Best Believe Her, Boy

THE CHANGING OF CLASSES AT WASHINGTON HIGH school was an orderly affair. We moved through the halls in single file, traveling in two opposing lines like cars on a highway. Posted in the median, in front of each classroom door, were senior students. They were the hall monitors who directed traffic and enforced the no talking rule.

One afternoon when I was in line headed to my next class, Mr. Leckey crooked his finger at me, indicating I should follow him into the library. He was a tall, prissy man with thin gray hair and a habit of speaking with his head tilted back, which made him appear to be talking down his nose to students. I was never sure if it was caused by his attitude or his bifocals. When he was first introduced to our class, he seemed aloof and serious, but as time went on we found out that he was actually friendly and had a good sense of humor. For some reason he liked me, which was fortunate because English Literature was not my best subject. Discussing *A Tale of Two Cities* on a pretty fall afternoon was nearly torture for me.

When I entered the library, Mr. Leckey motioned for me to sit at a table and he took a seat across from me. Mrs. Richards, the French teacher who also served as librarian, joined us. The chair creaked as she lowered her oversized body into it. Both teachers were wearing serious expressions, and I thought I must be in major trouble to warrant such a meeting. My mind raced back through recent events, trying to figure out what I had done, but before I found the answer Mr. Leckey spoke.

"Terry, I'm the faculty advisor for the yearbook and Mrs. Richards is my assistant. It's time for us to appoint a junior editor. The seniors on the staff have voted to offer the position to you, if you're interested."

His statement was totally unexpected, and my first thought was that at least I was not getting grief for some bad behavior. I didn't know much about how the yearbook was produced, but I was moderately interested.

"How hard is the job?" I said.

"This year you would be a general helper and observe how the book is put together," he said. "Next year it would be your responsibility to oversee the entire production, including design, layout, photography and ad sales.

"That sounds like a lot of work."

"We'll choose a business manager from your class to help with the finances and some other staff members to do much of the work."

I sat quietly for a moment, considering the offer.

"We don't need a decision for a few days. Think about it," he said.

I stood up and started to leave for my class. With some effort, Mrs. Richards turned in her chair and looked at Mr. Leckey.

"I mean no offense, but I don't think he's up to the job," she said. "It's not his cup of tea. We need someone with more artistic interests." Her snobbish tone irritated me. Ever since the day I chose agriculture instead of French class she had not been friendly, and her comment caused me to make an instant decision

"I'll be the editor," I said firmly.

Mrs. Richard's face revealed her disappointment. Mr. Leckey smiled.

"Good, I'll tell the seniors," he said. "Your first yearbook meeting is tomorrow at 2:00 PM."

Already I had a problem—the prom committee was scheduled to meet at the same time.

I moved the prom meeting to another day and we met in the cafeteria to begin work on the big dance. Our first job was to select the paper that would create a false ceiling in the auditorium on prom night. It had to be ordered months in advance and Page and two other girls searched through catalogs, trying to find a pattern. I could see that it was going to take awhile, so Jack and I went to measure the auditorium to calculate the number of rolls needed to cover the ceiling.

When we returned, the girls had chosen a dark blue paper with lots of silver stars.

"It will be romantic and look like the night sky," Page said. She blew me a kiss and I wiggled my eyebrows in response.

Unfortunately, the pattern they chose was the most expensive in any of the catalogs. It would take half the money in our treasury to pay for it, and I was reluctant to spend so much on our first purchase. I asked them to pick something else, but they held firm, sure that they had found the perfect ceiling.

I flipped through the catalog and found the same pattern in a non-flame retardant paper at half the price. I showed it to the faculty advisor and she said I would have to get the principal's approval to buy it.

Mr. Baughn had retired and Elmo Powell was our new principal. He was a tall, handsome man about my father's age. Shortly after he arrived at the school, someone found out his nickname was Buzz; after that the students called him Buzzy—except when he was around. My friends and I began testing him during his first week on the job. We quickly discovered that his face turned red when he got mad, and when he was extremely angry, two prominences on his forehead turned bright red. These bumps became known as Buzzy's horns, and when they appeared it was a warning for us to back off.

It had been a while since I had done anything to irritate Mr. Powell, and I felt comfortable going to his office. I found him sitting at his desk, making out the basketball schedule. I laid the catalog in front of him and pointed out what I wanted to buy. In a few seconds he looked up and shook his head.

"Terry, you're too young to remember the big nightclub fires, and the panic that resulted in so many deaths. There will be a lot of paper in that ceiling and I can't let you order something that will burn. You'll have to buy the flame retardant kind, no matter what it costs."

I went back to the meeting and filled out an order sheet for the more expensive paper. The girls were happy but I still wondered if we were wasting our money.

* * *

A few nights before Christmas, I was awakened after midnight by bang-ing noises and men shouting. For a few seconds my heart raced, until I recognized the sounds. The low growl of a truck engine confirmed that it was a chicken catching crew starting work and the banging was from wooden coops being unloaded.

When a flock was ready for market, the chicken company sent out a group of catchers with several tractor-trailers stacked high with coops. Most of the work was done at night when the birds were quiet. It was not a pleasant job; many of the men were drifters and some of them drank heavily. They labored in dusty, darkened houses, illumi-nated by one tiny bulb, appearing ghostlike as they waded among sleepy chickens. The men caught the birds by hand, usually ten or twelve at a time, and carried them outside to the coops.

My father seldom made me get out of bed on those nights. Usually he watched the operation alone after coming home from the factory. He was on hand to prevent his equipment from being damaged by the catching crew and to make sure the truck drivers stayed on our drive-way. In the winter the trucks sometimes got stuck in the mud and he had to call a wrecker to get them out.

On that night things seemed to be going smoothly and I drifted back to sleep, in spite of the din of chicken squawks, flapping wings and banging coops.

In the faint light of morning I went out to feed my pigs. Several chickens that had escaped the catchers were standing in the yard, unsure what to do with their new found freedom. One of them picked cautiously at the frost-covered grass.

The pig house was warm and cozy when I entered, and some of the occupants grunted softly while I searched for the light switch. When the bulb came on, I immediately had the feeling that something was wrong. The only animals in the building were weaned pigs that were ready for sale. There appeared to be more empty space in their pen than on the previous afternoon. I counted the pigs and four of the biggest were missing.

It wasn't obvious how they could have escaped but I thought they might be outside. I searched the pig lot but there was no sign of them. It was like the morning after the arrival of my first pigs years before, except there was no deep straw for them to hide under. Where these four pigs had gone was a mystery. I fed the remaining animals and went back to the house.

The aroma of French toast and scrapple filled the kitchen. Dad was at the stove pouring a cup of coffee. He had gotten out of bed with only an hour of sleep. There was a lot to do on the day after the chickens were caught.

"Four of my pigs have gotten out and I can't find them," I said, hoping he had seen them during the night.

"They wouldn't go far away from the others. You just haven't looked in the right place," he said dismissively. He dumped two teaspoons of sugar into his coffee. "I'll go out and find them for you."

After we ate, Dad went to search for the pigs and I went to the Ross place to feed the sows. When I returned, he was back in the kitchen, looking solemn.

"Those pigs aren't here. I think the catching crew stole them."

I stared at him in disbelief. Nothing was ever stolen in our community. Our neighbors might take an illegal oyster from the state, or shoot a few ducks over the limit, but they never stole from each other.

"I went to bed before the crew finished," he said. "I guess they hauled the pigs out in a chicken coop on the last load."

My disbelief turned to anger as I thought about the work and expense of raising the animals. Their loss would all but eliminate any profit from those litters. I pictured the thieves in my pig house with a flashlight, selecting the best animals.

"Those bastards," I muttered. Mom's jaw tightened.

"You're not going to talk like that in this house," she said.

"Why not? Dad swears here and he's even worse at the store."

"I might not be able to control your father, but you I can manage."

Dad glared at me from across the kitchen and I changed the subject. "Can't we call the chicken company and find out where those catchers live?"

"I'll call them, and the sheriff," Dad said.

When I got home from school that afternoon, my father had already left for work, but Mom told me the results of his phone calls. The chicken company manager said that the men on the crew lived all over the Eastern Shore, some as much as fifty miles away. He claimed to know nothing about the pigs and stated that his company was not liable. The response from the sheriff was almost as bad; he promised to look into the matter but he was not optimistic about results. I waited for a phone call from him but it never came.

After a few days, I realized that nothing was going to be done about the missing pigs. It was disappointing that adults were letting me down. Some had stolen from me and others were refusing to help. My view of people began to change.

By the time the holidays arrived, I was starting to forget about my loss. Christmas Day began like all others for our family; we gathered around the tree at first light to open presents. Dad gave me a canvas hunting coat and new hip boots. Mom came through with a sweater and a book.

As soon as the presents were opened, my mother went to the kitchen to begin preparing breakfast. It was a major event, with all the Shockley family attending, plus some neighbors who had no relatives in the area. The crowd overwhelmed our dining room and some of the children ate at card tables set up in the living room. When the food arrived, it appeared to be enough for a group twice our size. There were platters of fried eggs, scrambled eggs, biscuits and pancakes. On the meat tray was some of every part of a pig that could be fried. It was good food and nobody worried about clogged arteries.

When the guests departed, I drove to the Ross place to feed my sows. It was two hours after their regular mealtime, and they began squealing as soon as I pulled into the driveway. They got louder as I filled a basket with corn from the old house kitchen. My pile of grain seemed to be shrinking faster than I had expected but I told myself it was just natural settling over time. The sows became more vocal and I hurried to their pen; by the time I got there the noise was deafening. It ceased instantly when I tossed in the first ears, replaced by the crunching sound of sharp teeth biting dry corn.

In the adjoining pen, my newly purchased Duroc boar was pacing along the fence line. He was a beautiful animal, dark red and muscular, and in a few days I planned to turn him in with the females. It was time for him to breed the new gilts that I had added to the herd. My expansion plans were still on schedule.

When the work was finished, I hurried home—the best part of the day was about to begin. My father and I were going duck hunting, as we did every Christmas. For the first time Danny was old enough to go, but he decided to try goose hunting in a neighbor's field instead. My father and I would be alone together. Lately that had become more uncomfortable, but I knew we would be okay on the river.

Dad and I packed a lunch and assembled our gear. I was taking along the new 12-gauge shotgun I had purchased. It was a brisk, sunny day with a west wind and we put on extra clothes. I wore my new coat and hip boots.

We took the outboard skiff downriver to a large tract of publicly owned marsh where we rarely saw any other hunters. Dad eased our boat into a gut and I tied it to some myrtle bushes on the bank.

"Let's sneak up on the Cattails," he said. The Cattails was a brackish water pond where black ducks and widgeon liked to feed. He struck out in that direction and I followed, walking close to the gut, hoping to surprise a duck on the way. A hundred yards out, a clump of marsh grass collapsed as I stepped on it, and I slipped into a deep hole. A rush of cold water raced down both legs. My father moved on, unaware of what had happened. I pulled myself out and took off my boots. When I dumped them, water, mud and bits of chewed roots—the remains of some muskrat's breakfast—poured out. Nothing like breaking new waders in quickly, I thought.

I put the boots back on over my wet socks and pants; it was going to be a less than comfortable day. I was glad my father had not seen me fall in; there was no need to reinforce his suspicion that he was raising an imbecile.

He was now way ahead and I hustled through the needle reeds trying to catch up. Suddenly, he dropped to his hands and knees and began to crawl. He had spotted a duck and he was not going to wait for me. I kicked myself for falling behind. A black duck sprang into the air from the far side of the pond. My father's head and gun barrel rose above the reeds. When his gun cracked, the bird fell as if it was trying to drill itself into the soft earth. My father stood up and another duck took flight from a pothole to his left. It should have been an easy shot but the second barrel went off halfway through his swing.

"Damn it," he said, looking down at his right hand. It had been five years since he had been shot, but he still had trouble moving his partially numb finger to the gun's second trigger. Once before, I had seen him shoot a duck on the water and then take the head off a decoy with the second barrel.

"That's it, I'm getting an automatic," he said. "I've never liked them but I've got to have a gun with one trigger." He had said that before, but his love for the old double barrel always stood in his way.

We walked the marsh for another two hours. As long as I kept moving, my feet were warm. I killed a widgeon at the next pond. My father shot a black duck passing by at sixty yards. I am sure in its grape-size brain the bird thought it was out of range but when the gun went off, it cartwheeled out of the sky. The old man always had a way of surprising them.

Later in the afternoon we walked back to the river shore. Dad built a blind out of myrtle bushes and dried eelgrass while I put out the decoys. As usual, my arrangement did not please him and he made me move them twice. When he was satisfied with the spread, we settled in to wait for the evening flight.

The cold soon began to creep into my wet lower body. My toes went numb and I fought to keep from shivering, determined that my father would see no weakness out of me. Just before sundown, a flock of widgeon streaked in. The whoosh of air spilling from their wings announced that they had seen the decoys. The flock circled once and glided toward a spot of open water in front of the blind.

"Let them sit down," my father said. I knew what he was planning. When the birds were all on the water, we eased our guns through the blind.

"Take the ones on your side—wait for them to line up," he whispered. "The first of us to get three in a row takes the shot."

I looked down my barrel trying to find a pair that I could kill with one shot. I had just located them when Dad whistled. At the sound, all of the ducks raised their heads. We shot in unison. Five birds remained on the water. Neither of us shot again; we had enough meat.

"That's the way to do it," he said. "Five with two shots and not a pellet in their breast. They'll be good table birds." To my father the meat was the most important thing; he would never kill a bird just for sport. And he was frugal with his gun shells, from memories of the Depression, I suppose. If ducks came into the decoys and failed to sit down, forcing us to take our first shot on the wing, he considered the effort a failure.

I waded out to get the downed birds, glad to have an excuse to move my feet.

"Get the decoys while you're out there," he said. "We'd better head back if we're going to make it to Hilda's on time." The whole family was gathering again that evening for dinner at the Shockleys' house.

On the boat ride home I picked ducks, while my father sat in the stern operating the outboard motor. Lightheartedly, I let the feathers blow back in his face. He knew I was doing it on purpose and he pretended not to notice, but a hint of a smile gave him away. White tufts of down accumulated on his eyebrows. When they began to tickle, he wiped them off with the back of his glove. Things were different on the river; out there I could still joke with him a little.

* * *

On the first day back to school after Christmas break, our bus arrived earlier than usual. Don Rogers, a longtime friend, was one of the few students in homeroom when I walked in.

"Did you take Karen out during the holidays?" he asked. I was surprised that he had opened the conversation that way.

"We went to the movies one night but she was busy with her family most of the time." Karen and I had been dating for two months and I liked her more than any girl I had ever known. After her comment on our first date, we had never talked about going steady but I was not seeing anyone else and I thought she wasn't either.

"I wondered if you two were still dating, because I saw her with her old boyfriend." I had been keeping an eye on the door, waiting for Karen, but suddenly he had my full attention.

"It couldn't have been them, they're through," I said.

"Yes it was. I parked right beside them at the drive-in. Robert was home for the holidays and she was snuggled up under his arm."

A knot tightened in my chest. Don was not one to make jokes.

"They went out another night, too. A friend of mine saw them."

"It doesn't bother me," I said. I walked out of the room and into the hall. A sickness was developing in me like I had never felt before. At that moment, Karen came in from her bus.

"Hi, I missed you," she said. Her voice was as sweet as ever.

"Hi," I said weakly, unable to manage a smile. She looked at me curiously, before going in to put down her books. I went to the gym and shot baskets until classes started.

The morning passed slowly and nothing my teachers said registered in my over-active mind. I thought about the nights I had called Karen's house and her mother said she was out with friends. How often had she dated him? Who else had she dated?

I avoided Karen at lunchtime, but in history class her desk was right behind mine. I sat down and faced forward. She tapped me on the shoulder and I turned around.

"What's the matter with you?" she said, smiling.

"I heard you went out with Robert."

She looked surprised. "Does it bother you that I went out with him?"

"Well, I don't like it." It was hard not to show how much it bothered me.

"I told you I didn't want to go steady."

"But you said that you and Robert were through."

"We're just friends. He was home from college and feeling lonely. I just went out with him to cheer him up."

I wanted to believe her, in fact I did believe her—she and Robert were just friends—but I needed something more.

"I don't want you to go out with him again."

"Terry, we're *not* going steady." She sounded annoyed and I didn't want to make her angry.

"Okay," I said, weakly. I sounded like a wimp and I hated myself for it, but what else could I do.

For the next week, I resisted the strong desire to ask Karen out. We talked every day and she acted as though nothing had happened, but I never mentioned a date. When she asked what I was going to do on the weekend, I gave her a vague answer.

The weekend came and it passed slowly. On Friday night, I hung out in Princess Anne and played pool with two Deal Island boys. My mind was never on the game and I lost almost every rack.

Saturday evening, I rode to the Oaks Drive-In with Fred Miller, another classmate. He was also a soccer fullback and we were becoming friends. Fred was tall, athletic and had his own car, but his shyness around girls kept him from dating often. At the drive-in, I asked every-one if they had seen Karen but no one had.

Sunday was a dreary winter day and there was not much to do in the afternoon. Our one clear television channel was running the *Wizard of Oz*. It seemed that my life could not sink any lower.

On Monday morning I awoke with a new attitude, and I left for school thinking I didn't really care what Karen did. When I walked into homeroom, Mitch was sitting in Karen's desk and she was sitting on his lap. The knot in my chest tightened again but I pretended not to notice them and went to the closet to hang up my coat.

"Now are you going to give me my desk back?" she said.

"No, I'm going to keep you like this all morning," he said, putting his arm around her waist. She pretended to struggle and to be upset, but they were laughing when I left for the ag-shop.

The rest of the week was not any easier. The next day Karen spent time with Jack, teasing him about a girl he had been dating. She sat with him at lunch and giggled as they talked. I sat across the room with two other boys on the soccer team and tried not to look their way.

On Wednesday I was feeling isolated from my friends, and I was happy when Page walked up beside me on the way back from gym class.

"Why so quiet?" she asked, bumping me with her hip.

"No reason."

"Worried about Karen, huh?"

"No, not at all," I said, wondering how she always knew everything.

"Liar, I can see what's going on."

"What do you mean?" My life had never been so out of balance and I thought maybe she could explain why.

"You'll have to figure that out for yourself," she said. "But don't take too long, or you'll ruin a good thing."

"Why do girls talk in riddles?"

"That's part of our charm. By the way, did you hear that Karen asked Fred to drive her home after school?"

I stopped walking and looked into her eyes. "I don't believe that."

"What an innocent," she said over her shoulder, before disappearing through the classroom door.

Page's information was correct. At the end of the school day, I watched as Karen and Fred walked across the parking lot to his car. That was more than I could take. Pride overcame all other feelings and it removed any thoughts of asking her out again. I had been taught a painful lesson, and I vowed that no girl in the future would ever find me so gullible.

The next morning Mitch was waiting in the hall near the bus entrance.

"Are you and Karen going out again?" he said.

"No, I've finally gotten the picture."

A look of surprise crossed his face and he smiled. "It's about time. You've been looking like a fool."

It was embarrassing to hear what everyone must have known, "Those days are over . . . you can have her now."

"I'm not interested. I never have been," he said.

I looked at him in amazement, wondering what went on in his head.

25. A Thief Gets His Due

IT WAS A COLD, GRAY MORNING IN EARLY FEBRUARY AS I drove into the Ross place to feed my sows. They heard the truck approaching, and some began to come out of their A-frames, walking stiffly on the frozen ground.

Four of the new gilts had elected to sleep outside. They had rooted out a large hole in a dry part of the pasture and the excavated dirt was piled around the edge. The gilts completely filled the crater and their snouts poked out over the rim. They looked snug and warm and resembled a nest of giant birds.

The boar stepped out of an A-frame and stretched before walking to the feeding area. He had been with the females for several weeks, and half of them were pregnant. The first litters from my expanded herd would arrive in three months.

When I entered the old house to get corn and protein supplement for the morning feeding, I was again struck by the feeling that my corn pile was shrinking too fast. I had calculated that it would last until June but it was obviously going to run out sooner. It was hard to believe that someone was stealing from me again but I had to find out.

After delivering the feed to the sows, I returned to the house and smoothed out the corn pile so I could better determine if any was missing in the future. I located an ear with some husk still covering the kernels. I stripped back that outer covering, tied it in a knot and placed the ear in the pile close to the door. Next I removed a string from a feedbag and ran it across the open doorway at knee level. I tied one end to a nail and tucked the other into a crack in the doorframe. The string would come loose easily if anyone stepped into the room. If there was a thief, he was coming at night and my detection system would go unnoticed.

For three mornings I carefully inspected my setup and found nothing disturbed. As I approached the house on the fourth day, I saw that the string was down. My pulse quickened as I crossed the yard. When I looked through the doorway, the marked ear was gone and there was an obvious indentation in the corn pile. It appeared that someone had removed nearly two bushels.

I had suspected a thief but seeing the proof was shocking. Strangers had stolen my pigs, but this was someone local because the corn was disappearing a little at a time. The fact that it was someone I knew made me furious. The stealing had to end and I was determined to make it happen.

Stopping the crook would not be easy. I thought about sleeping in the old house at night, until I remembered how spooky it was after dark. Sometimes when I fed sows late in the evening, creaks and groans from the aging structure sent chills up my spine. I considered padlocking the house and putting plywood over the windows, but that would have cost money and may not have stopped the pilfering. The place was remote and it would have been easy to break into.

I drove home and told my father about the missing corn. He looked dismayed.

"I hate a thief—they're the lowest form of life," he said. He called the state police and they promised to make inquiries, but I knew it was not high on their list of priorities. Later in the day Mom saw a patrol car cruise slowly down Oriole Road, which was more response than I got when my pigs were stolen.

That night, as I lay in bed trying to figure out how to deal with the situation, I thought of the few stories I had heard about thieves. I remembered that when Dad was a boy, his father had suspected someone was stealing his firewood. My grandfather drilled a hole in a piece of wood, filed it with gunpowder and plugged the end. He put it back on the woodpile and a few days later his neighbor's stove mysteriously blew up. No one was injured and the wood stopped disappearing. I wanted to do something like that, something that sent a message directly from me to whomever was taking my corn.

One day in history class I found the answer. My mind was wandering and I remembered walking into my uncle's electric fence on a dark night. The shock gave me the sensation of being grabbed, but I couldn't tell where. My arms flailed wildly at the darkness as the pulses of electricity surged through my body. A demon had me and I could not get free. Finally I felt the wire and realized that I had to back up to stop the agony. When I broke contact with the fence, my heart was pounding like never before.

I began to formulate a plan using a new fence charger that I had recently purchased. It was powerful, and when sows hit the fence, the "zap" from the spark could be heard thirty yards away. I thought I might be able to give the thief a night to remember.

I arrived home from school and immediately headed for the Ross place. I moved the fence charger into the house and mounted it out of sight of the corn pile. After nailing porcelain insulators to the doorframe, I began stringing wire. When I finished, there were horizontal wires spaced to hit an intruder at his neck, waist and shins. Two diagonal ones would contact his chest and upper thighs. I smiled in anticipation.

For two weeks I checked my electrical trap every morning, but the wires were always in place and no corn was missing. I began to believe the thief had been scared off. Maybe word had gotten out that the state police were investigating.

One morning, I walked toward the Ross house still sleepy from a late night of working on prom decorations. Ten feet from the door I stepped on something hard and looked down. I saw an insulator with wire still attached. Farther on was a tangle of wire and insulators. The twisted mess was still connected to the doorframe by the one insulator not pulled loose.

I studied the scene, trying to imagine what had happened. Instead of hitting the wire and backing up as I had expected, the thief must have reached out and become entangled in it. During the struggle he had ripped the wire and insulators off the building.

I imagined him sneaking into the eerie, old house and being grabbed by the current. There wasn't enough electricity to do him harm, but for ten seconds he must have believed Charlie Ross's ghost had descended from the attic to devour him. I began to laugh aloud in sweet revenge. I felt as though I had gotten even with all thieves, including the ones that had stolen my pigs.

I never lost any more corn, and the thief's identity remained a mystery. He reduced my chance of going to college but the thought of him battling my hot wire eased the pain.

* * *

A few weeks after the theft problem was solved, I was sitting at my desk in school and a senior student dropped off an engraved invitation for me to be inducted into the National Honor Society. It was something I hadn't thought about or expected.

The induction ceremony occurred at an assembly in front of the entire student body. All of the members of the Society, including me, donned borrowed choir robes and marched on to the stage. Mrs. Richards played the piano and the faculty advisor, a gray-haired lady who taught Civics, gave a speech about pursuing academic excellence. When I stood to receive my certificate, I glanced toward the audience and saw Mitch and some of my other friends looking bored.

After the ceremony, the faculty advisor led us to the cafeteria where we were served hot tea and hard cookies.

"You've entered an elite group and set yourself apart from the other students," Mrs. Richards said to the new members.

The whole affair seemed snobbish and I took a hard look at the group I had joined. They were nice kids and some of the girls were good-looking. But to that point, the biggest risk any of the boys had taken was deciding to wear saddle shoes instead of loafers to a dance. I forced down my cookie and left the room, anxious to get back to the group I had been set apart from.

* * *

By late winter, work on the prom was well underway and it was keeping me busy. The yearbook was also taking more time than I had expected. To make matters worse, I had been elected as regional Vice President of the Maryland FFA. That position required me to make speeches at FFA banquets at other schools. I wanted public speaking experience but the preparation was time consuming. I was feeling pressure and wondering if I could get everything done.

The prom was less than two months away and I was concerned about our decorations. Would they be ready in time and would they be elaborate enough to satisfy the seniors? The prom committee had chosen *Three Coins in a Fountain* as the theme. Although the movie was set in Rome, some of the girls wanted a Venetian canal, complete with a gondola, for the stage decorations. For the rear of the auditorium they had plans for a fountain, surrounded by columns and an arched entryway. The boys were responsible for building whatever the girls designed.

Construction was taking place in a barn loft on the farm owned by the parents of Doug Gray, one of my classmates. The farm was located on Deal Island Road, about a mile from town. Doug was a sandy-haired boy who was one of the best athletes in the class. On two school nights per week, I met a group of other students at the Grays' barn to build and paint decorations.

On some construction nights, there was more partying than work, and I had to remind everyone how little time we had left before the prom. There was a small group of my classmates that I relied on to work steadily and Fred Miller was one of them. We were still friends even though he had given Karen a ride home from school. One afternoon, as classes were ending, Fred approached me in the hall with a sense of urgency.

"Noble, I just talked to a senior. A group of them is going to raid the barn tonight. They're going to see what we've built and tell the whole school." The prom theme and decorations were a closely-guarded secret, and normally the seniors did not find out until they walked into the auditorium on the night of the dance.

"They'll never try that," I said. In the past no seniors had ever shown up at a prom construction site.

"The guy I talked to said they're serious. We'd better get ready for them."

"Okay, barn defense is your job. Take care of it."

When I arrived at the Gray farm that evening, Fred was unloading tin cans from the trunk of his car and Jack Northam was helping.

"What are you planning?" I said.

"Seniors can only get into the loft by coming up the ladder and through the hole in the floor," Fred said. "I'm going to stack cans on each side of the walkway leading to the ladder and then I'm going to tie a string between the bottom cans in each stack. In the dark, they'll hit the string and we'll hear the cans fall." I suppose Fred and I had read the same boys' adventure books in which string was used to detect intruders.

"What will we do then, Sherlock?" I was impatient, hating to see so much time wasted preparing for an event that wasn't likely to happen.

"We'll put plywood over the hole and stand on it. They'll never be able to move us."

"Don't let them off that easy," Jack said. "Let's fill some buckets with water and set them near the hole. We can wet their asses before we put the plywood down."

"Right, it'll be like pouring boiling oil from a castle wall," Fred said. He was normally mild mannered but his enthusiasm for this job was growing.

I climbed the ladder to the loft and started work on the gondola, while Fred set up his can alarm and tested it. Jack and Doug filled some buckets and set them near the loft entrance. When their preparations were complete, they finally settled down to work.

Two hours went by with no sign of the seniors and the early excitement about the attack faded. Jack and Fred were joking about which girls they might ask to the dance, when the clattering of cans silenced everyone. I figured it was just a barn cat until I heard whispering at the base of the ladder. Doug turned off the light, and four of us picked up the buckets and moved toward the floor opening. In the shadows below several people were visible and one was starting up the ladder.

"Let 'em have it," Jack said.

We all dumped our buckets at once. A chorus of moans and curses erupted from below. Getting drenched on a cold night must not have been what they were expecting.

Jack and I covered the entrance hole. Instead of helping us, Fred opened the big hay door at the end of the loft. I could see his silhouette in the faint moonlight. Below him the seniors were running out of the barn.

"Let's get 'em," he said, and jumped out the door. It was more than eight feet to the ground.

Inspired by his action, we raced down the ladder to give him support. When we ran out of the barn, Fred and the seniors were nowhere in sight. We searched the outbuildings, not sure what we would do with a senior if we found one.

"This way, they're headed for the road," Fred yelled from a distance.

We ran down the farm lane toward his voice. When we caught up he was confronting six seniors standing beside their car on the shoulder of Deal Island Road. The car lights were on and I could identify all the boys.

Their leader was Calvin, a big red-haired boy with a reputation for fighting. He was unhappy about being outsmarted by a bunch of juniors. He and Fred were glaring at each other a few feet apart.

"This farm is private property—don't come on it again," Fred said.

"We're standing on public road. You juniors are all chicken. Step over here and I'll whip any of you."

"You don't scare me, fatso," Fred said, stepping forward. I was amazed; he had never been in a fight before and he was taking on Calvin, of all people.

The two boys circled each other for a moment and then Fred made a quick move, catching his opponent in a headlock. The senior was surprised. He threw body punches but he couldn't land anything solid from his subdued position. Fred tightened his headlock and the big boy's face turned red. He fought back, getting his hands between my classmate's legs and lifting him into the air. They fell to the ground and began to roll around. Neither of them was doing much damage to the other, but the gravel was taking its toll. They were both bleeding from multiple wounds on their arms.

After a couple more minutes wrestling on the ground, they were exhausted and everyone could see the fight was a draw. Slowly, they released their holds and stood up.

"You were just lucky," Calvin said.

"I'll take you on anytime," Fred shot back.

There was more tough talk before the seniors agreed to leave. When they were gone we went back to the barn but no work got done. We discussed every detail of the raid and we all had a new respect for Fred.

* * *

In March my father was out of work again. Business at the factory was bad. Throughout the previous year there had been several layoffs and this time the company was saying it might be months before the second shift returned to work. My father had the income from the three chicken houses but he was not satisfied. He had been a child during the Depression and he wanted a better life as an adult. I noticed him grow more irritable as money became tight again. We argued over my use of the pickup for prom work but I appealed to Mom and she convinced him to let me keep driving it.

The answer to my father's dilemma began to develop one afternoon as I was feeding sows. Low clouds had covered the sky all day and the wind was freshening from the northeast. Just as I finished dumping out the corn, a cold rain started to fall and the animals attacked the food with more enthusiasm than usual. As they got wet, I noticed that some of them began to shiver.

By suppertime the wind had gained strength, and the back screen door began slapping in its frame.

"It's going to be a real Nor'easter," Dad said. "Somebody will die on the water tonight." He was still sometimes called by neighbors to do rescues if one of their relatives was lost, because he knew the river and Sound so well.

After the meal I checked the conditions outside; the rain was heavy and the temperature had dropped ten degrees. This was no ordinary storm and my sows would need more straw bedding if they were to keep warm.

When I drove into the Ross place, the rain was traveling horizontally across the headlight beams, as though it had no plans to hit the ground. I gathered straw from the old house and ran to the A-frames. The animals refused to step outside, so I covered them where they lay with the bedding. They grunted in appreciation. I climbed back into the truck, wet and shivering, noticing that the rain was turning to snow. It was one of those times when I was thankful to be human and living in a warm house.

The storm roared for most of the night but the snow didn't stick. In the morning we found a few downed trees and some of our neighbors were without power. My sows came through fine, but their pasture was flooded and their houses resembled ships on a sea. The morning radio mentioned the possibility of damage in Ocean City and other coastal towns.

By evening the news reporters were talking about a major disaster along Maryland's coast. Ocean City had sustained millions of dollars in damages. Some low-lying towns were flooded and the residents were stranded. It had been the worst northeaster anyone could remember.

Two weeks after the storm, my father went to the unemployment office in Salisbury to apply for benefits. He had been reluctant to go, believing that no healthy man should ever take anything from the government. Mom reminded him that his employer had paid into the fund for him and that the money was his.

While my father was waiting at the office, a man walked in and asked if anyone had construction experience, saying that his company needed carpenters and concrete workers to help rebuild Ocean City. Dad mentioned that he had built chicken houses and the man offered him a job at one and a half times what he had been making at the factory. All his life he had tried to avoid walking in his father's footsteps, and now fate had served up that option again—this time he said yes.

Within two days my father was at work in Ocean City on a high-rise building. He took along my grandfather's old toolbox from the attic. From the start, he seemed to enjoy the new job. It was outdoors and he was being taught the construction of multi-story buildings. He must have learned quickly, because his employer continually increased his responsibilities and pay. For the next decade it would be his career, until he owned enough chicken houses to be a full-time poultry farmer.

26. Cinders, Alcohol and Fire

 A WEEK BEFORE THE PROM, I TRAVELED WITH OUR TRACK team to the state meet at the University of Maryland campus at College Park. The team had won the regional competition and I had qualified for the quarter mile and the long jump. For the first time we would be competing against larger, integrated schools from Baltimore and none of us was sure what to expect. Somerset County schools would remain segregated for several more years.

We arrived at the stadium in mid-morning and I had a long wait before my qualifying heat in the quarter mile. When we were finally called, I went to the starting area, which was hidden in the tunnel by the football locker rooms. The start was staggered and I drew the outside lane. That put me in front of the pack on the straightaway, where I was unable to see my competition.

The minutes leading up to a race always made me nervous, but this was worse than anything I had experienced. The big stadium, with its hard-packed cinder track, seemed far from the grass ovals on which I usually ran. As I stepped into the starting blocks my legs felt weak, but when the pistol fired, I took off with all the speed I could muster. Because of the staggered start, I appeared to be leading coming out of the tunnel. Some of my teammates were standing nearby and I heard them cheer. It was premature.

Going into the first turn, I heard footsteps. As I rounded the bend, two black boys from Baltimore sailed past me, their spikes throwing up cinders. I pushed myself harder and I did not lose any more ground until the next turn, but at that point they pulled away. When they crossed the finish line I was five yards back. Only the top two finishers went to the finals and my day at the track was over.

I walked to the infield with my head hanging low. Some of my teammates were standing by the high jump, including our shot putter, a slightly overweight senior.

"Noble, you looked pretty good until you picked up that piano on the first turn," he said. He laughed and put his arm on my shoulder.

"Those guys are fast," I said. "How would you like to run against them?"

"Oh, I never run, it's bad for my health." The other boys laughed and slapped me on the back. I began to feel better.

The story at the long jump was similar to the quarter mile. I was leading early in the competition, but near the end, three boys posted exceptional jumps and I finished just out of the ribbons.

On the first part of the drive home I thought about the track meet, vowing to come back in my senior year when I would be stronger and have more time to train. As we crossed the Bay Bridge my mind returned to prom work. The break from it had been nice, but the time for the final push was at hand.

* * *

We began setting up prom decorations on the day before the dance. That morning, all my classmates assembled in the auditorium in their work clothes. Many of the girls wore slacks, something the dress code did not allow on regular school days. It took a few minutes to get the boys' attention on the job that lay ahead.

Our first task was to begin hanging the ceiling. The school maintenance department provided a rolling scaffold for the job. The work went slowly because the edges of the paper strips had to be pinned together by hand. I quickly found out that the job was going to take much longer than I thought, maybe until late into the night. I was planning for that when Mr. Powell walked over to the scaffold and called up to me.

"Terry, you have to be finished with all decorations by 6:00 PM."

"We can't be done by then," I said, starting to feel panic.

"Find a way to do it. That's when I'm locking the auditorium."

I watched the girls laboriously pinning the paper, and thought we would be the only class to put on a prom with half a ceiling. The prospect of that embarrassment was crushing. Jack had overheard me talking to the principal and he climbed up to where I was standing.

"Maybe we can get it done," he said. He took the roll of paper from me and began supervising the work. I was trying to think of a way to speed up the process when Page called up from the floor.

"We need some vegetation to cover the entry to the fountain."

"What? We never planned for vegetation."

"Well, the arch you boys built doesn't look so great. If we could cover it with greenery, it would be acceptable."

"Okay, I'll have some English Ivy here by afternoon." I knew of a deserted farmyard on Deal Island Road where ivy grew to the tops of the trees.

The rumble of an engine drew my attention away from Page. Ricky Clark was backing his father's farm truck up to the side door of the auditorium. He and a couple of other boys were bringing the last load of decorations from the barn. They carried the gondola up to the stage, where Fred was building a frame for the Venetian canal. At least that part seemed to be on schedule.

On the far side of the room, some of my classmates appeared to be upset that the scaffold was interfering with them setting up the tables. I took another look at the ceiling crew. Jack and the girls were still struggling with the paper and the situation looked hopeless. It was a bad time for me to leave, but I had to get out of the building.

"Ricky, can we use your truck to haul ivy?" I asked.

"Sure, what are we waiting for?" Ricky was a friendly, cooperative boy with a crew cut. His father owned a large tract of land and he was destined to be a farmer. Two other boys volunteered to help. One of them was a tall skinny kid named Frank who had recently decided that life was all about good times.

The four of us got in the truck for what I thought would be a short trip. As we were leaving the school grounds, Ricky prepared to turn right.

"No, go left," Frank said. "Let's take Black Road—it's not much farther to drive."

"Why?" I said.

"You'll see." There was silly grin on his face.

Black Road was an unpaved sandy track that ran through heavy woods. There were only two farms along its entire length and at night it seemed dark and remote. Soon after we turned on to it, Frank directed us to stop beside a culvert. He got out and ran his arm into the pipe. When it reappeared, his hand was wrapped around a pint of bourbon. He got back into the truck carefully, protecting his prize.

"I couldn't take this home last night, so I stashed it here." He opened the top and took a swallow. "Man, that's good," he said. He thrust the bottle in my direction. "Noble, have a drink."

I had tried beer a couple of times but never hard liquor. "No thanks, there's still a lot of work to do."

He looked at me as if I were clueless and he had the answers. "Why do you try so hard? Are you aiming for the Mr. Responsibility award?" He elbowed me in the ribs. "Loosen up. Enjoy yourself once in a while."

He passed the bottle to the other boys and they each took a sip. From their expression, neither of them was experienced with hard liquor. As we rolled along, I thought about what Frank had to say. His words stung; maybe I did need to change. When he offered the bottle again, I took it.

"If the prom is only going to have half a ceiling, what difference could one drink make?" I said.

"Atta boy," Frank said, helping me tip the bottle. As soon as I swallowed, tears came to my eyes and I fought to catch my breath.

"It sure is warm going down," I said. My voice was so squeaky, it brought roars of laughter from the other boys.

By the time we arrived at the old farmstead, the bottle had been around three more times. We were as loose a group of ivy gatherers as the county had ever seen.

"Alright boys, let's get Page her vegetation and get back to school," I said, using the best leadership tone I could command under the circumstances.

Frank stepped out of the truck cab, missed the running board and fell on his face in the yard. That caused two minutes of uncontrollable laughter.

"Let's get to work," I said, trying to restore order. I was still laughing and it had minimal effect.

Eventually, they settled down and we got to the job at hand. Ricky backed the truck under the tallest tree and they began to strip the vines from the trunk. I climbed into the high branches, where the ivy was thickest. Courage from the liquor took me to places I would never have gone, normally.

I lost track of time as I scrambled around in the treetop cutting greenery and dropping it to the truck. My helpers finished their work on the tree trunk and lay down in the shade. From what I could see not much remained in the bottle. I continued to work three stories up without fear, until I slipped off the limb I was sitting on.

Somehow, my hand closed around a small branch. It held and I swung back and forth like a monkey. With the help of adrenaline, I hooked my leg over the main limb and pulled myself to safety.

My pulse was racing and my head had instantly cleared. We had enough ivy and I had to get back to school. It was time to face whatever embarrassment lay ahead.

I climbed down the tree and roused the other boys. "We've got enough greenery, let's go." They slowly stumbled to their feet and Frank gave me a sleepy grin.

"It looked like you were going to take the fast way down. What changed your mind?" he said.

"The thought of falling on you, jackass."

When Ricky drove into the school parking lot, my watch said 3:00 PM. It didn't seem possible that we had been gone so long. As I approached the auditorium door, my stomach churned from a mixture of liquor and dread. I hesitated a moment to gather some strength.

When I stepped inside the place had been transformed. To my amazement, the ceiling was almost complete and most of the tables were set up and decorated. The fountain and columns were in place. A Venetian canal had appeared on stage. A lot of work remained but it could be finished before our deadline. I did not have long to enjoy the scene before Page walked over with a frown.

"Where have you been? We need that ivy."

I pointed toward the truck, which Ricky was backing up to the door.

"It's about time," she said. She went off to direct the unloading. I was still enjoying the scene when Sally tapped me on the shoulder.

"Where are the souvenir booklets for the tables?"

"In the car—I'll go get them."

"Hurry up or the tables won't be finished." She rushed off to get more candles.

On my way out, I stopped by the scaffold to talk to the ceiling crew. They were obviously tired and their hair looked frizzy from rubbing against the paper. Their fingers were covered in tape to protect against the pins. I was amazed at what they had accomplished.

"Where did you disappear to?" Jack said.

"I had a little trouble getting the ivy." It seemed best not to discuss the details. "How did you get so much done?"

"We just got faster with every strip of paper."

"And we haven't been off this scaffold since you left," a girl said. "Except once to go to the bathroom." I felt as though I had really taken advantage of them. "Do you want me to get another crew?" I said.

"No," they all answered together.

"We've come this far and we'll finish it," Jack said.

Their hard work had saved me and they knew it. I owed them a tremendous debt of gratitude and my "thank you" did not seem like enough.

* * *

Prom night was better than I had anticipated. I relaxed for the first time in a month. My date said it was a special evening. We hired the most expensive band in the area to play for the dance and they were a hit. The seniors were excited about the music and the atmosphere we had created in the room. Some of the snobby ones even complimented our decorations.

Everything went smoothly until an hour into the evening. Just after the band returned from their first break, I noticed a burst of activity to their left. In a moment, flames rose from a table. A candle had been tipped over and it had ignited the paper on the table top, which was not flame retardant. One of the boys was beating at the fire with his white dinner jacket.

I hurried across the dance floor. On the way I could see the band gathering up their instruments, preparing for a quick exit. Mr. Powell came rushing in from the hallway and we reached the table at the same time. By then it was all over. The rented dinner jacket had done the job, though it was a bit blackened and Jim Tilghman would not be happy when it was returned.

Mr. Powell and I examined the ceiling above the table. The crepe paper was only scorched.

"Now do you understand?" he said.

I nodded my head, realizing how right he had been. "Thanks," I said.

27. Bittersweet Victory

 IT WAS A COOL JUNE MORNING AND I WAS STANDING alone in our front yard. The last drops of heavy dew were retreating, and a number of honeybees were at work, cruising the patches of white clover scattered through the grass. They delicately maneuvered between the small flowers, gathering a tiny drop of nectar at each one.

It had been a long time since I had stopped to watch the bees. I was facing the prospect of a summer day with no work to do. The pigs had already received their morning feed and I had nothing else on my schedule. My mood was good; the first six sows in my expanded herd had weaned an average of 9.5 pigs per litter. If the remainder of the group did as well, college would be a real possibility.

I sat down on the front steps and I tried to decide what to do with my day. Dipnetting crabs was out; runoff from recent thunderstorms had clouded the river water. Fishing was not good either; the first run of big rock was over and the sea trout were not in the Manokin yet.

A faint sound, like a honking goose, caught my attention. As I looked up I saw an old, green pickup truck rolling slowly up the road. It was Tommy Toots and the sound was his voice coming through the open truck window. Tommy had a passenger, another old bachelor named Richard Bedsworth, who lived alone in Champ. They were headed to their summer jobs at the plant nursery. As usual, Tommy was driving from the middle of the seat, making it appear that they were in a reversed dating position. As they drew closer, I could hear every word of the one-sided conversation.

"By God, Richard, them communists are going to get us. 'Tween the Russians and the Chinamen, we don't stand a chance," Tommy bellowed. Richard nodded politely, knowing better than to try to speak. His driver never left any openings when he was sure of his subject.

"By Jesus, I'm going to build me a fallout shelter, that's what I'm going to do."

Richard nodded again.

"I'll tell you the truth—when they drop that bomb, I'm going to be ready."

That was the last phrase I could make out as the truck moved on. I was surprised that Tommy knew about fallout shelters, since he had no television and his radio seldom worked. If he attempted to build a shelter, it would have to be above ground because of the high water table where he lived.

I still had no plans for the day so I walked to the Corner Store. It was too wet to work in the fields, so a large group of farmers was gathered there, including the Shockleys. A waterman from St. Stephens had stopped by for a soda on his way to Crisfield to buy net bags for his crab scrapes. Bobby and the waterman got into a friendly debate.

"There's a good run of small peelers out there now," the crabber said. "The state oughta reduce the size limit so we can sell them."

"If the state would let you, you'd catch the last crab," Bobby said, needling the hotheaded waterman.

"Damn it, the state is always costing us money with their rules. You might not know it, but times are hard on the water."

"That's typical . . . 'times are hard' is all I hear from you," Bobby said. "I wish farmers had it as good as watermen. All you have to do is run your boat out in state waters and harvest whatever is in season. The state even plants oysters for you and you still complain."

The crabber squirmed on his pop case seat, but my cousin was not finished.

"I believe farmers could make out alright if the state would plant corn on its land and let us drive our combines in the field to harvest it for free. You don't know how easy you've got it." Bobby had scored points and the man was at a loss for words. One of the other farmers piled on.

"You tell him. We're tired of his complaints. The state and county keep raising our taxes and spending money on the watermen and we get nothing."

The crabber had heard enough. "Screw you both," he said.

Everyone in the room laughed. The men would part friends, but the talk had revealed true feelings.

I went over to the ice cream freezer and began searching for a two-flavored ice cream cup. As usual they were under an endless pile of orange popsicles. The wooden spoons were hidden in a box of ice cream sandwiches. The freezer was a stainless steel chest with little black doors on the top, and it was not an easy place to find anything. The designer knew more about refrigeration than selling.

I had just opened my ice cream when Milbert walked over.

"How are you today, Captain?" he said.

"Fine, I need to cultivate corn but it's too wet."

"We're in the same boat. How would you like to help me clean out my Number 3 chicken house this afternoon? I can spread it on the pasture."

"Sure." I had hoped to find something fun to do, but I could not refuse my uncle.

"Louie Reid can help, but everyone else is busy. It will be just the two of you on the shovels."

"That's okay, there's no better working partner than him."

Louie and I worked together regularly, but he no longer had to help me, like he had done in the tomato field. We labored as equals, even though he always did a little more than everyone else to keep up his reputation as the hardest-working man. This would be the first time in a while that just the two of us were on a job.

We started on the chicken house in the early afternoon. Each of us was responsible for cleaning one-half of the floor; it would be hours before we reached the far end of the building. After thirty minutes Louie was a few feet ahead of me in cleaning out his side, which was the way he liked it. I worked at a steady pace, until he started shoveling on my side, as though I couldn't keep up. Those days were over and I felt a need to show him.

I began to work harder, loading my shovel more and walking faster on every trip to the spreader. By the time the next load pulled out, I was ahead. After that, I noticed Louie had stopped talking and there was a new quickness in his stride. I picked up my speed even more and he seemed to match it. A race was on to the end of the house.

It was a warm afternoon and rivulets of sweat ran down my back and legs. Once, during a break between spreaders, I glanced at my competitor and he was wiping his face and neck with his handkerchief. He put it away and tightened his belt another notch on his wasp-like waist. It seemed impossible that a body so thin could do that much work.

The battle went on for another hour, and as we neared the end, I sensed that Louie was struggling. For the first time I could hear him breathing. I kept up the pace and when I finished, he was still eight feet from the end. I was elated to have beaten my teacher and the man who outworked everyone.

Louie was leaning on his shovel, trying to catch his breath. When I looked into his eyes, I was immediately sorry for what I had done. He had an expression of real loss. His reputation for hard work was one of his most important possessions and a boy had beaten him.

There was an awkward silence until Milbert spoke.

"Well Louie, it looks like he got you this time." My uncle emphasized the last two words as though it would never happen again. That seemed to bolster Louie's spirits and he managed a smile.

"I suppose it's only fitting," he said. "His body is coming and mine is going." He looked over at me. "If you're so ambitious, why don't you help me finish?"

* * *

It was only a few days after my competition with Louie, when Bobby drove up to my farrowing house and got out of his car looking glum.

"I've got some bad news. Mr. Widdowson isn't going to buy any more of our pigs. His boss has decided to get out of the business."

The price of hogs had dropped, but I hadn't expected that. "Why is he quitting?"

"He says he can't make any money feeding our pigs to market weight."

Mr. Widdowson had been buying all of our pigs, even the runts, for two years, and he always paid a fair price. Finding another buyer like him would not be easy. I knew my college plans might be in trouble again.

"Where are we going to sell them?" I asked.

"I've talked to a livestock dealer near Salisbury who says he'll take them." The man he was considering bought from one farmer and sold to another, making a profit on each deal.

"How much is he paying?" I said, fearing the answer.

"Seven fifty per pig."

"That's twenty-five percent less than we were getting."

"I can't find anyone else who will take them." He looked dejected as he got back into his car.

I turned and gazed at the pen holding the six litters that were ready for sale. My chance for an education was starting to look slimmer.

Over the next few days, I called other pig buyers, but no one was paying over $7.50. For a while, I indulged in self-pity over the unfairness of the price dropping at the moment my operation reached full production. Eventually my optimism returned, and I decided to find a way to make up for the lost income. At the time I didn't recognize the valuable lessons I had learned about supply and demand, and that there was more to business than being good at production.

* * *

Even though I was still struggling to earn money for college, that didn't stop me from trying to have fun. One Friday night in late summer I met Fred in Princess Anne, and we spent the evening cruising the back roads in his car. We both had the desire to pull off a prank that would let the school know our class was a force to be reckoned with. For two hours we considered and rejected ideas; everything that came to mind seemed ordinary, or it had been done before. I was about to give up when Fred broke into a smile.

"Let's drop tires over the flagpole at school," he said. "They'll stack up at the bottom and look like a pile of donuts. It will be impressive on the first day of class, when everyone gathers on the lawn." His excitement grew as he described the idea. "They'll be really hard to remove and the teachers will wonder how we got them over the pole."

"Well, genius, that's what I'm wondering. How do we accomplish that trick? The pole is over thirty feet high and it can't be lowered."

"Between us, we can figure out a way. It's a minor detail."

"Yeah, sure." I had a feeling that I was going to wind up trapped in some uncomfortable detail. "If we do it, we can't let anyone know it was us. Buzzy and the school superintendent won't appreciate this stunt."

"It'll stay top secret."

With the decision made, we drove to the school to reconnoiter. It was located on Main Street, the only route through town, and the flagpole was separated from the road by only fifty yards of lawn. We rolled slowly through the circular driveway in front of the building, and I was surprised that lights near the front door illuminated the flagpole so well. We were going to be highly visible from the street. It was obvious the work would have to be done after midnight, when traffic through town was almost non-existent.

We parked on a side street and tried to come up with a plan. Fred thought he could pull the tires up the pole with the flag rope but that still left the problem of flipping them over the top. We decided that one of us would have to climb the three-inch pipe shaft. Extension ladders were rare and neither of our fathers had one. If we borrowed a ladder word would get back to the school. That left no choice but to shinny up to the top. I was the better climber so I volunteered.

Just after dark on the evening before classes started, Fred and I hid five tires in the bushes beside the school. We went to our houses to wait, having agreed to meet at the Corner Store at 2:00 AM. I went to bed at my regular time and fought to stay awake.

Thirty minutes before our meeting time, I opened the window screen beside my bed and lowered myself to the ground. Danny and Cindy continued to sleep peacefully. There was no moon and I had to feel my way along the darkened road to the store. A light was on in the building and I stood in the shadows until Fred's car pulled into the parking lot. When his open window was right beside me, I stepped out of the darkness. "Here I am," I said. He jumped sideways in his seat.

"Man, I'm nervous enough without you doing that," he said.

"Did you have any trouble getting away from home?" Fred lived in town on a quiet, tree-lined avenue, where an engine rumbling after midnight would be noticed.

"No, I pushed the car half a block down the street before starting it."

"Good. My father leaves for work early and I need to be home before he gets up."

The road was deserted as we drove to Princess Anne. Once there we followed a dimly-lit street, looking for Big Head Bill, the town's only police officer. We found the patrol car parked in front of the court-house and he was slumped behind the wheel, asleep.

Satisfied that he would not be a problem, we headed for the high school. Fred pulled into the Presbyterian cemetery, which bordered the school property, and we hid the car on a back road behind some large tombstones. After retrieving the tires, we sneaked along in the shadows toward the flagpole. When we got near, Fred hesitated on the edge of the darkness. He seemed to be having doubts.

"That's more light than I expected. Maybe we should forget about it," he said.

"It was your plan and you have to decide, but I think we've come too far to give up."

He was quiet for a moment as he considered the risk. "Okay, we'll do it, but if we get caught I'm going to tell the cops it was your idea."

"Right, just get your chicken ass moving." I ran toward the pole, lug-ging my tires, and he followed. It felt as though we were on a spot-lighted stage and everyone in town was watching. He hooked the first tire to the rope and tried to raise it, but the pulley had rusted during the summer and it would barely turn with so much weight. I joined him on the rope, and after a struggle we got the tire to the top.

I began to climb the pole but it was difficult to get a grip on the metal pipe. I squeezed tighter with my legs and slowly made progress. When I reached the tire, I unhooked it and flipped it over the top. Get-ting the tire past me was really awkward but I managed to hang on and let it drop to the concrete below. It made a satisfying thump.

Fred began to hook up a second tire and I waited at the top. The muscles in my arms were beginning to burn. The sound of a vehicle made me look toward the street and what I saw caused my heart to pound. A state police car was driving slowly out of town, and in a moment, it would pass in front of the school.

"Cop!" I said in a loud whisper. Fred dropped to the ground and tried to hide in grass that was three inches tall. I held on to the pole and watched the patrol car go by, expecting it to spin around and come racing up the school driveway. I thought of my father's often-repeated warning: "If you ever wind up in jail, don't call me. I'm not going to bail you out."

I couldn't believe it when the cop just drove on until he was out of sight. It was a few seconds before we realized our good fortune.

"How did he not see us?" Fred said.

"He was just sleepy and didn't look this way." My arms were beginning to shake. "Get that tire up here, I can't hold on much longer."

He pulled on the rope but the tire only went a few feet above his head before stopping.

"I can't move it," he said.

I slid down to the ground and helped on the rope. The tire moved a few more feet, and then the rope slipped off the pulley wheel and jammed. Nothing we did would break it loose. I went back up the pole and disconnected the tire, thinking I could climb with it over my shoulder, but it was not to be. My muscles refused to do the work and I slid back to the ground. We were out of options.

"One tire will still be pretty impressive," Fred said.

"Yeah, let's get out of here before that cop comes back."

At home I managed to get back into bed without anyone waking up.

The next morning, when Fred and I arrived at school, a few of our classmates were on the front steps speculating about how the tire got there. We smiled enough to raise suspicion, but when they asked about it we denied any connection.

Charlie Somers, the school maintenance man, and Mr. Powell were standing at the base of the pole. The principal looked irritated. Charlie's glasses were resting halfway down his nose and he was staring up the pole, scratching his gray head. He liked to joke with students as long as he came out the winner, but I questioned how he was going to take our prank.

When first period class was over, I looked out the front door of the school and Charlie was on his hands and knees, cutting the tire with a hacksaw. His red face indicated he had been at it for a while. When he stopped to wipe away the sweat and looked toward the building, I ducked behind the doorframe, trying not to be seen.

In gym class, I told Fred about Charlie cutting the tire. He laughed, and we agreed that putting one over on the maintenance man was a bonus. Neither of us suspected that, in less than a year, Charlie would have his revenge.

* * *

My father never found out about the prank but there was still trouble between us. It flared up one night at supper.

"I've decided to sell the big boat," my father said, between bites of his soft crab sandwich. We were in the middle of the meal, and up until then, there had been little talk.

"Why? I might want to work on the water if I don't go to college," I said.

"If you take up crabbing, you can buy another boat. I want the money now. Besides, the deal is already done."

I had only used the bateau twice that summer but I was annoyed that he sold it without telling me.

"That's not fair. When I have a family, I won't do things like that."

My father stopped eating and his eyes narrowed. "Well, good for you," he said.

For a minute the conversation ceased, but the boat sale was still irritating me. In fact, a lot about my father was irritating me. I was fed up with him making rules and giving orders, and there was another subject where I felt I was being treated unfairly.

"I'm a senior now and I don't see why I can't stay out until midnight. None of the other boys have to be in at 11:00 PM."

My father's eyes were growing dark; he was obviously unhappy that I was spoiling his meal—they were the last crabs of the season. I didn't care; I wanted more freedom and things had to change.

"Jack worked at a hotel in Ocean City this summer and he didn't have any curfew for three months," I said.

My father began to bite the inside of his lip. My mother could see trouble coming and she spoke up. "Terry, I don't want you staying out too late—boys can get into a lot of mischief. And you haven't been to church lately. I want you there on Sunday."

"I'm not going to spend two hours sitting with that bunch of hypocrites." The hurt look on Mom's face made me instantly sorry; the church meant a lot to her.

I had also insulted the people of Oriole and that was more than my father could take. Out of the corner of my eye, I could see him preparing to backhand me. It had been years since I had received any physical discipline, and in a fraction of a second, I decided it was not going to happen again. As his hand came forward I grabbed his wrist, stopping his arm in midswing. It was his good arm. It had been a while since he had felt my strength and he looked surprised. I pushed his hand back toward his face, just to show him I could.

"Let's go outside," he said.

"Fine with me." I released my grip and we stood up.

"THOMAS, NO! IT'S NOT WORTH IT. BOTH OF YOU, SIT DOWN," Mom said, in a growl that came from somewhere deep inside her.

My father and I stared at each other for a few seconds and then he took his seat. I stood a little longer, just to let him know that I was never going to back down. We finished the meal in silence.

From that day on, my relationship with my father was different. He was still the boss, but there were more negotiations and fewer orders. I went to church the next Sunday and Mom seemed happy. In a few weeks my curfew was changed to 12:30 AM.

28. Plastered

 NO ONE HAD FIGURED OUT THAT FRED AND I WERE responsible for putting the tire over the flagpole, and we were busy getting ready for soccer season. Practice had gone well and the coach was satisfied with my play. On the day before the first game, he called me into his office.

"Noble, you're going to start tomorrow at center fullback. Think you can handle it?"

"Yes sir."

"You'll be the last defender before the goalie. Anyone getting past you will have a good chance of scoring. Remember, if you can't get the ball at least get your man."

I had heard those instructions before. If I couldn't turn the ball back upfield, I was supposed to collide with the opposing forward hard enough to take him out of the play.

"I won't let anyone get by me," I promised.

"Another thing—when basketball practice starts be sure to come out. Last year you played well enough in gym class to make the team."

His invitation surprised me and I left his office excited about the possibility of a three-letter year. With no prom work to get in the way, I could concentrate on sports.

Our opponent for the first game was Deal Island. They were a small school but the boys played tough. At the start of the game, I was nervous and I made some mistakes. Twice, I missed the ball and my man, but neither error resulted in a score. By the second half, I settled down and began to play a respectable game. We won 2-1.

The second match was at home against Marion High School. Those boys were the sons of watermen and farmers from the southern part of the county. Their center forward was fast and always on the attack. During the first half he was constantly making a run at our goal. Each time I managed to stop him but we had several bruising collisions where he hit the ground hard. By halftime he was frustrated and on the way off the field he threatened me. I promised him more of the same treatment in the second half.

When I reached the sideline, the coach walked over to me. "Noble, it looks like you've finally learned how to play your position. Keep it up."

The second period was much like the first. Their center forward led the attack and I continued to take the ball away from him. He grew more irritated and pressed harder, refusing to pass to his teammates. With less than a quarter to go, we were leading 1-0.

The forward made another fast break toward our goal and I went out to meet him. We kicked at the ball at the same instant and I made solid contact, sending it back upfield. When my left foot came down, an awful pain in my shin caused me to collapse to the ground. Nothing had ever hurt so badly and I lay on the grass writhing. Fred came over to help me up.

"That guy didn't go for the ball. He kicked over it, straight at your leg."

Fred got me to a standing position, but as soon as I put weight on the leg I went down again. Two other teammates came from the sideline and assisted me off the field. They lowered me to the ground behind the coach and began to remove my shoe and shin guards. I was wearing two pairs of heavy canvas guards with wooden dowels sewn inside for strength.

"Look, they're broken," one of the boys said, bending the guards back and forth. All the dowels were snapped.

The county truant officer had come by to watch the game and he was standing nearby. "So's his leg, I heard it crack. Someone had better call his parents," he said.

While the game concluded I sat alone behind our bench, trying not to move my leg. If I remained still the pain was bearable. Even though my shinbone had a lump and a slight bend, I figured the truant officer must be wrong—I had never had a broken bone before.

We won the game and my mother arrived just as the teams were leaving the field. She drove me to the office of a popular surgeon in Salisbury. Office hours were over, but they agreed to see me. After my leg was x-rayed, the doctor came into the examination room.

"You have a fractured tibia," he said.

"Are you sure," I said, desperately wanting him to be wrong. "It doesn't feel that bad."

He put the film on the view box. "Do you see this fracture line?" He pointed to the bone and there was a crack all the way through. "You're lucky the ends are in such good position. I can fix it with a cast."

The fact that my leg was broken started to sink in. "How long will the cast stay on?"

"About seven weeks. It depends on how fast you heal."

"No, you've got to do it faster. Seven weeks will wipe out the entire soccer season."

He put his hand on my shoulder and looked me in the eyes. "Son, you'd better forget about soccer." The finality of his words was crushing.

While I contemplated life without the game, the nurse laid out the cast material on a stainless steel tray. She dropped a roll of plaster into a pan of water just as the doctor returned.

"Are you ready?" he said.

"I guess so." I was not sure what I had to get ready for.

"Hold still until we're finished." Without warning, he pushed down hard on the broken bone and pulled up on my foot. I was not ready for that and I bit my lip while they applied the plaster. It wasn't long before a hard, white shell covered my leg.

My mother drove me home and, as we pulled into our driveway, I could see my father standing on the back steps. It was an hour after his suppertime and he was not happy. Mom got out quickly and walked toward the house. I struggled to exit the passenger's side but the full-length cast made everything awkward.

"Where have you been, I'm hungry," my father said.

Mom explained to him what had happened as I made my way up the sidewalk, fighting with the crutches. My father had a look of disbelief.

"What's the matter with you, have you got weak bones? I've never had a broken bone in my life." He seemed embarrassed to have raised such a fragile son. It didn't matter that I was the second strongest boy in the entire high school. "Who's going to do your work?" he said.

Up until then, I hadn't thought about my chores. "I'll do them on crutches."

"Not likely." He frowned and headed inside to wait for his supper.

The doctor had sent me home without any medication. As the evening went on the pain increased and by midnight sleep was impossible. I spent the night in my father's recliner, trying to ignore the throbbing in my leg. In the early hours of the morning, sitting alone in the darkness, I was overwhelmed with self-pity.

By morning the pain had subsided, but the doctor had instructed me not to go to school and to keep my leg elevated for a few days. I tried sitting up in a chair, but the toes sticking out of my cast turned purple and I went back to bed.

That evening at supper my father and Danny decided how they would divide my chores. No sows were due to farrow and my only regular work was feeding them and the chickens in number two house. Danny agreed to take over part of the chicken feeding and my father made me promise to pay him back when I recovered. Dad said he would take full responsibility for the pigs.

When the meal was over I went back to bed. In a few minutes the phone rang and Mom brought me a message. "Page is going to come over and sit with you for a while." It was welcome news. I was tired of being alone with no television.

Page was the first girl to ever enter my room. It was exciting, but my mother instructed us to leave the door wide open. Page sat in a chair beside my bed and we talked for hours about school and our plans for college. The evening ended too early when Danny came in and announced that he was ready for bed. We were still sharing the room and he ignored my dirty look. Before leaving, Page leaned over and kissed me on the cheek. I started to think there may be benefits to having a broken leg.

At school on Monday morning, I was the center of attention until everyone had signed my cast. After that I was just the guy who slowed down the cafeteria line. In a few days Mitch began to amuse himself by jerking one of my crutches from under me while I was walking. He would catch me at the last second, before I hit the floor. I soon took the fun out of that by cracking him across the shins with a crutch every time he came near.

* * *

Thankfully, I had a diversion from my disappointment about the soccer season. The Livestock Show, which had been renamed the Somerset County Fair, was approaching, and the FFA boys still did much of the work. Before the previous year's show, I had helped Dr. Johnson blood test all the animals that were exhibited, but that was impossible now with my cast. I volunteered to help with the Fair Queen Contest. Most of the contestants were from our end of the county, but the runner-up was a pretty, brown-haired girl from Crisfield, named Beverly.

During the fair, I worked closely with Beverly. Nothing about growing up in Crisfield had prepared her for dealing with livestock—to her, all cows looked the same. My job was to direct her to the right show ring and make sure she gave the correct ribbons to the winners. Farmers with prize dairy cows objected if their ribbon said "Grand Champion Steer."

Beverly was fun to be with, and we laughed about her confusion over the animals. I was disappointed when the fair ended, but a few days later I called to ask her out. She said yes. It felt good to be planning a date and not thinking about my leg.

All that remained was convincing my father that I could operate the car with a full length cast. Surprisingly, he was sympathetic. After giving me a short driving test he acquiesced, without complaining about the long trip to Beverly's house. I was grateful.

* * *

A week later I was doing my homework on the dining room table, when I heard a solemn television voice announce that President Kennedy would address the nation.

"I wonder what this is about?" my father said.

I picked up my crutches and made my way to the living room. Our family listened in silence as the president told us about the Soviet missiles in Cuba and his plans for a blockade.

"This is serious. If we start boarding Russian ships, it could easily lead to war," my father said.

Civil Defense films had given me a pretty good idea what war would be like and I decided there was no reason to finish my homework. For the rest of the evening, I listened to my parents speculate about what might happen.

At school the next day, the talk was about nothing but missiles and possible war. We calculated the straight-line distance from Washington D.C. to Princess Anne and discussed the prevailing winds. If the Capitol was bombed, we would be out of the blast zone but heavy fallout would drift across the Bay to us. Tommy Toots had not yet built his shelter and I wondered if he was at work in his backyard.

Our teachers were uncertain if we would be able to see the flash from the explosions. Our first warning might be the siren on top of the fire station in town. No one talked about it, but we all spent the day listening for that steady wail we had heard so often in drills. Somewhere during the war talk, the promise of our senior year slipped away. It would be a while before we found it again.

That afternoon when Danny and I came home from school, Mom had just returned from the grocery store. She was in the pantry, filling the shelves with extra canned goods.

"Your father wanted me to stock up," she said.

In a little while my father arrived home from work, carrying boxes of shotgun shells and .22 caliber bullets. "The hardware store was almost sold out. You never know what might happen—it's best to be prepared."

"Prepared for what?" I said.

"We might have to live off the land for a while."

I hated that I was injured and desperate times may lie ahead, when I would be of little use.

As the days passed, everyone watched the news closely. When Khrushchev announced that construction on the missile sites had stopped, the men at the Corner Store were suspicious. They expected some sort of trick from that "lying communist." Gradually, it was accepted that the threat was really over.

At school things returned to a different normal. The crisis had brought home the real possibility of nuclear war. My classmates stopped talking about it, but we all felt a new urgency to get out of school and on with our lives.

* * *

When I began dating Beverly, it was soon obvious that her father was a serious man who planned to protect his daughter from the likes of me. The first night I arrived at her house, he gave me the "I know what you're after" look. The fact that I was wearing a full-length cast didn't seem to matter. He questioned me for half an hour before Beverly and I could leave. It wasn't that his daughter was wild; she was more than attentive to his rules. I took her home two minutes after curfew and she was noticeably upset about being late.

Obedience was not Beverly's only good quality; she was a determined girl who already had her life well planned. As a straight "A" student, she had selected her college in the tenth grade. On our second date she described what her married life would be like—it involved a brick rancher with two kids playing in the yard. There was no question that she would make her dream come true; her husband would have no choice but to sign on. By the time it was clear that I was in an audition, I was having doubts about the part.

Beverly and I dated for more than a month, until I was sure that ranch houses didn't suit me. She was having doubts too—I was just not trainable enough. She was a nice girl who went on to win several beauty pageants but we were not meant to be.

29. Snapping Yellow Teeth

IN NOVEMBER, MY MOTHER DROVE ME TO THE DOCTOR'S office to have my cast removed. It was a cold, dreary day but my mood couldn't have been better. This unexpected interruption in my life was about to end. I was impatient as I sat in the waiting room and looked at an old *Life* magazine.

Before long, the nurse placed me in an exam room and the doctor breezed in to inspect the cast.

"Are you ready to get this thing off?" he asked.

"Will it hurt?" I remembered the day he applied it.

"No, this is painless."

"Then I'm ready. I'm tired of scratching my leg with a piece of wire and basketball practice is about to start."

He gave my mother a warning look and then turned back to me. "Let's see how it healed before we talk about basketball."

The doctor began to cut the cast with a noisy saw, and plaster dust filled the air. I squirmed, certain that he was going to slice my leg. The nurse assured me that the blade only vibrated and it would not hurt my skin. When the two halves of plaster split apart, I was startled at the sight of my leg. It was so shrunken that if it had not been attached to my pelvis, I would have believed it belonged to someone else. The thigh muscles were only half their normal diameter.

"What happened?" I said in disbelief.

"Don't worry, it's just muscle atrophy," he said. "You haven't used the leg for seven weeks. It will come back to normal in a month or so."

He took an x-ray and left the room while it was being developed. I studied my withered leg, determined to get it back into shape before basketball season no matter how much effort was required. In a few minutes he called my mother into the hall. When they returned he was wearing the expression of someone bearing disappointing news.

"It's healing okay, but I'd better cast it again for another month. If I don't, I'm afraid you'll put too much stress on it."

"Wait, you said seven weeks . . ."

"It won't be bad—just a short cast below the knee. You'll still need crutches but four weeks isn't long."

At that moment it seemed like forever.

* * *

In spite of the new cast, I could not avoid going back to work at home. My sows were beginning to have their fall litters and there were already two groups of pink, little pigs tugging at their mothers' teats. The workload was more than my father could handle and I had to take over some of the chores. The short cast had increased my mobility, but the crutches still got in the way.

One afternoon, I was giving iron injections to baby pigs as a protection against anemia. Prices were still down, but those animals remained my only hope of going to college. Richard Tyler, the boy who had been with me during the shark episode, was helping by holding the pigs.

Sows were never happy when humans were handling their offspring. That day one of the females was especially protective, and she tried to bite us every time we got near. I lured her out of the building with feed and Richard closed the door behind her, trapping the pigs inside where we could safely get to them. As an extra precaution before starting work, we moved the babies out of their pen and into the aisle way.

The pigs squealed when we injected them, and their mother became agitated hearing their cries. She paced outside, making deep-throated grunts which got louder with every pig we handled. We hurried to finish the litter but we weren't fast enough. I was on the last pig when the sow crashed through the door.

For a moment, Richard and I froze. The sow ran across the pen and launched herself halfway over the waist high partition. Richard jumped back just in time to avoid the snapping yellow teeth. I was caught fumbling with my crutches and she bit me hard on my chest. The force of the attack knocked me to the concrete floor. As soon as I was down, she slid off the partition and began searching for her pigs. Richard quickly placed two in the pen with her and she started to relax.

I got up carefully, afraid that my leg had been re-injured, but I was glad to see that the cast was still intact. I stood for a few seconds and there was no pain at the fracture site, so I decided it must be okay. My chest was a different story; there was a large tear in my shirt and long bloody gouges in my skin.

Richard inspected my wounds. "Aaah, we're not going to quit work for those little scratches. I've hurt myself worse than that combing my hair." The long, carefully contoured wave on his forehead made me think he might not be kidding.

He searched through the cabinet and found the iodine that I used to disinfect pig navel cords.

"I'll put this on it," he said with a grin.

"No way." I knew he would apply it liberally to produce maximum discomfort. I took the bottle and dabbed the brown liquid on carefully.

"You're a bigger wimp than my sister," he said.

"If you had fastened the door right, none of this would have happened," I said, knowing it was not his fault. After I gathered up my crutches, we moved on to the next litter.

"From now on, I want hazardous duty pay," he said.

"What makes you think you're getting paid?"

He faked surprise. "You mean I'm doing this just for the experience?"

"Yes, hasn't it been worth it so far?"

The banter went on until the job was finished. I could always count on Richard for help, and a little fun along the way.

* * *

Eleven weeks after my leg was broken, the cast was finally removed. By that point my limb was almost unrecognizable. Dark and scaly skin covered a tiny calf muscle that hung loose and flabby. I could hardly bear to look at it.

The doctor x-rayed it once more and pronounced the bone healed.

He sent me home with instructions to continue using the crutches, but to bear as much weight on my foot as the pain would allow. Physical therapy was never mentioned; I'm not sure it existed on the Eastern Shore in 1962.

That evening I walked around the living room with crutches, putting my foot on the floor for the first time in almost three months. Everything about the leg hurt, especially the ankle, which had been locked in the same position from the start. I wondered if it could ever be normal.

For the next week I pushed myself, using the leg more each day, and gradually it began to limber up. One afternoon I decided the crutches had to go. On my way across the backyard, I stopped and leaned them against the maple tree. My first stride was a bold one, but the pain was more than I expected and I almost fell to the ground. I hobbled to the back steps and sat down. Tears filled my eyes as I realized how long it would take for my leg to recover. It was already December and basketball season was slipping away.

30. A Price on My Head

 FRED HAD A LOOK OF CONCERN AS I ENTERED THE auditorium. The Christmas Formal was only two days away and he was chairman of the dance committee.

"Where's my tree, Noble?" he demanded.

Two weeks earlier I had promised to find a large cedar tree to use as a centerpiece for his decorations.

"I searched the marsh edge on our side of the river, where the best ones grow," I said. "But they were all too small or too ugly."

"Don't give me excuses, I need a tree."

My friend was in a jam, and that caused me to make a suggestion I knew could lead to trouble. "There is one tree growing on Champ Road that's tall and thick and a nice shade of green."

"Let's go get it."

"There might be a problem—it's growing on county property. The road mowing crew has left it alone for years because it's so pretty, but Dad says it's interfering with traffic and they will soon have to cut it."

"I don't see the problem, let's cut it for them," he said.

"There's one other thing. The man who owns the Champ store really likes that tree. It's standing less than fifty feet from his yard. I've heard him tell my father how beautiful it is." Mr. Albert had died and a new man, Mr. Bradshaw, had purchased the store. He got along well with my father but he was cool toward me.

"Let's go look at it tonight," Fred said. He was anxious to have the problem solved.

That night turned out to be perfect for questionable activities. There was no moon, and warm air had blown in from the south, over-running the frozen ground and producing a low fog. I shut off the truck engine at the end of the road leading to the harbor. Frank, the boy who had helped gather ivy for the prom, had joined Fred and me.

"We'd better push it from here," I said.

"How far to the tree?" Frank asked.

"One hundred fifty yards."

"Jesus, is this the best plan you could come up with?" He was not a fan of unnecessary work.

"You're the muscle, not the brains of this outfit," Fred said.

I removed the bulb from the truck's interior light, seeing no reason to announce our presence. The little pickup rolled easily down the dark macadam. I pushed on the doorframe with one hand and steered with the other. Fred and Frank shoved against the fenders. The road was almost invisible in the mist and our only guide was the faint glow from the lights of Mr. Bradshaw's house.

"Does the old man have a gun?" Frank whispered.

"Yeah, and he's already shot one man at the store," I said, lying.

"Oh damn." I felt the truck slow down.

"Keep pushing," Fred said. "He'll probably never hit your skinny ass in this fog."

When we arrived at the tree, the house seemed much closer than I remembered. Silently, I retrieved one of my father's handsaws from behind the truck seat. I lay down on the frozen ground and began to cut while Fred pulled on the upper branches to take the pressure off the saw. In a minute the tree lay across the road and the aroma of cedar filled the damp air.

The Bradshaw home was quiet until we began to load our prize. As Fred lowered the tailgate, a support chain rattled and a little dog began to bark inside the house. The noise added urgency to our work. Frank got in the truck bed and pulled on the tree while we pushed it from the road. It suddenly moved toward him and he fell backwards, disappearing under the branches. Fred and I laughed as he grumbled and wiggled his way out. The porch light at the house came on and we all fell silent.

"What's going on out there?" a gruff voice said.

The three of us scrambled into the pickup cab. The engine started on the first revolution and I sped off, hoping the fog would make the truck hard to identify. Frank slid down low in the seat, keeping his head below the rear window. We made our escape and drove to town, where we hid the tree behind the school. On the way home, I wondered if we had really gotten away so easily.

The next morning all of my classmates were in the auditorium, getting it ready for the dance. The decorations were not as elaborate as they had been for the prom, and the job was more relaxed. It was good to be a worker and just having fun; the stress was on Fred's face this time. I set up our tree in front of the stage while other boys lined the walls with pine and holly boughs. The girls made fluffy artificial snow by whipping together soap flakes, salt and water, and they applied it everywhere. Mr. Powell unlocked the storage room where the Christmas lights were kept. Fred and some girls began to trim the tree.

In the rear of the storage room was the school's only vending machine, which the principal brought out for special occasions, such as Friday night dances. It was just an insulated box on four spindly legs and the entire top opened to reveal rows of bottles hanging by their necks in metal racks. To buy a drink, it was necessary to drop a dime in the slot and then slide a bottle over to a little gate, which opened to release the soda.

I decided to have a drink, even though there was no ice in the machine and it was against the rules for students to have sodas during school hours. I deposited my dime but when I tried to pull the bottle out, the gate jammed. Not wanting to lose my money, I went to my father's truck and found a bottle opener. On my return, I slipped into the cafeteria for a straw.

Back at the vending machine, my soda was still hanging in the rack. I opened the top, leaned over and drained it dry with the straw. It tasted good and I drank another one, figuring the machine owed me that for trying to beat me. Satisfied, I joined Fred and helped decorate the tree.

In a short time, I noticed a group of my classmates hanging around the storage room. When I looked in Mitch was leaning over the vending machine, draining the last soda. He straightened up and burped.

"Thanks Noble," he said.

"Mr. Powell isn't going to like this," I said, looking at the rows of top-less bottles, some with straws still sticking out.

"He won't find out for a while. We're serving punch tonight and the next dance isn't for a month."

He closed the lid and I helped him stack boxes on top of it but I was sure we had not heard the end of the incident.

My date for the formal was a cute blonde from Crisfield. She liked to dance and we had fun, even though I was still limping. The tree was beautiful, and it gave the auditorium a warm Christmas glow that put everyone in a holiday mood. For that evening, the nuclear threat of October was a distant memory.

I slept late the next morning and when I came out of my room, my parents were talking in the kitchen.

"Someone cut that cedar tree on Champ Road," Dad said. Mr. Brad-shaw is furious and he has a reward poster in his store."

"Who did it?" Mom said.

"Nobody knows, but it was too large to fit in most houses."

I suddenly felt uneasy—a reward poster was something new—maybe I had strayed too far this time. I eased into the kitchen attempt-ing to be inconspicuous.

"Did you have fun at the dance?" Mom asked.

"Sure, it was great."

"You took that girl from Crisfield?" Dad said.

"Yeah, I like her."

"Why can't you go out with somebody closer to home? Do you know how many miles you're putting on our car?" He had recently purchased a new Ford Galaxy 500, which was a sharp looking car, and I was grateful.

"I'm thinking about dating Page," I said, hoping to calm him. He looked pleased.

"Now you're making sense for the first time since you got your license." He picked up his paper and turned to the sports page.

Mom poured a yellow circle of pancake mix into a black, iron fry-ing pan. "Do you want scrapple too?" she said.

I nodded yes. My father was intent on his reading, but I needed to know about the reward.

"Did you say Mr. Bradshaw is mad about someone cutting a tree?"

"Yes, the pretty one on the road near his house," he said.

"What's he going to do about it? Wasn't it on county land?"

"It was, but he says he's taking whoever did it to court."

I started to lose my appetite; winding up in court could cost me a chance at college. "How much is the reward?"

"Ten dollars."

Immediately, I felt relieved. No one would give me up for just ten dollars.

That afternoon I went to the Champ store on the pretense of buying a candy bar. The reward poster was displayed prominently near the door. On it was a picture of the missing tree and a promise to pay ten dollars for the name of the person who took it. As I paid for the candy bar I searched Mr. Bradshaw's eyes for any sign that he suspected me. He stared back with his usual grumpy expression.

Outside the store I broke into a grin—being the subject of a reward poster, even a ten-dollar one, was exciting.

* * *

For a month after Christmas I partied hard. Any weekend night that I did not have a date, I was out drinking with several of my classmates. We parked on back roads and drank beer until all of us were in a daze. Everything that was said on those evenings was funny, no matter how stupid. When I drove home late at night, our rural roads were devoid of traffic, which allowed me to survive. My parents were always in bed when I arrived home and I managed to hide my behavior from them.

At school I often felt angry, and I quit doing anything in my classes except disrupt them with a wisecrack if the teachers called on me. When I thought about my plans for college, I felt bitter. With the low pig prices, the chance of my having enough money was slim. In the past I had always had a positive attitude, but that was changing. Maybe it was missing out on basketball season, or maybe I was just tired of being Mr. Responsible. Whatever the reason, something inside was driving me to take risks with my future.

On one cold Saturday evening, a late farrowing sow delivered her pigs and I sat with her until she finished, which made me late to a party at the Princess Anne Firehouse. When I arrived in town some of my friends, including Frank, were already past happy and on the way to insane. Alcohol was not permitted in the building but they had a bottle stashed in a bush outside. Before I could get to it, a junior girl came in and announced that the police had heard about the drinking, and they were on their way to raid the party.

I loaded Frank and two other friends, Dale and Matt, into the car and drove them out of town. Matt, a good-looking boy with curly black hair and an athletic build, could be charming and funny, but there was always anger close to the surface. He was often in fights, sometimes taking on two or three boys at once. Mom said his childhood had been hard and that he deserved a break. He was a math whiz and the teachers were frustrated by his lack of interest in school. Something about his attitude drew the girls to him, even the prudish ones.

I convinced my passengers to go to a dance in Crisfield. On the way, Frank leaned his head out the window and threw up. When we arrived he couldn't get out of the car, and we went inside without him.

There were a lot of girls there that night, and I was having fun until I noticed a group of boys gathered around Matt and Dale. When I walked over to see if there was trouble brewing, I heard Matt's voice.

"You're as ugly as a frog peeping through ice," he said to a Crisfielder, six inches taller than he.

I stepped in between them, and using all the goodwill I had built up with those Crab-town boys, I eased my friends toward the door. Matt protested but I kept him moving; Dale seemed happy to be rescued. When we got to my parents' car, I noticed that much of Frank's supper was stuck to the rear fender. His mother had served green beans and something that looked like chicken. I tried to wipe it off with a paper towel, but it was frozen to the paint.

I loaded my passengers into the car and drove to the only open gas station in Crisfield. The thermometer by the door registered 2 degrees. The attendant said his hot water pipe had just frozen but he gave me a bucket of cold to wash the fender. When I poured it on, Frank's lost meal became encased in a thick layer of ice, making it impossible to remove.

I drove back to Princess Anne and we heard that the party had been raided, but things had quieted down. Big Head Bill was parked by the courthouse, asleep. I had kept my friends out of trouble but I vowed never to babysit for drunks again. Everything in town was closed, and my only option was to clean off the car in the morning before my parents got out of bed. At first light I went outside with a pail of hot water, and began to wash the fender. Steam rose up in the frigid air as I worked. The job was half finished when I noticed my father at the kitchen sink filling the coffeepot. He spotted me and came outside, walking on the frozen ground in his bare feet.

"What's going on?" he said.

"Something spilled on the car and I'm washing it off."

He took one look at the frozen mess and knew what had happened. "You were out drinking and got sick."

"It wasn't me, I didn't drink anything."

"Somebody in the car had alcohol and that's just as bad."

"I was just helping a friend . . ."

"I don't want to hear it. Clean this up good, your mother has to drive the car to church. I'll deal with you later."

After washing the fender, I went to the Ross place to feed my sows. When I returned to the house, my parents were sitting at the kitchen table. For the first time in my life, Mom looked at me with disgust and it hurt.

My father studied me for a while with his jaw clenched.

"Terry, you're too young to be drinking, and I'm going to do whatever it takes to stop you. For a start, you're grounded for four weeks."

"That's not fair . . ."

"I think it's what you need. If you challenge me on this, you'll be sorry."

A month with no social life in the middle of my senior year was worse punishment than I had expected, and I resented getting it because of someone else's drinking. My teenage logic ignored the fact that I had been drunk the previous four weekends.

Anger at my father for the perceived injustice caused me to avoid him even more, and we spoke only when absolutely necessary. I began to think that he no longer mattered in my life; he was just someone to be endured for a few more months. The University of Maryland had accepted me, but even if I didn't make it to college, I was determined to leave home soon after graduation.

* * *

At school things were almost as bad. One morning Mr. Powell stopped me as I was coming out of the locker room.

"Terry, I hope you enjoyed your Cokes," he said, sarcastically.

"What do you mean?"

"I know you led the raid on the vending machine."

It had been so long I had forgotten about the incident, but it was new to him and he was upset.

"Do you realize the profit from that machine goes to the PTA? I'm going to have to tell the parents what happened and who was involved."

"But I only took. . . ." I stopped; he had made up his mind and any explanation I offered would make me seem weak.

The next morning I gave Mr. Powell three dollars to cover the loss of the drinks. I couldn't have all the parents thinking I was a thief.

"You did the right thing this time," he said. "I won't tell the PTA but if you don't change your ways, you're headed for big trouble."

After what felt like a lifetime, the four-week grounding was over and I was careful to avoid alcohol and the boys who were drinking. My relationship with my father was still cold, and I was happy to get out of the house on weekends. I started dating a petite, blonde cheerleader from Crisfield named Gloria. On our first date, I went in to meet her parents; I liked her Dad and we talked for a while about fishing.

"Who's your father?" he asked.

"Tom Noble. He used to work for the Tidewater Fisheries, but now he raises chickens and does construction."

He paused and looked at me curiously. "Tidewater Fisheries, you say?"

"Yes sir," I answered nervously, afraid that Dad may have arrested him.

A faraway look came to his eyes. "Your father saved my life one night, years ago, in Holland Straits."

"He did?" I was relieved he was not holding a grudge.

"I used to work for the Holland's Island Gunning Club."

"What happened?" The story was one I had never heard.

"Ask your father," he said in a wavering voice. Then he turned to Gloria. "He's okay—you two go out and have fun."

The next day was Saturday and I helped my father ready the chicken houses for a new batch of baby chicks. He was lighting gas heaters while I put down feed trays. For a long time there was silence between us, but curiosity made me ask about what I had heard the evening before.

"I remember that night," Dad said. "He was in a bad fix."

"Tell me about it."

"It was cold . . . sometime in late December. My mate and I were anchored near Spring Island, spending the night to watch for hand-scrapers. Just after sundown, I stepped out of the cabin and heard the whine of an outboard motor. With binoculars I could see a boat turning in a tight circle, and there didn't seem to be anyone aboard."

My father halted as he went back in time for the memory. I tried to hurry him along.

"Had he fallen overboard?"

"Not completely. We pulled anchor and headed his way. When we got close, I could see him dragging through the water behind the boat. Just the heel of his hip boot was hooked over the stern."

I imagined the man's desperate situation, with the cold water stealing life from his body, clinging to his only salvation but unable to pull himself aboard.

"How did he wind up like that?"

"His motor wouldn't start in the cold, so he put it in gear to get a higher throttle setting. When it fired, the boat lurched forward and threw him out the back."

I thought of the times I had started our motor in gear and decided not to do it again.

"How did you get him in?"

"I brought the *Somerset* up beside his boat, matching the speed and turn radius the best I could. When I was close enough, my mate jumped aboard and shut off his engine."

I pictured that maneuver in the near darkness of Holland Straits, and I knew it could not have been easy.

"With all of his heavy, wet clothes, it took both of us to pull him into his boat. He was barely able to talk. We warmed him up with coffee and took him back to the Gunning Club. I think he quit that week, deciding he would rather work on land."

With the story over I went back to my chore, throwing the feed into the trays with more force than was needed. Strangely, I felt annoyed. I had written my father off as someone different from the man I had known as a young boy. I didn't need my old hero coming back to confuse me.

31. The Prom and Rotten Eggs

WITH THE FIRST WARM DAYS OF SPRING, I BEGAN TO TEST my leg on the track. I had been walking without pain, but running was different; on the first day out my leg hurt with every step. Weeks passed before I could finish a quarter mile at anything other than a jog. When I finally made a timed run, the results were not good. The coach frowned when he looked at the stopwatch and he said that I limped all the way down the stretch.

The long jump was even worse. My leg had lost its spring and the fracture site throbbed every time I hit the take-off board. Jumping with the other leg felt unnatural and I could never get the timing right. After a few practices, I reluctantly turned my back on that event.

My only hope was the quarter mile, and I worked hard at it, running more sprints and laps than ever before. Gradually, my time improved and I made the team. At the first meet I placed second to my teammate, a junior I should have beaten. Things continued that way throughout the season, a string of second place finishes. Late in the spring the coach said he could still detect a limp when I was in the stretch. It should have been my year but I could not make it happen.

I began to feel sorry for myself more than at any time since the injury, and my attitude at school got worse. In the past I had never studied for a test; I had always been able to pick up what I needed from the class discussion. Now when a test was handed out I began to write down ridiculous answers to the questions, and my grades soon reflected my efforts.

One day during the noon hour, I sat in a car with Frank and drank malt liquor. It was the first alcohol I had consumed since my grounding and I downed several of the short cans before going back into the school.

A yearbook meeting was scheduled for that afternoon, and when I arrived at the cafeteria, the room seemed distorted and out of square, something I had never noticed before. I spoke little during the meeting, choosing my words carefully when it was necessary. Mr. Leckey was not fooled and he called me aside as the other students were leaving. There was a look of genuine concern on his face.

"I am very disappointed in your behavior. You have great promise, but if you don't clean up your act, everything is going to slip away from you."

I moved quickly toward the exit before he could say anything else. On the way out I collided with the doorframe, bruising my shoulder.

That evening, when my head was clear, I thought about Mr. Leckey's warning. Perhaps my future was slipping away. I wasn't sure that I cared, but I did regret betraying his trust. No doubt Mrs. Richards would enjoy saying, "I told you so." I resolved to give the yearbook my full attention.

* * *

It was difficult to keep my balance, as I crouched in the back of the farm truck, bouncing up the gravel lane. A half-moon illuminated my classmates huddled in the shadows against the wooden rails. We were on our way to raid the barn where the junior class was preparing their prom decorations. A foul smell filled the air around us.

The raid had been planned that afternoon in advanced math class. Our teacher had gone to the office for a meeting, leaving the blackboard full of equations for us to solve. Matt finished the problems in a few minutes and showed his solutions to the class. He was the best math student the school had seen in years, but the only things that mattered to him were girls, drinking and fighting.

With the assignment complete, the boys around me began to discuss what we might do for excitement.

"We should pay an unexpected visit to the juniors tonight," I said. "They're working in the Williams' barn off Polk's Road."

"Excellent idea. We need to keep up the tradition," Jack said.

For a while, we talked about what to do when we got to the barn. Water balloons, firecrackers and loosening the coil wires on their cars were considered and rejected.

Matt appeared to be ignoring our discussion, but he spoke up. "You are a bunch of pansies. Why don't you do something that will really be remembered?"

"Like what, tough guy?" I said.

"Like driving up to the barn and rotten egging the whole place."

"Okay genius, where do we get rotten eggs?" Jack said.

"My uncle raises geese and he just emptied his incubators. He has bags of eggs that didn't hatch, and most of them are rotten."

The boldness of his proposal surprised all of us and we paused to consider it. Jack was the first to speak.

"We're not taking my car."

"Mine either," three of us said, almost simultaneously.

Without transportation, it looked like the idea was dead.

"I'll drive my father's grain truck," Doug said. That settled the matter. If ever there was a born getaway driver, it was Doug. He was so fearless behind the wheel I had quit riding with him.

As the truck rumbled on toward the farmhouse, I had second thoughts about our plan. Many of the junior boys were my friends, and none of them had ever done anything to deserve what they were about to get. The attack was going to be a major escalation over last year's raid and I was not sure how they would react.

When we passed under the yard light, my classmates' faces were clearly visible. All of them had serious expressions, except Matt, who was grinning. The truck wheels hit a pothole and an egg exploded in one of the bags. The pop was followed by a terrible stench.

"Man, that's ripe," Jack whispered.

Doug stopped the truck in front of the barn. There was a light on above the big door. He sat alone in the cab while the rest of us remained crouched behind the rails, out of sight. I had a view through a small knothole.

The juniors heard the engine and swarmed out of the barn, like bees defending their hive. When they were close to the truck, Doug blew the horn, which was our signal to rise. We appeared from behind the rails and astonishment filled the faces of our victims. That changed to disbelief when the eggs started to fly. At first they just stood there as though paralyzed, but when we went back to our bags for more ammunition, they came to life and ran toward the barn. We pelted their backsides as they went.

Once inside the shelter of the building, they began to curse us with a vigor I had never heard before, stringing together words in truly original sequences. Doug drove away, leaving them swearing and he spun the truck around in a field behind the barn. Our only escape from the farm was back the way we had come in.

As we approached the barn a second time, three junior boys ran out determined to attack us, but they fell back under an awesome barrage of eggs. Our driver stopped, trying to lure more of them out of hiding. The barn light abruptly went off. Bottles and boards began to smash against the rails and we ducked for cover.

"Let's go, before they block the road," I yelled.

Doug jammed the accelerator to the floor and sped out the lane. When we were back on Polk's Road, he stopped and we talked excitedly about what had occurred. No one had been hit with the debris thrown at us, but Dale and Jack had eggs explode in their hands. They were reeking and I figured the juniors couldn't smell much worse. Matt wanted to make another attack on the barn, but we overruled him and headed for the Esso station in town to wash up.

The next morning when I entered the school, three junior boys met me at the door. They made threats but I pushed passed them and walked toward the senior end of the hall. Halfway there, I found Matt surrounded by another group of juniors.

"Okay, meet me behind the gym at lunch," he said to them, as I approached.

"Are you guys really all that mad?" I asked, trying to ease the tension.

"Are you kidding, you clobbered us with those eggs," a boy named Mike said. He was one of the most likable members of the group. "It took me two baths to get rid of the odor, and Mom threw my clothes out. Even worse, Jimmy found a partially hatched, dead goose draped over his shoulder."

Matt and I roared with laughter, imagining the scene. The junior boys began to chuckle, admitting that it was pretty funny. They were good guys and I figured they would soon get over it. I walked away thinking everything was settled.

Just before classes began the principal's secretary appeared at our homeroom door and handed Mr. Leckey a note, which he read aloud. "The following are to report immediately to Mr. Powell's office." He read off the names of everyone on the raid.

The six of us assembled in the hall and began to joke nervously about what was coming. There was always the thrill of the unknown preceding a trip to the office. I doubted that we could be punished; the whole incident had taken place off school property.

"Don't admit to anything," Matt said. "He doesn't have any proof it was us."

"Only twenty eye witnesses," Jack said.

Mr. Powell was seated at his desk and there were six chairs lined up in front of it. I took a seat on the end.

"Boys, what you did last night was despicable," he said, looking straight at me.

"What do you mean?" I said, taking Matt's advice.

"You know what I mean," he shot back. The horns on his forehead were more prominent than I had ever seen them. "Mrs. Williams called me at home first thing this morning. The roaring truck engine and all the yelling last night really upset her. She had no idea what was happening."

I glanced at the other boys and they were all looking at the floor, feeling as guilty as I did for disturbing Mrs. Williams.

Mr. Powell continued to look mainly at me. "I may not be able to punish you because of where the act took place, but let me make one thing clear—in the future, if I hear of even the slightest bit of trouble concerning this prom, I will cancel it. Do you understand?" We knew he wasn't bluffing; he had cancelled the traditional senior trip to New York because of the wild behavior of the previous class.

"Yes sir," six voices said together.

"Go back to class and think about it. I'm going to be watching you all closely," he said.

I figured he was going to need a microscope to watch me any closer.

By noon, news of the raid and Mr. Powell's threat had spread throughout the school. The girls were furious that we had put the prom at risk. Most of them had already bought their dresses. The six of us sat in the lunchroom together, feeling like outcasts.

One of the junior girls, who some boys would have given a body part to go out with, glared at us as she walked by with her tray and said, "You boys are so stupid."

That afternoon it was a relief to go out to the shop for agriculture class. The building was a refuge from the main school and the dirty looks from the girls.

Mr. Anderson arrived a few minutes late, carrying a stack of soil test results from his farms. He passed them out and went to the blackboard, where he wrote down the crop to be planted in each field. Our assignment was to calculate the fertilizer requirements for each one. We were to figure the pounds of nitrogen, phosphorus, and potassium that he should apply for optimum plant growth. The nutrient requirements for corn, tomatoes, snap beans and small grains were all different and had to be considered.

For two hours we worked on the calculations and I made multiple trips to the pencil sharpener. It was good to have my mind away from the troubles of the morning, but when the class was over, Mr. Anderson called me to his desk. I expected him to talk about FFA business; I had been re-elected as state vice-president and we were planning the summer convention.

"What's happening with you?" he said. "I spoke to Buzz Powell today and he thinks you're going to wind up in the state penitentiary. I'm not sure I disagree." Hearing Mr. Powell's prediction was a shock, but deep inside I thought he must be wrong.

"We threw some eggs at the juniors."

"It's not just that, it's your whole pattern of behavior." Mr. Anderson appeared angry with me for the first time. "Your future was as bright as anyone I ever taught, but you seem determined to throw it away."

His words were painful and I avoided his eyes. He had always been my biggest supporter and, in many ways, a second father. I could think of nothing to say and I headed for the door.

"Boy, you need to straighten up, I've got too much invested in you," he said, in a softer tone.

"Okay." I did not look back.

Walking away from the shop, I wondered if he and Mr. Powell

really believed I would wind up in prison. Could they see something in my behavior that was leading to serious trouble, or was it just a scare tactic?"

That question stayed in my mind for days. I thought they must have been truly worried about me, to make such a statement. Maybe I had been pushing things too far. After a week, I decided that my future mattered, and it was time to start acting like it.

For the next month I did what was expected of me, and there was little trouble at home and none at school. Page and I dated a few times, which pleased my father, but we had been friends too long for there to be much of a spark. Soon I was putting too many miles on his car again.

The junior boys wanted to retaliate for our attack, but Mr. Powell's threat kept them at bay. In May, the prom came off as planned and the girls got over their anger that we had almost ruined it.

By graduation I had repaired my relationship with Mr. Powell and the teachers. I was amazed at how easily they forgave my behavior. After the commencement ceremony they all smiled and shook my hand; even Mrs. Richards managed a pleasant word. They all showed genuine interest in my plans for college which were still uncertain. The conflict between us, that I had felt was necessary a few months before, now seemed silly. They were nice people and I was glad they had been part of my life.

It was good that only Fred and I knew about the game warden firecrackers and fuse under his graduation gown. We had planned for him to drop the lit package into a trashcan in the dressing room as he came off the stage, but surprisingly, the janitor was stationed there. Maybe someone had overheard us making plans. If the administration won the last round, it was all right—I was glad we had not disrupted the ceremony.

32. Why is Your Face Black?

WITH THE END OF THE SCHOOL YEAR, I BEGAN TO dissolve my farming operation. The sows had farrowed their last litters under my ownership and I got their pigs ready for sale. Danny, at twelve, could not take on the entire herd, but he bought two sows with a loan from my parents. I sold the remainder of the animals to the livestock dealer and he parceled them out to other farmers. My father bought the tractor for work around the chicken houses, and our neighbors purchased my remaining implements.

When I sold all the livestock and equipment, I was holding enough money for two years of college. Mr. Anderson helped me find a job at the University of Maryland dining hall, which would stretch that a bit further, but it still felt insufficient. Starting college and having to drop out for lack of funds was not something I wanted to do.

Part of the answer to my problem came at church on a Sunday in early June. The first service had ended and I was standing in the slow-moving line leaving the building. Up ahead near the door, I could hear a sonorous male voice like that of a radio announcer.

"My, that's a pretty dress, Eva."

"Oh, it's an old one I've had for years," a female voice said.

"Well, keep wearing it. You look lovely in it."

There was a pleased laugh and the line moved forward. The male voice spoke again.

"Hello, Mary, that's a beautiful hat. You look more gorgeous than ever."

"Why, thank you, Harry," another female voice said with a hint of flirtation.

By now, it was clear who was holding up the line. It was Senator Harry T. Phoebus, an Oriole resident and member of the Maryland legislature. He was a debonair man and the only person I knew who wore double-breasted suits. He had been in office since before I was born.

As young boys, my friends and I often stood in the churchyard, listening to the Senator compliment every female that came through the door. In a low voice, he often told a dozen or more women that they were the best-looking one there. We snickered, unable to believe our ears; no other man in the community paid compliments like that. When I grew older, it was obvious that some women went to church more to hear the Senator than the preacher.

He also paid plenty of attention to the rest of the congregation, always asking the men about their farming or crabbing and whether he could do anything for them in Annapolis. No matter what the problem, he promised to look into it. When I came through the line, he usually shook my hand and asked about school. His palm was the softest I had ever felt and I was afraid my calluses might scratch it.

On that Sunday he had new information about me.

"Young man, I hear you are soon off to college."

"Yes sir, if I can find the money."

"Well, I can help with that," he said, loud enough for everyone to hear. "With your grades, I can easily give you a senatorial scholarship which will pay for tuition."

"I don't know," I said. Taking money I had not worked for seemed like begging, and I enjoyed doing things on my own.

"Don't be silly. Come by my office next week and I'll fix up the paperwork."

When I arrived home from church, I told my father about the offer.

"I believe I'd take the scholarship," he said. It was the only advice he ever gave me about college.

The next day I went to see Senator Phoebus at his car dealership in Princess Anne. His office had a bare concrete floor; an old oak desk flanked by two chairs and a green filing cabinet were the only furniture.

On the walls were photographs of the Senator meeting with political figures. One showed him shaking hands with a smiling Richard Nixon. They proved what everyone knew—Harry Phoebus was a powerful man who had once been considered a leading contender for governor.

We were half way through the paperwork when Judge Mac Duer walked in. He was a middle-aged man with a stern look, made more pronounced by his thick glasses. It was a warm day and the sleeves of his white shirt were rolled up.

"Harry, I want to talk politics but I'll wait until you're finished there." He took a seat in the only guest chair and read the paper. The Judge was a strict enforcer of the law and a fearsome presence on the bench. Every boy knew it was a big mistake to land in his courtroom.

When we had completed the scholarship form, the Senator spoke.

"Judge, do you know this fine young man?"

Mr. Duer looked up over his glasses. "What's your name boy?"

I told him, and, for no reason, I was instantly nervous.

"Who's your father?"

"Thomas Noble."

"I know Tom, he was a good officer for the Tidewater Fisheries." There was a hint of a smile and I took it as a good sign.

"Terry is going to the University," the Senator said.

"Humph," the Judge responded. He paused and looked me up and down before fixing his eyes on mine.

"Let me tell you something, boy. If you go up to the University and study hard every night, including weekends, and don't mess with any women or alcohol, then maybe you'll stay there. Otherwise, they're going to send you home. Come January, you'll be back here shucking oysters or doing something worse. Do you understand?"

"Yes sir." It was impossible to answer him any other way.

I turned toward the Senator to get away from the Judge's eyes. The Senator was smiling.

"Don't scare him too much, Mac."

"Harry, he needs it. I can tell by the look of him."

I thanked them both and backed toward the door. The Judge pointed his finger at me. "Take what I said to heart, now boy."

I took his advice and it turned out to be the best I ever received about college.

* * *

Two days after my meeting with the Senator, my father received a call from Mr. Bond, the superintendent of schools. Dad had recently become a member of the school board and I had applied for a summer job there. The board always hired a few teachers and college bound students to paint, cut grass, and do minor repairs. The work was steady and it paid better than farm labor or crabbing. When my father hung up, he confirmed that I had a job and it would begin the next day. He mentioned that Fred had also been hired, which was good news; if the work was boring, I was sure we could find a way to make it interesting.

The next morning we met Mr. Bond in town. He was a balding, middle-aged man from out of the county. His manner was genteel but there was tension in his eyes. He assigned Fred to the painting crew, and I was given a job as assistant to Charlie Somers, the chief maintenance man. It was disappointing not to be working with my friend but the superintendent seemed to think it was better that way.

I climbed into Charlie's yellow truck and we headed for the elementary school. Before we had gone a block, he asked, "Who put the tire over the flagpole?"

"I don't know," I said, stifling a grin.

"Come on, you can tell me. You're out of school now."

I gave in and admitted that it was Fred and me.

"Hah! I told Buzz Powell that it was you." He sounded tickled to have solved the mystery and to be proven right. "You're going to pay for it," he said, and laughed heartily.

I learned the first day that Charlie thought having an assistant meant that he did no physical labor. He saw his job simply as managing me, his one-man work force. My first assignment was to clean the interiors of the furnaces in all the schools in the county.

Each morning for the next few weeks, I crawled through the narrow firebox door of a furnace. When I was inside the combustion chamber, Charlie would hand me a scraper and wire brush. I spent the day crouched in there, removing soot and fire deposits from the steam pipes. He would place a portable radio nearby, tuned to a station of my choice, and then disappear.

In two hours, he would return and bring me a soda. Usually he looked into the furnace with a smile and said, "Good work, keep it up." Charlie believed motivation to be an important part of management.

At other times he might say, "Gee, you aren't very neat. You've got that stuff all over you." By then my clothes and exposed skin would be black with soot.

At the end of the day, the only place where I could clean up was the lavatory sink in the school bathroom. There was never any hot water; it had been turned off for the summer. With just cold water and bar soap, it was hard to remove even the outer layer of grime. I changed into clean clothes before leaving work, but my face and arms were still as black as any coal miner's when I walked out to the river bridge to hitch a ride home.

I had hitchhiked to and from town for years, whenever there was no vehicle for me to drive. Everyone living down Deal Island Road knew me and it was usually only a few minutes before I caught a ride. But with my face black, I wasn't so recognizable. Many people stared as they drove past; some looked so long they almost hit the bridge railing. Most of my rides came from individuals whose curiosity overwhelmed their caution. They would slam on their brakes and back up to see who or what I was. At first it was embarrassing, but after a while, watching their reactions became a real source of entertainment.

One afternoon a black man slid his car to a stop in front of me. His name was Anthony but everyone called him Ant'ny. I had worked with him in the tomato fields, but it was obvious he didn't recognize me. I got into the car and thanked him for picking me up. By that point I no longer told people immediately why I had a black face and arms. It was more fun to wait and let them work their way around to asking me.

Ant'ny drove off slowly, seldom looking at the road. He always had a powerful stare, and when he locked his eyes on a person they knew they were being looked at by an expert. That day I got the full treatment.

"Nice day isn't it," I said.

"Yeah." The car drifted on to the shoulder and he jerked the wheel to bring it back.

"We might have a shower this evening," I said, looking out the window at the clouds.

"Maybe."

"I'm going fishing before the storm."

"Uh-huh." His fingers began to tap on the steering wheel.

"I think the rockfish . . ."

"Whose boy are you?" he blurted out.

I told him and a light of recognition crossed his face.

"I know you," he said. For another minute he studied me intently, during which time we almost went off the road on a turn. Finally he could take it no more. "Why the hell is your face black?"

I explained about my job and the lack of a good place to clean up. He was silent for a while and I wasn't sure he believed my story. As we neared the Corner Store, he began to laugh.

"I thought maybe you were trying to come over."

"What do you mean?"

"You know, come over to our side."

I realized that he was joking and took a chance, "Do you mean become a colored person?"

"Yeah, we have a lot more fun than whites."

"I've heard that, but I guess I'm stuck where I am."

He turned into the store parking lot and cut off the engine.

"If you change your mind, we'll take you in," he said, with a devilish grin.

"I'll remember that, thanks for the ride."

I walked home and filled the tub for the first of two baths I took every afternoon.

Ant'ny gave me a ride several times that summer.

* * *

By mid-July, the furnaces were all clean and my work situation improved. I spent most days mowing grass with a tractor or doing minor repairs, such as replacing cracked windows. It was an enjoyable time; Charlie kept me amused with jokes and funny stories from his youth. We became friends and it was all right with me that I was doing all the labor. I would have been content to finish out the summer that way. But one morning when I reported for work, Charlie appeared sad.

"Mr. Bond wants you and Fred to put a coat of tar on the high school roof and you start today. I'll be working in Crisfield for a while and he'll be your supervisor."

When the superintendent arrived, Fred and I were hauling five-gallon cans of tar up a tall ladder to the roof. Mr. Bond removed some long-handled brushes from the trunk of his car and followed us up the ladder. He began to show us how to apply the tar, and it was soon obvious that the job wouldn't be a quick one. He brushed for several minutes and only covered a tiny area. Drops of sweat appeared on his bald head and his face reddened.

"The salesman said it went down easier than this," he muttered. After a bit more struggle, he handed me the brush. "Well, that's how it's done. You boys get on with it. I'll be checking on you regularly."

For a few days, Fred and I worked diligently through the withering mid-summer heat. Each afternoon the thermometer nudged 100 degrees and the roof neared cooking temperature. The breezes all departed for cooler latitudes and the leaves on the big pecan trees were still. The old tar surface melted and our tennis shoes stuck to it with every step.

Each day at quitting time, we climbed down from the roof, discouraged at how little we had accomplished. Once on the ground, we began removing the dried tar from our skin using kerosene. We wore shorts and getting the sticky coating out of our leg hair was difficult.

Fred and I became sluggish and worn down by the constant heat. We began to take longer breaks on the ground, sitting in the shade. We both decided that it was the worst job we had ever had. Mr. Bond checked on our progress regularly, sometimes frowning at what he saw.

Relief came one evening when a thunderhead began to build out over the Bay. It grew closer to our house and bolts of lightning began to play tag across the sky. The break we had been hoping for arrived. The storm lasted for hours and when it was over, the air was cool and fresh for the first time in weeks.

The next morning Fred and I were in good spirits. As he climbed the ladder above me, I decided to paint the back of his shorts with tar. I coated his butt as he scrambled upward, trying to escape. Once on the roof, he pulled his shorts around and examined my work.

"You jerk, there's only one way on to this roof and you're going to pay to get here." He filled his brush and positioned himself at the top of the ladder.

I removed my shirt and tied it around my head for protection. Slowly I moved up the ladder, thrusting with my brush to keep him off balance. I felt like a medieval warrior assaulting a castle wall. Seeing an opening, I swiped my brush across his legs, coating the hair above his knees.

"You jackass," he said. His attack intensified and I continued to parry with my brush. I was still free of tar and he was getting frustrated.

The battle ended when I stepped up a rung on the ladder just as he swung downward. The wooden corner of his brush hit my head with full force, knocking the shirt off. The world began to spin and I slid down the ladder, fighting to stay conscious. At the bottom I sat down on the ground.

"Are you okay?" he yelled.

I touched the top of my head and there was a wet spot. I thought it was tar but my fingers came back red. "I'm bleeding."

Fred hustled down and looked at my head. "Stay here. I'll get help." I wasn't going anywhere. He ran into the auditorium where the painting crew was working and came back with Jim Henderson, one of the younger teachers.

"How did this happen?" he said, looking at the wound. Fred explained the accident.

"How bad is it?" I asked.

"Not good. It needs to be sewn up," Mr. Henderson said. "And if Bond finds out, he'll fire both of you."

"He can't find out—I need the money. Take me somewhere to have it sewn up."

The most trusted doctor in our area practiced in the small community of Dames Quarter, ten miles away. It was too far to drive with the possibility that Mr. Bond might stop by the school any time.

I decided to take my chances with a physician who had an office a few blocks from the school. He had come to town as a brilliant young doctor, first in his class at medical school. In a few years, alcohol and his own drugs had reduced him to sleeping in his car. Periodically he would dry out, open a new office and resume practice. When he was "right" the adults said there was no one better. This time he had been straight for just a few weeks.

Mr. Henderson parked his car in front of the doctor's office and went inside. He came out shaking his head.

"I don't think I'd go in there. He's talking fast and his hands are trembling."

"What am I going to do?"

"How about Dr. Marksman?"

"The colored doctor?" I had heard of him, but no one that I knew was a patient.

"He's old, but people say he's good."

"Okay, I'll try him."

Dr. Marksman's practice was located on his farm, which was a large piece of land bordering Maryland State College. His house and office sat pleasantly in a grove of tall trees. Mr. Henderson drove into the yard and I went to the door. I knocked several times before a courtly black man appeared behind the screen door. His hair was mostly white and he appeared to be near seventy.

"What can I do for you, son?" he asked in a kind voice.

"My head is cut. Can you sew it up?"

"Maybe. I don't do too much of that anymore but I'll take a look." He led me to his office and pointed to a chair. I sat down and he began to examine me.

"That's quite a gash. What's this black stuff?"

"Tar, I guess." I explained a little of what had happened.

"It's going to be hard to clean up."

He began to slowly and meticulously cleanse the wound. He tried to cut the hair with scissors, but sometimes the tar interfered, and when he pulled the scissors away the hair ripped out.

"Never seen such a mess," he said.

The process was painful, but he was such a gentleman I couldn't complain. Two quail were calling to each other out in his yard and I concentrated on their song while he worked. After he was satisfied with the condition of the wound, he injected a local anesthetic and began to suture. The work went on for most of an hour before he finished and applied the bandage.

"How much do I owe you, Doctor?"

"Would five dollars be too much?" he said, hesitantly.

"No sir, not at all." I paid him, happy to have the job done and to have met him.

I hurried out to Mr. Henderson's car and he drove fast back to the school. Fred was waiting with a concerned look.

"How are you?" he said.

"Not bad, just a headache. Let's get back to work."

I noticed that the tar was still coating his leg hair. We climbed the ladder and resumed our work but Mr. Bond never made an appearance that day.

When I arrived home, my parents saw the bandage and immediately started asking questions. I was vague with my explanation, trying to prevent my father from having to keep a secret from the superintendent.

"Fred's brush accidentally hit me," I said.

"How did that happen?" Mom asked.

"He was on the roof and I was climbing up the ladder."

"Did he drop it?" my father said.

"Yeah, sort of."

Dad looked unsatisfied, but before he could ask any more questions, I went to the bathroom to examine my head in the mirror. When I lifted the bandage, I saw a long horseshoe-shaped line of stitches. Fred had raised quite a divot.

Mr. Bond was at the school when we arrived for work the next day. I was wearing a hat and he gave me a knowing look.

"Boys, I'm closing down the roof project and I don't have anymore work for you this summer."

Fred and I were startled; someone on the painting crew must have talked. I was sure it was not Mr. Henderson; he was a solid guy. We tried to appear unconcerned about the news.

"That's good, I needed a little vacation," I said to Mr. Bond.

His face tightened up like there was something crawling in his underwear.

"You'll get your final check in the mail. Good luck at college," he said with a forced smile.

That evening I casually asked my father if there were any jobs at his construction site. He closed his paper and looked at me with suspicion.

"What happened to your job?"

"They ran out of work."

"There's something I'm not being told." He got up from his recliner and went to the phone. When he came back, he was biting his lip. "I talked to Mr. Bond and he said your head got cut because you were involved in horseplay. From what I gather, not much work was getting done. Here I am a new member of the school board and you go and embarrass me like this. Sometimes I wish I could disown you."

He seemed to really mean his last statement and I went outside and sat on the back steps. Cindy came over and put her head in my lap; I could always count on her. As I rubbed her ears I thought about the superintendent. Had he ever engaged in horseplay or had any real fun? I couldn't picture it. I could picture him spreading tar on that 100-degree roof and passing out by noon.

The next day I got a job at a tomato cannery, stacking cases in the warehouse. It paid the same as the school board and the working conditions were better.

For over a week I avoided my father. One evening he asked if I wanted to dipnet crabs with him on the following morning, and I said yes. It turned out to be a good day for both of us, even though he did take a short spill overboard.

33. Witnessing a Miracle

I SHIFTED THE OUTBOARD MOTOR INTO NEUTRAL AND let the boat coast toward the wharf. Five nice rockfish were laying in a bushel basket at the bow, and one was still flapping its tail. Bruce was at the gas dock filling his boat's tank for the next day's work. His crab scrapes were gone and there were tong shafts protruding from the cockpit. I steered my skiff alongside his boat and shut off the engine.

"Need a fish for supper?" I said.

"I could use one. Who gave them to you?" He could see my rod leaning against the boat seat.

"Are you doubting my skill as a fisherman?"

"I know that you and your old man would starve if you had to live off what you could catch."

I laughed and tossed a fish on to his culling board. Talk like that meant we were still friends, even though I had not seen him for a month.

"Looks like you're ready for tonging," I said.

"Crabs are about done for this year. I suppose I'll go out and hunt for the few oysters left in the river."

He sounded concerned about what the winter may hold in store and I remembered the game he and my father used to play.

"You've probably got enough oysters around your stake to get by for a while."

271

He threw back his head and laughed. "Don't worry about what's around my stake. That's between me and the Lord. And he doesn't eat oysters so he doesn't care." His gas tank became full and he hung the hose nozzle back on its hook. "It shouldn't matter to you anyway. I hear you're leaving."

"I have to be at the University one week from today."

A look of sadness came to his face. "Well, go up there and show them what a marsh boy can do. Hell, if I was a few years younger I'd go with you." There seemed to be regret in his voice about the way his life had turned out. All his years had been spent in Champ, working alone every day on his boat.

I looked at his lively blue eyes, set wide in that river-weathered face. "I bet you would have done just fine in college."

That seemed to please him and his warm smile returned. "Maybe so. I was a good student." He untied the rope holding his boat to the piling and prepared to leave. "You could have cleaned that fish before delivering it, you know."

* * *

During the week before I was to leave home, I visited with most of the adults who had been important in my life. I said goodbye to the Shockleys and the men at the Corner Store. I even bid farewell to Tommy Toots, who was now driving his gray Ford tractor everywhere he went because the judge had taken his driver's license. Everyone agreed that he was more of a hazard on it at 10 mph than he had been in his truck at 25 mph.

On my last Sunday at home, I accompanied my mother on her regular visit to my grandparents. When we arrived, Grandma seemed upset and she spoke to my mother in low tones as they warmed up dinner. I sat on the porch and talked with my grandfather about the merits of salted eel as trotline bait. He was then over seventy and he had given up crab scraping for the easier job of trotlining.

From the kitchen, I overheard my grandmother say, "And he could have drowned." I saw my grandfather wince.

"What happened?" I said.

"Nothing much, but Ruth thinks it's the end of the world."

"Tell me about it," I urged. He was usually happy to tell a story, but there was reluctance about this one.

"On Friday, I fell overboard out in the Sound," he said, as if it was a regular occurrence.

I knew it was serious. "How did you manage that?"

"I had pulled up my line and was headed home, running about one third speed. Like every day, I was standing on the washboard, scrubbing it with my mop. For some reason, on Friday, I left my bucket on the washboard. The boat hit a little sea and I stepped backward and tripped over it. First thing I knew, I was in the water."

He paused to fill his pipe and I waited until he had tamped down the tobacco. "Were there any other boats around?"

"No, that was the problem. I had been on a right smart crabs for this time of year, and I had stayed later than the others."

At that point, I realized how much danger he had been in. "How did you get back aboard? Didn't your boat keep going?"

"Aye, she went off and left me all right. I treaded water and watched her go—it wasn't a good sight." He lit his pipe and took several puffs before going on with the story. "In a little bit, I could see that she was turning and would eventually make a big circle. I waited until I could figure the spot where she would come closest to me and then I struck out swimming."

"Could you still swim?"

"Boy, you should have seen me. I was still pretty good," he said, proudly.

I imagined him in the water, stroking hard, knowing he had only one chance to catch the boat.

"I got to her just as she was passing," he said. "I reached up and grabbed the washboard rail. One less stroke and I would have missed her."

"How did you get back in?"

"I hung on until I got my breath back. Then I worked my way to the stern and pulled myself aboard."

I was impressed; it was hard to get back into a moving vessel and my tough grandfather had done it.

"Now Ruth wants me to sell the boat and quit the water. What would I do with myself?"

For the first time I saw uncertainty in his eyes. I was struggling to answer his question when my grandmother called us to dinner.

After the meal, I told my grandfather about my plans for the University and he listened with interest. When I finished, he lit his pipe again and then spoke seriously.

"T, I don't know much about college, but I know educated men have an easier life. You're doing the right thing." He went on to tell me about some men he admired, including Teddy Roosevelt, whose hand he had once shaken in Philadelphia.

As he talked, I noticed Grandma pouring an inch or so of a green liquid into a water glass. I recognized it as her Spirits of Peppermint, a medication her doctor had been prescribing for over a year. She claimed that it calmed her nerves. A month before I had discovered the formula in an old pharmacy book. Unknown to my liquor-hating grandmother and the rest of the family, the mixture contained 80% alcohol. I was the only one besides the doctor who knew that she was having two drinks a day.

My grandfather and I continued to talk and he began to tell the story of his days on the schooner. After a while Grandma came over and sat on the side of his chair. She put her arm around his neck and hugged him. It was good to see affection between them after nearly fifty years of marriage.

When we were ready to leave, my grandmother hugged me. "Remember, saving your soul is the most important thing."

"I know. I'm working on it." It made her feel good to hear me say it.

* * *

For several weeks I had been having second thoughts about pursuing a veterinary degree. After graduation from Washington High, it felt great to be free of school and the thought of committing to eight years of college was daunting. I paid a visit to Dr. Johnson at his animal hospital in Pocomoke, hoping that a talk with him would help me decide.

I arrived at his office just before noon and the blinds on the windows were closed. I knocked on the door and his assistant, a slender gray-haired man, led me to the surgery room where a large female Chesapeake was on the operating table. Dr. Johnson was putting the last suture into her abdominal incision. His hands were almost a blur as he tied the knot and I wondered if I could ever learn to do that. He put down his instruments and looked up from his work.

"Are you still around? I thought you were off to College Park?"

"In a few days," I said. "What did you do to this dog?"

"Spayed her. She was in heat, and that always makes it harder. Look at the size of that uterus." He pointed to a lump of tissue lying at the end of the table. To me it looked small. The only other uterus I had seen was in the gilt that had the cesarean. I was amazed that the two organs could look so different.

He removed the drape and wiped a small amount of blood from the skin around the incision.

"A good piece of work if I say so myself." He turned to his assistant. "Are there any more surgeries for today?"

"No sir, that's it."

"Not a bad morning's work. I might be able to pay the mortgage this month," the doctor said. His assistant winked at me as he lifted the unconscious dog from the table.

The doctor turned around and began to wash his hands in a nearby sink. "Tell me again when you're leaving?"

Before I could respond, the phone on the surgery room wall rang and he answered it. I listened to his side of the conversation.

"This is Leroy, what can I do for you?"

"Is she down?"

"How bad is it?"

"I'll be right there."

He hung up the phone and turned around.

"Well, there goes lunch. That's a shame—I was going to let you buy. Now I've got a milk fever to deal with. Would you like to ride along and make yourself useful?"

I said yes without hesitation, thinking the trip might help me with my decision.

We traveled the few miles to the farm in the doctor's new station wagon. He had given up the Volkswagen to have more space for his equipment. As we pulled into the farmyard, a man was standing in a little pasture next to a tall, gambrel-roofed barn. A black and white Holstein cow was stretched out on the grass in front of him.

"Hurry up! She's almost gone," he yelled, as we got out of the car.

Dr. Johnson searched through the back of the station wagon and retrieved two bottles of fluids, a rubber IV tube, a large needle and nose tongs. The latter was a set of clamps to be inserted into the cow's nostrils as a way to hold her head still.

We hurried to where the patient was lying, but her breathing could be heard long before we got there. She was making a desperate grunt with each exhalation. The farmer, a round-faced man in his thirties, had a frantic look as he paced around the animal.

"She's the best cow in the herd, Doc. I'm expecting 80 pounds of milk a day out of her."

The cow appeared to be near death. She was lying flat on her side and her eye had a blank stare. It didn't blink, even when a fly came to it for moisture. Her long tongue was hanging out the side of her mouth. Except for the breathing, there was no sign of life.

"Put the nose tongs in her and stretch her neck out," Dr. Johnson said. I had done it a few times before, helping him test cows for the livestock show. This one was easy because she was unaware of what I was doing.

He knelt beside the patient and plunged the needle deep into her jugular vein. Dark red blood spurted out onto the grass. After hooking up the IV tube, he released the fluids and bubbles rose up in the bottle.

"This is a balancing act," he said. "She needs the medicine fast, but if I run it too quickly it will stop her heart." He must have been concerned about it, because he lowered the bottle to reduce the flow.

The cow's pitiful breathing began to wear on my nerves. Each effort sounded as though it might be her last. The farmer stared across the field, unable to watch, but Dr. Johnson remained calm.

"This is caused by low blood calcium. It usually happens shortly after calving, when these high-producing cows start putting so much mineral into their milk."

Just as he finished his explanation, the patient's eye blinked. In a few moments, she moved her tongue. Life was coming back into her face as though someone was turning the power on after an outage. In a short time her breathing became easier. When the second bottle of fluids was half-empty, the doctor removed the needle from her vein.

"Help me roll her onto her chest," he said.

The three of us pushed and pulled to move the 1,100-pound animal into a normal resting position. He administered the remaining fluid under the loose skin behind her front leg. The cow was now aware of her surroundings and she was looking better by the second.

Five minutes later Dr. Johnson slapped the cow hard across her back, and with that stimulation, she attempted to stand. He lifted on the base of her tail, and magically, she rose to her feet.

"Thank God," the farmer said.

The cow's first strides were wobbly but she quickly gained more control of her legs. All over her body muscles twitched as the nerves were resupplied with calcium. She began to wander about the pasture and it was not long before she put her head down for a bite of grass.

"I think she'll make it now," Dr. Johnson said. The farmer agreed and he began to gently guide the cow toward the barn.

As we rode out the farm lane, I could sense that my driver was pleased with himself.

"What did you think of that?" he asked.

"It was the most amazing thing I ever saw. That cow went from near death to up and grazing in twenty minutes. You're better than Oral Roberts."

He cackled with delight. "Didn't I look good, though?"

I assured him that he did.

"I love cases like that. They make me look smart."

Back at the office, we said our goodbyes. "Keep in touch," he said. "I might have a job for you when you graduate."

On the drive back to Princess Anne, I played the scene at the farm over in my mind. It still seemed like a miracle; maybe eight years in college wasn't so long after all.

34. Shoving Off with No Boat

 IN THREE DAYS I WAS TO LEAVE FOR THE UNIVERSITY, BUT I still did not have a ride. My dining hall job required me to be there forty-eight hours before most students. No one I knew who owned a car was going to campus so early. It looked as though I was in for a long bus trip. One evening, my father overheard me on the phone searching for transportation and when I hung up he made a surprise offer.

"I'll take the day off and drive you up to the college."

I had never considered asking him; if I was leaving home, I thought it was up to me to find the way.

"You don't have to do that. I'll take the bus."

"I've already decided, we're driving," he said, with finality.

I was glad to have my transportation problem solved, but the thought of spending three hours alone in a car with my father made me uncomfortable. How would we pass the time without something to hunt or catch?

The day of my freedom finally arrived and I got up early to do some last minute packing. Danny went out to feed his pigs and then returned to get ready for school. As I stuffed the last items into my footlocker, I felt sadness about leaving my little brother. We had shared the room for thirteen years and it was hard to remember a time when he was not there. As I rearranged items to find a spot for my desk lamp, I tried to find words to tell him my feelings, but all that came to mind made me look soft. I abandoned the idea and just gave him a shove on the arm. He grinned and shoved back with more force than was necessary. I put him in a headlock and scrubbed his scalp with my knuckles. When he yelled loud enough, I released him.

I went back to packing and as I closed the footlocker lid, there was a stinging blow to my upper arm. The little runt had hit me with one of his best punches. As he ran out of the house laughing, a walnut-sized lump was developing in my triceps. I chased after him, but when I got outside he was boarding the school bus. He smiled and waved at me just before the bus door closed.

Even though I was leaving home, that was too great a challenge to my position as older brother. After the bus was out of sight, I rode his bicycle to the far end of chicken house number two and hid it in the tall grass. It would take him a couple of days to find it, and he would have something to remember me by.

When I returned to the house, my father was pacing in the living room, anxious to be on the road. He had already loaded my luggage into the car. Mom had decided not to make the trip, and I had the feeling it was easier for her to say goodbye to me at home than to see me dropped off at a strange place. She was standing in the kitchen with a hurt look.

"I'm ready to go," I said.

She took my hand and held it tight. "Don't forget us. I want lots of letters."

"I'll be busy with classes and the job, but I'll write every week."

Tears filled her eyes, and for a moment I felt guilty for leaving.

"I'll come home in a month or so."

"Okay," she said softly, letting go of my hand.

* * *

It was quiet in the car as my father and I started toward College Park. Even though we had had a good day crabbing, talk between us was still not easy and we drove a long distance in silence. Finally, my father opened the conversation with a comfortable subject.

"Will you get home at anytime during duck season?"

"Thanksgiving and Christmas."

"Good. It would be a shame to miss out on hunting for the whole year."

For a while we reminisced about our best duck hunts, but the conversation eventually stalled and it was quiet again. As we crossed the Choptank River Bridge, an angler on the walkway pulled an eighteen-inch rockfish over the rail beside our car. Its flipping tail almost slapped the window.

"That's a nice rock," my father said.

"Are you going to fish anymore this fall?"

"I'm taking Danny trolling in Holland Straits."

That was one of my favorite trips and a twinge of jealousy ran through me. I was anxious to get on with my life but there were some things I regretted leaving behind. To feel better, I reminded myself of the excitement that lay ahead.

Dad stopped for coffee at a restaurant in the town of Easton. I bought a milkshake. "Here you go, honey," the waitress said, handing my drink across the counter.

My father liked to make good driving time and we were soon back on the road. I risked a question about work; lately we had been able to discuss that without a disagreement.

"Who's going to feed the chickens in house number two now that I'm gone?"

"Nobody. I'm getting an automatic feeding system."

His answer was totally unexpected; I thought he would take over the job himself. "Why didn't you get automatic feeders while I was home?"

"Didn't need them. What do you think boys are for?" he said, with a laugh.

I felt tricked and annoyed. "I wanted you to feed them so you would appreciate how much work I've been doing."

He stared at the road ahead and spoke in a fatherly tone I had not heard for a while.

"Son, I appreciate everything you've done. You've been a big help to the family. Sometimes, I don't know what I would have done without you."

He had no idea how my heart soared hearing those words. It had been a long time since he had said anything close to complimentary. We crossed the Bay Bridge in a better kind of silence. I hardly noticed the skipjacks working on an oyster bar north of the span.

Not much else was said until we neared the turnoff to College Park. I directed him onto Palmer Highway, a route that Mr. Anderson had taught me on our trips to FFA meetings. My father seemed impressed that I knew the area so well. I told him about a new road called the Washington Beltway that was being constructed nearby. It was supposed to simplify the trip and eliminate all traffic congestion in the area.

The Maryland campus was almost deserted as we drove through the narrow roads. Only a few people were on the sidewalks, and they appeared to be the graduate students who served as dormitory faculty residents. We parked on the back side of the quadrangle near where my dorm was located. Dad and I carried the footlocker and my one small suitcase toward my new home—a four story, brick colonial building that was well maintained but far from new.

Inside the lobby, a sign directed me to the first floor room of the faculty resident. He gave me a room assignment and a key, saying that except for him, the building was empty.

My father and I climbed the stairs to the second floor, carrying the footlocker between us. When I found my room and opened the door, he grunted in surprise.

"I thought it would be bigger," he said. "Can you live in this confinement?"

The room was small, with just two bunk beds on the right side and two undersized desks, plus a bureau and a closet on the left. A narrow walkway ran up the middle from the door to the window. It looked adequate to me and I tried to ease my father's concern about my living in such cramped quarters.

"I'll bet it's larger than what you had in the Navy."

He nodded his head. "I guess it is and I had fun there."

We set my luggage on the tiled floor and Dad walked over to the window. I sat down on the lower bunk to test the mattress. It was four inches of cotton padding resting on a flat spring. He gazed out over the quadrangle for a while before turning to face me.

"Well, I've gotten you this far, son. The rest is up to you."

"I know it is, Dad. I can do it."

Our eyes met for a moment. There was more to say, but neither of us could say it. He looked toward the door.

"I suppose I'd better be getting home. The chickens will need feeding this evening."

"Yeah, they're eating a lot with these cool nights."

There was no hug or even a handshake; it was not our way. He walked toward the hall and stopped in the doorway.

"You can come home anytime you want," he said. His voice wavered a little and I noticed that his eyes were glistening.

"I'll be there before too long and we'll hunt some ducks."

He turned and disappeared down the hallway and I heard the metal fire door slam as he entered the stairway. The sound, echoing through the empty building, gave me a feeling of loneliness. I half-heartedly began to unpack, but after several minutes I gave up and went to the window. To my surprise, Dad was just crossing the quadrangle. He must have paused in the lobby for some reason.

With his long stride, my father quickly overtook two graduate students walking along in conversation. His suntanned, muscular arms stood out in sharp contrast to the soft white ones on the men he passed. He looked out of place; this was not his world. But as he disappeared from view, I had the feeling I was watching a strong man, one who had done his best to raise his first-born son.

I turned away from the window and began to unpack the footlocker. I carefully arranged my lamp and clock on one of the desks, and with that act, the room began to feel like mine. As I hung up my clothes the loneliness faded. It was replaced by the excitement of being free and on my own in a different world. I lay down on the bed for a while to enjoy the sensation. My thoughts were interrupted by the banging of the fire door and the voices of young men in the hall. Other students were arriving early and I went out to meet them. My new life was beginning.

Terry Noble received his D.V.M. degree from the University of Georgia and practiced for twelve years. In 1983 he founded a company in Raleigh, North Carolina, devoted to the research and manufacture of animal vaccines. After selling the company, Terry and his wife moved to a ranch in Montana where he began writing. Today, they divide their time between the ranch and a home on Maryland's Eastern Shore, beside the river where he grew up.

If you would like to know more about Terry, or how to schedule him for an event, go to his website at: TerryLNoble.com.

Author photo: Aileen Noble